K·I·S·S

D1471924

£6·00

DK

The Only Guides You'll Ever Need!

THIS SERIES IS YOUR TRUSTED GUIDE through all of life's stages and situations. Want to learn how to surf the Internet or care for your new dog? Or maybe you'd like to become a wine connoisseur or an expert gardener? The solution is simple: just pick up a K.I.S.S. Guide and turn to the first page.

Expert authors will walk you through the subject from start to finish, using simple blocks of knowledge to build your skills one step at a time. Build upon these learning blocks and by the end of the book, you'll be an expert yourself! Or, if you are familiar with the topic but want to learn more, it's easy to dive in and pick up where you left off.

The K.I.S.S. Guides deliver what they promise: simple access to all the information you'll need on one subject. Other titles you might want to check out include: Yoga, Gambling, The Internet, Sex, Weight loss, Sailing, and many more.

GUIDE TO

Massage

CLARE MAXWELL-HUDSON

Foreword by **Tiffany M. Field**
Director of the Touch Research Institutes, Miami

A Dorling Kindersley Book

LONDON, NEW YORK,
MUNICH, MELBOURNE, DELHI

Dorling Kindersley Limited
Senior Editor Caroline Hunt
Project Editors Julian Gray, Jane Sarluis
Designers Martin Dièguez, Robert Bennett, Claire Watson
Managing Editor Maxine Lewis
Managing Art Editor Heather M^CCarry

Picture Researcher Cheryl Dubyk-Yates
Picture Librarian Hayley Smith
Production Heather Hughes
Category Publisher Mary Thompson

Text edited by Mary Lindsay

DK Publishing, Inc.
Senior Editor Jennifer Williams
US Consultant Jennifer Quasha

First published in Great Britain in 2001
by Dorling Kindersley Limited,
80 Strand, London WC2R ORL
A Penguin Company

2 4 6 8 10 9 7 5 3 1

A CIP catalogue record for this book is available from the British Library

ISBN 0 7513 3437 5

Colour reproduction by Colourscan
Printed and bound by Printer Industria Grafica, S.A., Barcelona, Spain

For our complete catalogue visit
www.dk.com

Contents at a Glance

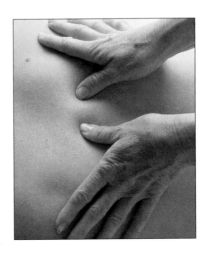

CONTENTS

PART ONE The Basics of Massage

Chapter 1   The Mystique of Massage   22

Chapter 2   Before you Start   34

PART THREE Massage Around the Body

PART FOUR Massage for all Occasions

Foreword

THE GROWTH of the massage therapy profession and the increasingly widespread adoption of massage therapy in the medical community has been supported by massage therapy research. Data, now, from thousands of studies highlight the effectiveness of massage therapy for maintaining health and decreasing chronic illness.

Psychiatric conditions, most notably depression, have been alleviated by the use of massage therapy. One possible explanation for these findings is the increase in serotonin levels noted following massage therapy. Serotonergic drugs such as antidepressants are noted to have similar effects. Increasing the body's natural production of serotonin by massage therapy reduces the need for these antidepressant medications. Similarly, addictive behaviours involved in eating disorders and substance abuse have also been ameliorated by massage therapy. The reduction of stress and stress hormones such as cortisol may lead to a reduced need for addictive behaviour. Similarly, the increase in antidepressant natural hormones in the body such as serotonin may alleviate the intensity of the craving.

Pain syndromes have also been reduced by massage therapy including chronic fatigue syndrome, premenstrual syndrome, lower back pain, and migraine headaches. Several theories exist as to why massage may alleviate pain. In the "gate theory" the notion is that the pressure receptors stimulated by massage therapy are longer and more myelinated (better insulated) than pain receptors, so that when pain is experienced and the painful part is rubbed, the pressure message gets to the brain more quickly than the pain message and the gate is shut, thus preventing the entry of the pain message. Much of this undoubtedly occurs by biochemical messages. Another possibility is that the pain syndrome is being mediated by sleep disturbance. In the absence of adequate amounts of deep sleep, substance P (which transmits pain) is emitted. If massage therapy can enhance deep sleep, which we know it can, than substance P levels and the pain it causes should be lower.

Autoimmune and immune disorders have also benefited from massage therapy. Autoimmune conditions including asthma, dermatitis, and diabetes are reduced possibly because negative immune functions are reduced, which may be secondary to the reduction in stress hormones. In our studies on immune disorders including HIV and cancer, we invariably note an increase in natural killer cell activity. Natural killer cells, being the frontline of the immune system, are critical for killing off viral cells and cancer cells. When cortisol levels are decreased, immune cells are invariably increased because cortisol typically destroys immune cells.

In one of the most exciting prevention studies, we have provided hospital employees with 10-minute massages during their lunch hour. The massage not only led to decreased stress, but the subjects reported a sense of heightened alertness, much like a "runner's high". When we then monitored their EEG waves, we noted that the EEG patterns also conformed to a state of heightened alertness. In addition, performance on a mathematical computation improved, with subjects performing the tasks in half the time with half the errors.

These data highlight the importance of massage for wellbeing and suggest that it is a good thing that massage therapy is one of the fastest growing professions in the world. Following reports that some 48 per cent of people are now buying alternative medicine out of their own pockets, with one of the most popular being massage therapy, insurance companies will presumably take this consumer preference seriously and cover these forms of therapy. They may not only be effective as treatments, but as potentiators of drug effects and as prevention measures to help people find wellbeing. In my view, massage therapy should be right up there with good diet and daily exercise. Books such as this help bring these techniques to therapists and the lay public alike so that massage can be practised in a very effective, high quality fashion.

TIFFANY M. FIELD

Introduction

SIMPLE MASSAGE is something that we already do every day. We stroke our foreheads to soothe away headaches, we rub our aching shoulders and feet, we pat children on the head to reassure them, and we hold a friend's hand to give comfort and support. It is the most natural of human instincts to reach out and touch, and massage is merely an extension of this intuitive response.

Massage may be defined as any systematic form of touch, which is found to give comfort and promote good health. Touch is the first sense to develop in the human embryo and there is increasing research to show that we all benefit from it. Research on premature babies indicates that massage can significantly aid their physical and mental growth and wellbeing. It even appears that the way we are touched as infants can affect the way we interact socially for the rest of our lives. Because touch is such a powerful way of communicating, it makes us feel accepted and helps us to form strong social bonds.

Historically there are records of athletes having massage to keep their muscles flexible and relaxed before an event and to eliminate stiffness after exercise. Massage, as a therapeutic tool, has, throughout history, been an integral part of medicine. Once more it is being appreciated as a complement to the scientific approach to healing.

Sadly, all too often we are scared to touch each other. The fear of accusations of inappropriate touch, of sexual abuse and harassment, has led to fear about touching, and we are increasingly finding touch-taboos in the workplace. Even in schools many teachers are reticent about touching the children in their charge. But, it has been found that the use of appropriate touch with young children has led to behavioural improvements. In a recent survey, the simple act of holding patients' hands improved patient morale and hastened recovery rates. The list of benefits is endless, showing us again and again that we all need to touch and be touched. Massage is formalized touch, with clearly defined boundaries, thus giving us the licence to touch and reassure.

Yet with all these advantages massage is easy to learn. All you need is your hands and the desire to make someone feel better – and the aim of this book is to help you develop this natural capacity.

I have been a professional massage therapist and teacher for over thirty years, and I love it just as much now as I did when I began. In writing this, my fifth book on the subject, I have once again rediscovered how much there is to learn about this simple art and its healing potential. My research has taken me all over the world learning different massage techniques, from the flowing strokes of Swedish massage to the deep-pressure therapy of the Orient. For centuries massage has been used to improve the quality of our lives. In the busy, modern world we need it more than ever before.

My hope is that with the assistance of this book you can develop the therapeutic powers in your hands, so that when you put your newfound skills to use on your family and friends you will, like me, agree that massage enhances the lives of us all. Remember – life may take it out of you – but massage puts it back.
Happy Massaging.

*Clare
Maxwell-Hudson.*

CLARE MAXWELL-HUDSON

Dedication
To all my clients, without whom this book would never have been written.

What's Inside?

*THE K.I.S.S. GUIDE TO MASSAGE starts with an historical
introduction to the subject, then delves into the techniques of massage,
leading you from the basic strokes to more exotic applications.*

PART ONE

In the first part of this book, I will introduce you to the history of massage and its part in the lives of ancient Egyptian, Greek, and Roman civilizations. I will also advise you on how to prepare to give a massage, and just how to set the scene.

PART TWO

Massage movements can be extraordinarily precise, ranging from the lightest brush in the air above the skin to deeply modulated pressures and sweeps. In Part Two I'll show you, step-by-step, how to carry out each of the chief massage strokes and discuss their benefits.

PART THREE

Now that you've learned the strokes, you can put them into practice. Dip into Part Three one chapter at a time, and follow the instructions to concentrate on just one part of the anatomy – like the back or the hands – or treat your partner to a full body massage.

PART FOUR

No matter what your age or condition, there's a type of massage out there for you. Part Four shows you how massage can be the perfect antidote to everyday problems: from soothing a baby in the womb, to tempering stress in the office, to providing comfort for the infirm and elderly.

PART FIVE

Although massage retains similar principles across the globe, its application differs with continent, culture, and climate. In Part Five, take a tour from Sweden through China to Japan, for an introduction to three different massage techniques.

The Extras

THROUGHOUT THE BOOK, *you will notice a number of boxes and symbols. They are there to emphasize certain points I want you to pay special attention to, because they are important to your understanding and improvement. You'll find:*

Very Important Point

This symbol points out a topic I believe deserves careful attention. You really need to know this information before continuing.

Complete No-No

This is a warning, something I want to advise you not to do or to be aware of.

Getting Technical

When the information is about to get a bit technical, I'll let you know so that you can read carefully.

Inside Scoop

These are special suggestions that come from my own personal experience. I want to share them with you because they helped me when I learned to give a massage.

You'll also find some little boxes that include information I think is important, useful, or just plain fun.

Trivia...

These are either fun anecdotes about the application of massage or interesting "Did you Know?" facts from studies and experts.

DEFINITION

*Here I'll **define** words and terms for you in an easy-to-understand style. You'll also find a glossary at the back of the book with massage jargon.*

INTERNET
Useful web links

I think the Internet is a great resource if you want to learn more about massage, so I've scouted out some web sites that will add to your understanding.

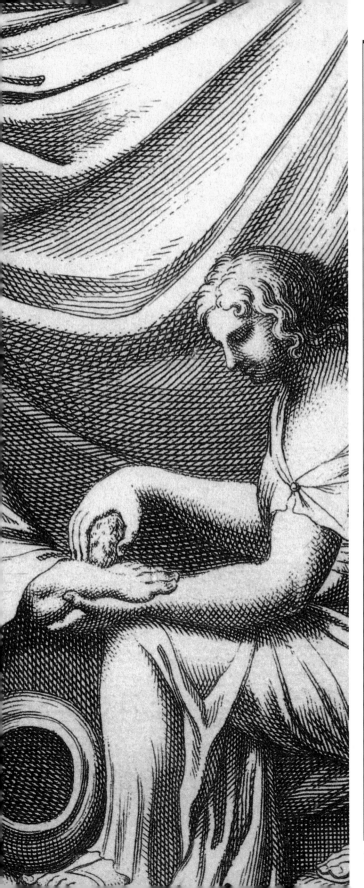

THE ROMANS BROUGHT MASSAGE TO THEIR BATHS

PART ONE

THE BASICS OF MASSAGE

BELIEVE IT OR NOT, MASSAGE is something we all do *naturally* every day of our lives. Whether it's rubbing an aching shoulder or stroking a furrowed brow, we all try to alleviate our aches and pains with our hands and we've been doing it *for centuries*. Take a look at Egyptian tomb paintings, Greek effigies, or Roman carvings, and you'll see how far back this *healing art* goes.

In Part One, I'll lead you gently into the *world of massage*, touching on a little history along the way. You'll come to understand the essential requirements of giving a good massage, what type of equipment you'll need, and how to create the right scene. I'll also show you a *basic massage sequence*, which you can adapt to suit your needs. Finally, I'll introduce the subject of aromatherapy and show you how it can increase the beneficial effects of massage.

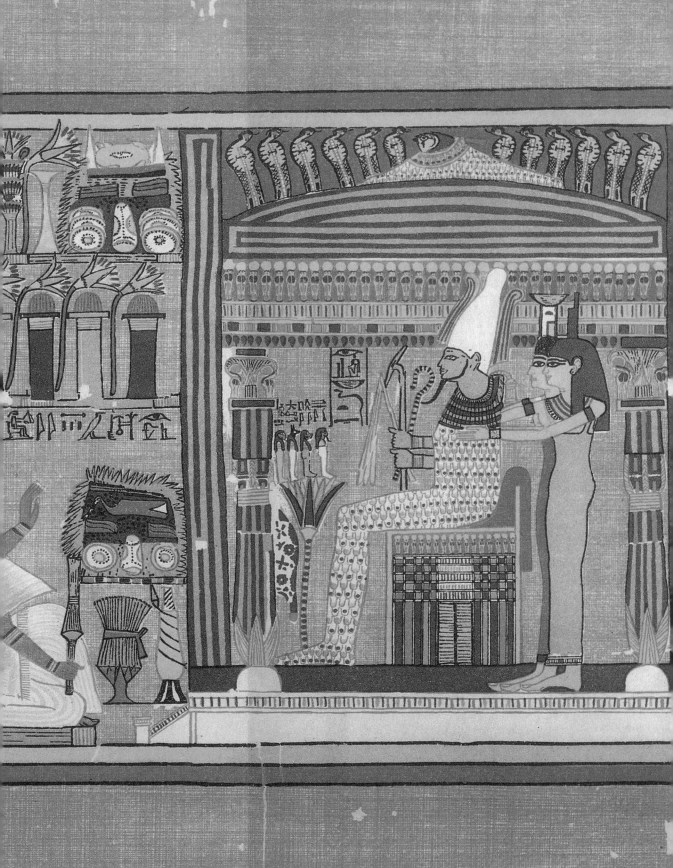

Chapter 1

The Mystique of Massage

O N THE ONE HAND, massage is simplicity itself – what could be simpler and more rewarding than touching someone to make them feel better? On the other hand, it is a highly developed skill that has evolved over many centuries into one of the most popular complementary therapies. The good news is that you don't have to be a qualified massage therapist to give a good massage; all you need is someone to practise on and a willingness to learn. Before I go into how you do it, I would like to start with some background information on the history and development of massage as a healing and relaxing therapy.

In this chapter...
✓ What is massage?
✓ Touching on history
✓ The power of touch
✓ Types of massage

THE SIMPLE POWER OF TOUCH GOES BACK A LONG WAY IN HISTORY

What is massage?

PROBABLY ONE OF THE OLDEST healing therapies known to man, massage is an extension of a basic instinct seen in animals and humans alike: apes groom each other, animals lick their wounds, humans rub away their aches and pains. The basis of massage is touch – the most fundamental of human needs; in fact, touch is so important that if it is absent or withdrawn it can lead to all sorts of problems, ranging from failure to thrive in babies, irritability and bad behaviour in children, and depression in adults.

■ **Basic instinct:** *from the moment we're born our first instinct is to touch. The sense of security that touch brings is the basis for all massage techniques.*

The profound effects

Massage relaxes, stimulates, comforts, soothes, shows caring and empathy, relieves stress, anxiety, and depression, alleviates pain, reduces symptoms of minor illnesses, and improves emotional and physical wellbeing.

The important thing about massage is that anybody can do it, anybody can have it done, there are no side effects, it can be adapted to individual needs, and most importantly it makes both the receiver and the giver feel good.

Linguistic origins

There is evidence of massage in ancient and more recent cultures. The fact that it has survived for so long and evolved into different branches reinforces its reputation as a universal panacea. However, the actual word "massage" is relatively new, but no one is sure about its derivation. It may originate from the Arabic word *masah*, meaning "to stroke with the hand"; or the Greek word *massein*, "to knead"; the Latin root *massa* has the same meaning as the Greek; a French word *masser*, "to shampoo"; and there's a Sanskrit word *makeh*, which means "to press softly".

Trivia...

Touch can be heard in our everyday language. We talk of "rubbing someone up the wrong way". We keep "in touch" and want to stay "in close contact"; we can be "out of touch" with a situation. We even describe each other in terms of touch: someone can be a "soft touch" or "thick skinned". The French have a lovely saying: bien dans sa peau (literally "well in your skin"), which means that you are feeling good about everything.

Touching on history

THROUGHOUT HISTORY, *and all over the world, we have used our hands to promote healing. Although it is safe to say that the use of massage preceded written history, it is more difficult to say when it was first mentioned.*

Ancient Egypt and Greece

The Ancient Egyptians used massage extensively for health and beauty as can be seen from tomb paintings dating back to 3,000 BC. Recorded comments about massage were made by the Greek physician, Hippocrates, who noted in the 5th century BC that "rubbing can bind a joint that is too loose and loosen a joint that is too rigid … hard rubbing binds, much rubbing causes parts to waste, and moderate rubbing makes them grow".

Early written evidence

One of the earliest references to massage in a written form can be found in a book on traditional Chinese medicine dating from the 3rd century BC, *The Yellow Emperor's Classic of Internal Medicine*. It tells us that massage as a form of medical treatment was used for patients with "complete paralysis, chills and fevers, most fittingly treated with breathing exercises, and massage of the skin and flesh".

■ **This tomb painting shows** *the Egyptian King Tutankahamen and his wife Ankhesenamon, thought by scholars to be anointing her husband with perfumed oil.*

Massage in the East

In India, massage plays an important part in Ayurvedic medicine dating back over 3,000 years. The Ayur-Veda (Art of Life), a sacred Hindi book written about 1860 BC, describes shampooing (massage) to reduce fatigue and promote well-being: "Rise early, bathe, wash the mouth, anoint the body, submit to friction and shampoo and then exercise." Avicenna, the great Persian physician (AD 980–1037) wrote: "The object of massage is to disperse the effete matters formed in the muscles and not expelled by exercise. Massage removes fatigue; such friction is soft and gentle and best done with oil." The relevance of this statement is seen today in the increasing number of athletes who use massage as part of their fitness regimes.

Roman baths

The Romans developed the use of public baths for health and social relaxation, and wealthy Romans had daily massages there given by their servants.

A lovely story goes that the Emperor Hadrian saw a veteran soldier rubbing himself against the marble wall at the baths and asked him what he was doing. The soldier replied that he couldn't afford a slave to give him massages. Immediately Hadrian gave him two slaves and enough money for their keep. The next day several old men were rubbing themselves against the walls in Hadrian's presence hoping for similar good fortune – but he told them to massage each another!

■ **The Roman baths** *were the forerunners of modern health spas; here people bathed and had oil rubbed into their skin.*

The rise and fall of massage

After the fall of the Roman Empire the love of physical beauty was frowned on and the use of massage was suppressed, although the use of the baths was retained in Turkey and brought back to Europe.

Massage was kept alive in Western regions of Europe and became part of folk medicine, but practitioners were often persecuted by the Church who thought their healing powers came from the Devil.

Trivia...

The Roman writer Pliny, who was also a renowned naturalist, was regularly massaged to relieve his asthma. Julius Caesar was "pinched" daily by a specially trained slave to alleviate his neuralgic pains.

During the Renaissance, the ancient knowledge of the Greeks and Romans was reintroduced to Europe, and with it came a renewed interest in massage as a medical treatment. The French surgeon, Ambrose Paré (1517–1590), who was personal physician to four kings, promoted the use of massage. In the 18th and 19th centuries, massage grew in popularity in Europe under the influence of Per Henrik Ling, whose system of Swedish massage spread from Stockholm and could be found as far away as Russia, France, and the US.

Trivia...

Captain Cook recorded how in 1779, his painful sciatica was cured when 12 women in Tahiti massaged him from head to foot.

A mixed reputation

At the end of the 19th century, massage was a popular medical treatment, performed by physicians and surgeons, but "houses of ill repute" also used the word "massage" as a cloak for their own activities. In London in 1894, eight professional women who were trained in the art of massage banded together to form the Society of Trained Masseurs. They were the founders of what is now known as the Chartered Society of Physiotherapy.

During World War 1, patients suffering from nerve injury or shellshock were treated with massage. In fact, St Thomas' Hospital, London, had a department of massage until 1934. However, when the pharmaceutical revolution arrived, massage was relegated to a back seat and its use was considered indulgent rather than therapeutic.

An all-round remedy

Today, massage has just about shaken off any dubious connotations to become one of the fastest growing complementary therapies. Its therapeutic benefits have been recognized by a new generation, wanting to find natural ways to achieve good health. Trained massage therapists now work in hospitals, hospices, psychiatric units, neurodisability centres, schools for children and adults with learning difficulties, special-care baby units, intensive-care units, old people's homes, and complementary medicine centres. They may be attached to sports centres, dance centres, football, rugby, and cycling clubs, health clubs, and spas. Many massage therapists also run private practices.

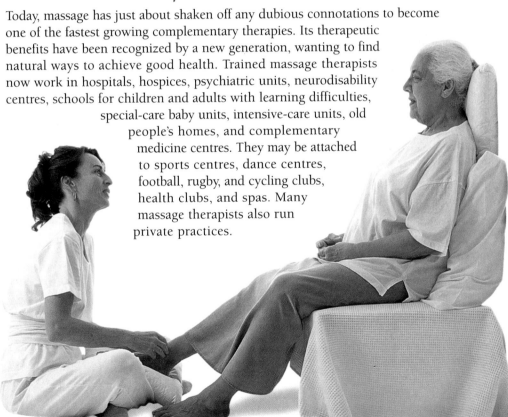

■ **Whatever your age or condition,** *there's a form of massage that can alleviate your suffering, help you to relax, and generally improve the quality of your life.*

The power of touch

THE FIRST SENSE TO DEVELOP *in the embryo is touch, and it is highly developed in even the youngest fetus. If you watch a baby on an ultrasound scan it very soon becomes apparent that the sense of touch is present. The skin develops from the same embryonic layer as the nervous system, and this has led one doctor to say: "It would improve our understanding of the skin if we think of it as the external nervous system."*

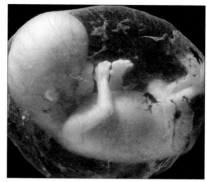

■ **After only a few weeks** *of growth, a young fetus is able to respond to touch in the mother's womb.*

Interesting skin facts

The skin is the largest organ in the body and all forms of touch are perceived through it. Thousands of specialized receptors in the **dermis** react to external stimuli, such as heat, cold, and pressure, by sending messages through the nervous system to the brain. An area of skin the size of a coin contains over three million cells, 50 nerve endings, and 90 cm (35 inches) of blood vessels.

> **DEFINITION**
>
> *The second layer of the skin – that is the layer containing most of the living elements, such as blood vessels, sweat glands, and nerves – is called the* **dermis**.

The sensitivity of touch receptors in different areas of skin can be measured by how far away two stimuli, for example pencil pricks, have to be before being felt as separate points. Middle of the back: 63 mm; forearm: 38 mm; palm of the hand: 13 mm; tip of the nose: 6 mm; fingertip: 2.5 mm; tip of the tongue 0.6 mm. This is why a tiny cut to the tongue seems to possess the dimensions of a canyon!

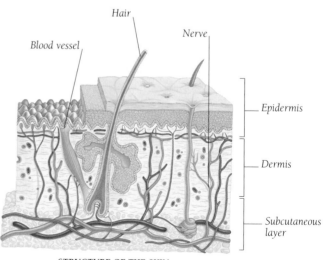

Hair

Nerve

Blood vessel

Epidermis

Dermis

Subcutaneous layer

STRUCTURE OF THE SKIN

Pain relief

Massage or stroking triggers the release of *endorphins*, and induces a feeling of comfort and well-being. Endorphins also play an important role in pain relief. Stronger, more vigorous massage helps to stretch tense muscles and ease stiff joints.

> **DEFINITION**
>
> *The body produces its own painkillers, with a chemical structure similar to morphine, that are called* **endorphins**.

Massage aids relaxation, directly affecting the body systems that govern heart rate, blood pressure, breathing, and digestion. There is lots of scientific evidence that shows that massage lowers the amount of stress hormones circulating in a body; as well as making you feel better, reducing stress hormones is beneficial because their presence in high quantities can weaken your immune system.

What the experts say

Here is an explanation of what happens to us during a massage from Dr Candace Pert, a neurochemist from the US: "When people feel pleasure, as they usually do during a massage, they focus on the present moment rather than staying involved with worries and preoccupations. An interesting scientific fact is that there are neurons containing peptides in every organ and throughout the body. One end of these cells is heading into the central nervous system, leading to the brain. The other end is located in the skin – when you manipulate skin, the peptides are released; you are programming the whole body – not so much just the brain area."

Cultural differences

There is no doubt that touch is a very touchy subject! There are striking differences in the way different cultures touch one another; in some countries it is even taboo. People from lands in the northern hemisphere are far less touchy-feely than people from warmer climes; however, they are more likely to cuddle and stroke their cats, dogs, and horses. So it seems that touching is such an over-riding human need that if you can't touch other people you'll find touching an animal is a fine substitute.

Why don't you carry out your own research and people-watch? See how many times different groups of people, for example couples, mothers, and siblings, touch each other. The point I'm trying to make is that massage is a form of touch and if you have a problem with touching people *per se*, you need to overcome this to reap the benefits of massage. I think these social inhibitions are due to a confusion between sensuality and sexuality, and as a result we have formalized touch. Massage can remove the taboos of touching, and allow people to touch in a positive way.

Did you know?

Various cross-cultural studies have been carried out to assess touchability. In one study conducted in cafés around the world, the researchers observed the number of times couples touched each other over the period of 1 hour. The results were 0, 2, 110, and 180, and the respective countries were UK, US, France, and Puerto Rico.

BODY SYSTEMS

Virtually every system in the body can be helped by massage, either directly or indirectly. This chart illustrates the various systems of the body and explains how massage can be used as pain relief or general relaxation. Use it for your reference.

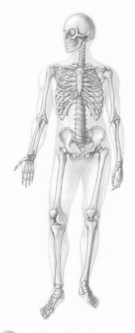

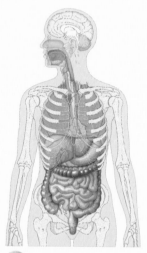

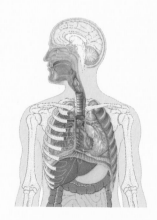

a **Skeletal system**

Bone is affected indirectly by massage. Improved circulation of blood brings oxygen and nutrients to the bones. Joint stiffness and pain can be reduced – as the muscles become more flexible, joint movement increases.

b **Muscular system**

Some massage movements relax and stretch muscles, reducing muscular tension and cramp. Massage also makes muscles more flexible by reducing muscle tone. Muscles tired by exercise are more quickly restored by massage than by rest.

f **Respiratory system**

As you become more relaxed during a massage, respiration may become slower and deeper as you are using your diaphragm for breathing and expending less energy. Physiotherapists use cupping movements over the base of the lungs to relieve chest congestion.

g **Digestive system**

Massage aids relaxation and therefore can help to increase the movement of food and waste products through the digestive system. This relaxation can have a balancing effect on the digestive system.

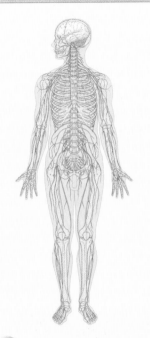
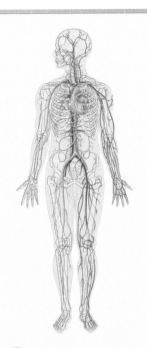
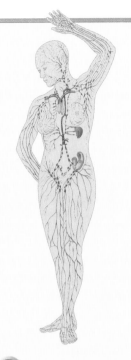

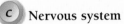

c Nervous system

Soothing massage can provide relief from nervous irritability and stress-related conditions, such as insomnia and tension headaches. When used energetically to stimulate, massage may relieve lethargy and fatigue.

d Circulation system

Massage can improve the flow of blood, which can help poor circulation. This is especially useful for anyone who is immobile.

e Lymphatic system

Gentle massage stimulates the lymphatic system, which helps clear the body of a build-up of waste products. The relaxing effect of the massage can relieve stress, which in turn can boost the immune system.

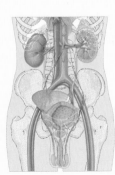

h Urinary system

Waste products that have been released during massage find their way via the blood to the kidneys where they may be filtered out and eliminated.

i Female reproductive system

Menstrual problems, such as period pains and PMS, can be alleviated by the relaxing effects of massage, as can menopausal symptoms.

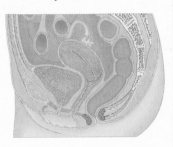

Types of massage

MASSAGE CAN BE ROUGHLY DIVIDED
*into two kinds – one that emanates from the East
and one from the West.*

INTERNET

www.worldofmassage
museum.com

*For some interesting
information on the history
of massage, check out the
World of Massage Museum's
web site.*

Eastern massage

Eastern massage is based on the premise in traditional
Chinese medicine that the body is made up of vertical
lines or meridians though which life energy flows.
Disease is the manifestation of a disrupted or blocked
flow of energy, and massage works by restoring the
movement and thus relieves symptoms. Many varieties of massage follow
this basic principle, for example Chinese massage, reflexology, and shiatsu.

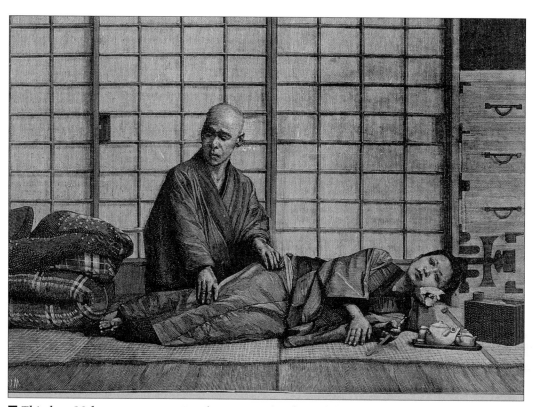

■ **This late 19th-century engraving** *depicts an earlier form of shiatsu massage popular in Japan,
known as* anma.

Western massage

The type of massage used in the West has its roots in anatomy and physiology, and is usually based loosely on Swedish massage. Simply speaking, the theory is that stroking, pressing, and squeezing the flesh stimulates the circulation, thus supplying more blood to the muscles and removing waste products of metabolism more effectively to prevent or remove a build-up.

A final note

In the frantic, materialistic, and technological age in which we now live, many people have lost touch with their inner feelings and in particular how to feel good about themselves. Massage is an excellent way of rediscovering yourself – so next time you feel you need some retail therapy, try having a massage instead. That item you left in the shop will soon be forgotten, but the feel-good factor from the massage will last a long time.

Did you know?

For many years, not much scientific evidence was available to support the claims of massage therapists, but the Touch Research Institute, founded in Miami in 1992, changed this. It studies the effects of touch on human beings, and has shown that HIV patients, premature babies, abused children, depressed teenage mothers, adolescents with eating disorders, drug addicts, people with cancer, asthma, diabetes, and various other illnesses, can all be helped by massage.

A simple summary

✓ Massage is simply an extension of the basic human need to touch and be touched.

✓ Evidence of massage exists from records of many ancient cultures, making it the oldest of all the healing therapies.

✓ A universal preventive and curative treatment, massage is today practised in all corners of the world.

✓ Massage is a panacea for many problems of the human body, mind, and soul.

✓ There are two basic variants of massage – one based on the oriental view of the body and the other founded on our knowledge of anatomy and physiology.

Chapter 2

Before You Start

THIS CHAPTER LETS YOU KNOW WHAT YOU NEED to have in order to give a massage – both in terms of your attributes and in terms of fixtures and fittings. In fact, you could have absolutely nothing besides a pair of hands and still be capable of giving a very good massage. I'll talk about the ideal situation, and you can adapt any of the elements to suit your circumstances.

In this chapter...

✓ Am I qualified to do massage?

✓ Setting the scene

✓ Bare essentials

✓ At ease with yourself

✓ Oiling the wheels

✓ Tailoring massage to your partner's needs

✓ When it's all over

Am I qualified to do massage?

IT IS NOT MY INTENTION to talk about professional courses and qualifications here. I am going to help you decide whether you feel confident about giving a massage to someone you know fairly well, or at least about practising on them.

If at first your movements feel awkward don't worry, just keep trying. Remember, practice makes perfect. If it turns out that you and massage don't go hand in hand, there's no need to despair because there are ways of learning. To begin with, it might help if you do the mini-questionnaire in the box below.

MASSAGE SUITABILITY QUESTIONNAIRE

To score, give yourself one point for every time you answered "yes".

1. Do you feel comfortable with your own body?
2. Do you feel comfortable with other people's bodies?
3. Do you feel comfortable touching other people?
4. Do you empathize easily with others when they tell you of their physical or emotional pain?
5. Do you spare the time to talk over someone else's personal problems?
6. Do you have the ability to make others feel calm and peaceful?
7. Are you interested in helping people feel good?
8. Do you have good powers of concentration?
9. Are you generally a positive and encouraging person?
10. Are you able to keep relatively quiet or silent for an hour or more?

The higher your score, the easier you will find giving a really good massage, and you can have a go immediately – or at least when you've finished reading this book. If you have a low score, the chances are that like many people brought up in a culture where touch is taboo, you need to relax your inhibitions about it before proceeding with massage.

Before you start

Try some of the simple exercises below to help overcome any fear of touching you may have. Then we can move on and find out more about massage.

a Shake hands with the next person that you are introduced to

b Experiment and increase your touch sensitivity by feeling different textures. Close your eyes and feel, for example, silk, velvet, cotton, stainless steel, plastic, wood, and even jelly

c Try touching different bits of your body and feel how different they are: your face, palms of your hands, inside of your arm, your legs, and the soles of your feet

d Stroke a variety of different animals, for example a cat, dog, horse, rabbit, hamster

e Take off your shoes and socks and walk around your home registering the different textures of the carpets and floors

f Help an elderly person to cross the road and have a chat

g Make the effort to talk to someone you don't know very well – a neighbour, for example

h Volunteer to help at a nursery, a school, a hospital, or an old people's home

i Have a massage yourself and really let yourself relax

j Give yourself a massage – yes go on, have a try!

■ **Helping out at a local school,** *or anywhere you come into regular contact with people, can help you overcome your fear of touching.*

What other attributes do I need?

Once you feel happier about simply touching, there are a few other qualities that help when it comes to doing massage. The following list is adapted from a book written in 1934 by James Mennell, who was Head of the Department of Massage at St Thomas' Hospital, London. Although written many years ago in relation to professional massage therapists, the points are no less true today and apply equally if you are doing massage for a hobby.

1. No great power or muscular development is required; knack can affect more than force and skill replaces physical strength

2. Self assurance that is not aggressive is a valuable asset, just as timidity and lack of firmness may be the reverse

3. You should never appear to be in a hurry. While treating someone, the whole world should cease to exist except for that person. Entire concentration should be your aim and anything irrelevant to this one objective should be discouraged

4. In all treatments, even of the most vigorous type, the massage at the beginning and the end should be of the gentlest and most soothing nature, rising in crescendo and passing off in diminuendo

5. The comfort of the patient throughout the treatment is worthy of the closest study, but only slightly less so is that of the masseur. You cannot perform massage efficiently while in a cramped position, or in discomfort from any other cause

6. Human life, its functions and actions, are subdued to a natural rhythm. Our objective in massage being to restore function, it is obvious we must maintain and perhaps assist in the restoration of rhythm. Let us see to it then, that our movements are rhythmical

I would like to add one more quality to Mennell's invaluable list – that of perseverance.

Most people are able to give a massage but to be good you really need to persevere. I have noticed time and time again that people who are persistent, succeed.

When one idea doesn't seem to work out, try another. This applies to life in general as much as to massage!

Now that we have established that you are a patient, relaxed, giving, caring, intuitive, empathetic, confident, self-assured, tactful person who is able to focus on the task in hand, I can proceed to the next stage of the perfect massage. This involves the surroundings in which you intend to do your massage.

Setting the scene

THERE ARE MANY WAYS *to enhance your*
surroundings so they are perfect for massage; while some
of these are the icing on the cake, others are really essential
to make the massage an enjoyable and relaxing experience,
for example, making sure there are no disturbances.

■ **Phones** *can be a nuisance*
– take them off the hook.

Timing

As already touched on by Mennell, it is very important that you are not rushed when doing a massage. This means you need to pick a time during the day when you know that for the duration of the massage there is no danger of being disturbed. This is often easier said than done when you are doing the massage in your own home, but there are a number of steps you can take to maximize the chances of peace and quiet.

SIMPLE TIPS FOR AN UNDISTURBED MASSAGE

a Turn off pagers and mobile phones and turn down your answering machine

b Don't drink too much or have a heavy meal immediately before the massage

c Make sure you and your partner go to the bathroom before starting the session

d Ensure you don't have anything pressing to do immediately after the massage – it will be at the back of your mind during the massage and affect relaxation

e If applicable, ensure child care arrangements are taken care of so you can be at ease while giving or receiving the massage

f If there are other people in the house, tell them what you are doing and make sure they know not to disturb you; hang a "do not disturb" notice on the door

g Don't underestimate the time the massage will take; if it runs over the anticipated time, you might become jittery, which will be conveyed to your partner as you tense up (incidentally, your partner will be blissfully unaware of the time and that the peace is about to come to an abrupt end!)

There will be many times when your partner or someone else needs a massage when the ambience is far from perfect, for example, in a noisy office or in a hospital, but don't ever let that put you off.

Location

If you are practising massage on a partner with whom you are romantically involved it is perfectly acceptable to use the bedroom as a location; for anyone else, it is probably better to avoid this area as there might be confusion about intention. In any case, beds are not the perfect massage surfaces as they are usually too soft and yielding and at the wrong height. The only time I would recommend using a bed is if your partner is suffering from insomnia and you want to give him or her a soporific massage to encourage sleep.

Unless you have a hard, thigh-high surface – yes, you could use the kitchen table – the floor is your best bet. Use any room, apart from the kitchen or bathroom, and make sure you place enough padding down. If you are only doing a hand or foot massage or an on-site massage, your partner just needs to sit in a chair.

Ambience

Creating a perfect massage setting involves practically all your senses – touch is taken care of, but stimulating the senses of smell, sight, and hearing, and having an appropriate room temperature, can really enhance the effects of massage.

Smell

Smell is a powerful and evocative sense and is important for healing and relaxation. You can use incense, scented candles, and flowers to create a beautifully-smelling room. However, you do need to plan this because bombarding your partner's olfactory system with too many different smells will actually defeat the object.

You also need to think about the kind of atmosphere you want to create – sensual, calming, uplifting, or whatever – and choose the scents you use accordingly. Think about the oil you will be using and make sure the background perfume of the room doesn't clash. If your massage partner is a man, he probably won't respond as well to feminine, floral smells so stick to woody or citrus notes. Most importantly, make sure you only use natural products, as synthetic perfumes won't have the same therapeutic effects.

MOOD-ENHANCING
SCENTED CANDLES

Sight

You might think that there is not much point in trying to stimulate your partner's visual senses as he or she will probably have closed eyes during the course of the massage. That's true, but for initial impressions, and to lull your partner into a relaxed state, it can really help. It will also help you, the person doing the massage, to get into the right mood. Keep lighting low, and draw the curtains or blinds if you are doing the massage during the day. Candlelight really adds to the atmosphere – there's something about the flickering flame and low light that is extremely relaxing.

Try to introduce warm colours – reds, oranges, yellows. Even a bunch of flowers in the right hues can give the impression of warmth; you could use dried or artificial flowers, if necessary.

A "WARM" FLORAL ARRANGEMENT

Hearing

As far as sound goes, this is very much a personal thing. You and your partner may prefer absolute silence so there are no distractions. On the other hand, that may not be possible and you might need to mask your neighbours' noises or the traffic outside. Choose from musical – something soothing and calming and not too avant-garde – or non-musical sounds, such as wind chimes or other Eastern sounds, or natural sounds, such as water running or birds singing.

Temperature

It is very important to get the temperature of the room right for your partner. Remember that he or she will be naked, or almost naked, with only a towel for warmth, while you are fully clothed, albeit dressed lightly for the job. Also, the person receiving the massage is lying still for up to an hour and a half and will therefore feel the cold much more than you. Your partner won't be able to relax fully if he or she is cold. In winter, make sure the central heating is on; for additional warmth, a small electric heated pad under your partner's back or a hot water bottle under their feet will feel really good. Use heated towels or blankets to add a real touch of luxury.

Although you want the room to be warm during the massage, it mustn't get stuffy; make sure you have a window open slightly to let in fresh air.

Bare essentials

I WILL NOW TOUCH on the basic equipment that you will need for a massage. The most important thing you need, however obvious it might seem, is a place for your partner to lie down in comfort.

A firm base

Your partner should lie on a firm, padded surface. I like to massage on the floor for several reasons: everyone can find enough space on the floor, so there is no excuse not to massage, and you can practise just about anywhere at any time. I also like the fact that the person being massaged can spread out and that there is plenty of space around me. Pad the floor with a piece of foam rubber, a futon mattress, or a couple of thick blankets, and kneel on something soft, to avoid sore, calloused knees. Use cushions and rolled-up towels to make your partner is comfortable.

INEXPENSIVE PADDING DEVICES

Some people don't like the sensation of lying face down – a primitive fear of suffocation – and may not be very relaxed in this position. Try putting a rolled-up towel under the top of your partner's chest to make a bit of breathing space, or ask your partner to put their head to one side.

What else could I use?

If you suffer from painful knees or a bad back, you will probably find it easier to work at a table. It should reach about the top of your thighs, and it must be sturdy enough to hold your partner's weight and your weight as you lean into the massage. Pad the table with foam rubber or some blankets.

■ **Whether it be on the floor or on a table,** *your partner needs a firm base as a platform for the massage.*

If you see yourself becoming serious about massage, it's worth investing in a portable massage table. They are about 2 m (6½ ft) long by 60 cm (24 in) wide and roughly the height of a normal table. You can buy one from a specialist outlet (see Appendix).

Make sure you have a couple of towels or blankets available to keep your partner warm and to preserve his or her dignity – only expose the parts of the body you are working on. Many people feel vulnerable enough just lying down, so being naked as well can increase feelings of insecurity and you must respect this – even in someone you know very well.

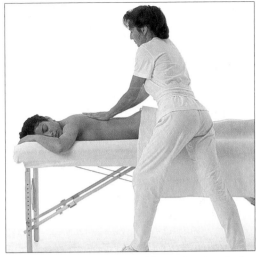

■ **A portable massage table** *makes the ideal base. Just be prepared to make lots of house calls!*

At ease with yourself

IN ORDER TO MASSAGE really successfully, your own personal comfort is as important as that of your partner. If you are comfortable you can really concentrate on your partner, but if you have the odd ache or pain, you are more liable to focus on yourself. When done correctly, massage is as relaxing to give as to receive.

Your posture

Good posture is absolutely essential if you want to avoid backache and fatigue. Make sure that your partner is close enough so that you don't have to stretch to reach his or her body. Always face in the direction of your massage strokes – face your partner's head when working up the body, and face across the body when working across.

Never stay in one position for long: move your whole body as you move your hands around your partner's body.

If you are working on a table, keep your feet about 30 cm (12 in) apart and bend your knees so that you can lean into the strokes. Your feet should be pointing in the same direction as your strokes.

If you are working on the floor, kneel with your knees apart or, if you find it more comfortable, have one knee on the floor and the other one up with your foot on the floor. To distribute your weight evenly, shift from one foot to the other if you are standing, or from one knee to the other if you are on the floor.

Keep your back as straight as possible and use your body weight to apply depth and pressure; brute force will only tire you and will hurt your partner. Using your body correctly will help the massage to flow and leave you feeling refreshed rather than tired.

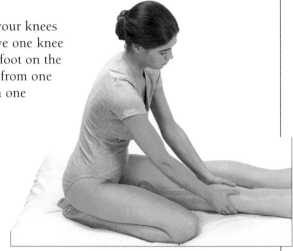

■ **Distribute your weight evenly** *with your knees apart, and keep your back as straight as possible.*

Your breathing

I think of massage as active meditation: even if you are feeling stressed or rushed, once you start to give a massage, these irritations disappear. The soothing, hypnotic strokes not only calm your partner but will also be relaxing for you. Centre yourself and focus on your partner. Make a conscious effort to breathe slowly and deeply throughout the massage; really be aware of your breathing and keep it flowing at a consistent pace. It is not uncommon for a person to hold his or her breath when they are trying to concentrate, and I frequently have to remind new students to breathe properly when they are learning to massage. To check whether you are breathing properly, put one hand on your chest and the other on your stomach and breathe normally. Which hand moves?
   It should be the one on your stomach.

To practise breathing correctly, sit or lie comfortably and put your hands on your abdomen. Breathe in for a count of three and feel your abdomen expand. Then breathe out for a count of four, and feel your abdomen contract.

Your clothes

Wear loose-fitting clothes – but not so loose that they fall onto your partner – made of natural, washable fabrics. If you are a woman, trousers or shorts are obviously more practical than a skirt or dress. You need flat shoes, or preferably go barefoot. Remove any jewellery before doing a massage: rings can scratch the skin, and bracelets or necklaces may jangle or trail over it, which can be irritating. Watches can make irritating noises. You can keep your earrings on (but if your partner is wearing any, remove them if you are going to do a face, neck, or head massage).

YOUR HANDS

You can compare your hands to a tradesman's tools – so it is important that you keep them in good, working order. Your massage tools need to be strong, flexible, relaxed, and sensitive. To keep your hands strong and supple try the following exercises.

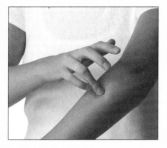

a Drum your fingers

Drum your fingers up and down your forearm to improve their strength and flexibility. Vary the depth and speed of the movement, and try not to tense your hands. Continue for about 30 seconds.

b Press and hold

For greater strength and flexibility, place your hands together in a praying position, then lift your elbows up so that your palms separate. Press your fingers against each other and hold for 10 seconds.

c Squeeze a ball

Strengthen your hands by holding a small rubber ball in one hand, and repeatedly squeeze and relax your fingers. Continue for about 30 seconds, then repeat the exercise with your other hand.

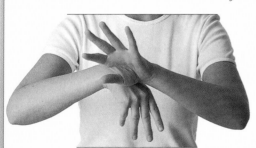

d Roll and stretch

Improve flexibility by placing one wrist on the other, with your elbows sticking out. Roll your hands around one another in a large circle, stretching your fingertips. Continue for 10 seconds.

e Heighten sensitivity

Hold your hands close together without touching. Draw them 5 cm (2 in) apart, then back until they almost touch. Repeat, drawing your hands further apart until they are 25 cm (10 in) apart. You may experience a warm or tingling sensation.

Oiling the wheels

USING OIL IN MASSAGE helps your hands glide over your partner's skin and generally enhances the whole experience. I have devoted a whole chapter to the subject of aromatic oils (Chapter 4) so I will only touch on the practical aspects of using oils here.

Never pour the oil directly onto your partner's body as it will be cold. Pour about a teaspoon of your chosen, diluted oil into the palm of one hand and rub your hands together to warm it. Then stroke the oil onto your partner's body. During the massage, one hand should always remain in contact with your partner's body, so when you need to use more oil, follow the sequence below.

1 Pour a little oil onto the back of one of your hands, still stroking slowly with this hand.

2 Continue stroking your partner and place your free hand lightly on top of the one doing the massage.

3 Stroke the oil onto the body from the back of your hand, and continue your massage.

Keep your oil in a plastic bottle with a narrow opening so that it is easy to add a few drops of oil during the massage, and so that you don't spill much if you accidentally knock the bottle over.

While doing a massage, you should always keep the top of your oil bottle off. If you keep it screwed on, you will have to interrupt your flow to open the top each time your hands dry up and they need replenishment.

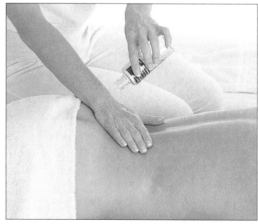

■ **If you find you need more oil,** *drizzle it on the back of one hand and stroke it on with the other.*

Two final tips

Make sure to keep your bottle of oil within easy reach throughout the course of the massage to minimize disruption. And don't forget to replace the top and return the oil to its storage place when you've finished the massage.

One of the side-effects of using oil is that a lot of it ends up on the towels. I've experimented with different methods of removing this and have found that adding about a quarter of a cup of washing soda to the powder you normally use in your washing machine helps.

BOTTLES OF OILS

Tailoring massage to your partner's needs

HOW DO YOU DECIDE what sort of massage to give your partner? Although there are no real rules and every single massage is unique, there are a few things you should know about your partner before starting. I have compiled a short checklist of questions that should go through your mind before you start the massage (see box overleaf).

So many variations

You can tailor a massage to suit any need: even a single technique can be stimulating or soothing, depending on how you do it. The fun of massage is experimenting. You need never do the same massage twice – your feelings and needs will change, as will your partner's, so the combinations are infinite. There is more on this topic in the next chapter where I show you the rudiments of a massage sequence.

Trivia...
The importance of being guided by your partner's needs are wittily illustrated by this epigram by J.B. Morton:
Bruised by the masseur's final whack
The patient lay without a sound
Then coming to, he hit him back
Now masseur's in the cold, cold ground.

WHAT YOU SHOULD ASK YOURSELF OR YOUR PARTNER BEFORE GIVING A MASSAGE

Some of these questions will be answered by just looking at your partner or by your previous knowledge of him or her. Others require you to pause for thought before you start. And others you will need to verbalize.

1. Are there any obvious physical problem areas, e.g., injury, pain, swelling, etc? (See Chapter 3 for a list of medical questions you should ask before massage.)

2. Are there any obvious emotional problems, e.g., stress, depression, anxiety, etc?

3. Is the massage solely for relaxation or pampering?

4. Are you doing the massage for a specific, therapeutic end?

5. What body characteristics does your partner have – muscular, hairy, skinny, hunched up, flabby, well-toned, confident, low self-esteem, bony, frail, etc. You may have to adapt your massage accordingly

6. What does your partner have to do after the massage, i.e., can he or she be in a soporific state or is it in the middle of a working day and your partner needs to return to work alert?

7. Does your partner have any likes or dislikes as regards the aromas of essential oils? Is he or she allergic to any oils or do they suffer from a nut allergy?

8. Does your partner have any body piercings, old scars, or burns? Ask if the areas are tender, and avoid them if so

9. Is your partner very hairy? If so, you will probably need to use more oil – or you could try using talcum powder

10. Does your partner have any views about the kind of massage he or she wants?

Don't use talcum powder if your partner is allergic to it – use a cornstarch-based powder instead.

When it's all over

AT THE END OF A MASSAGE, I like to give a client time to "come round"; I cover him or her with a towel and leave the room for 5 or 10 minutes, which gives them a chance to adjust to being back in the real world and get dressed in privacy.

Some people, particularly the elderly (or anyone after a long massage), may feel slightly light-headed after lying down. Others might have trouble getting off a high table or couch. If you think either situation is possible, stay with your partner until he or she is safely sitting upright or standing.

If you have done a massage on only part of the body or through clothes, you need to allow your partner a similar period for re-orientation. Both giver and receiver are often thirsty after a massage so have a couple of glasses of water ready.

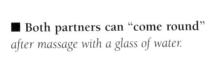

■ **Both partners can "come round"** *after massage with a glass of water.*

A simple summary

✔ Every massage is a unique experience.

✔ Comfortable working conditions and peace of mind are essential ingredients for a good massage.

✔ Little details and extra touches in the surroundings can enhance any massage.

✔ You can tailor your massage technique to suit different circumstances.

✔ Finishing off a massage in a sympathetic way is just as important as the actual massage routine, and it's a good idea to have some water handy to cool down and combat thirst.

Chapter 3

Having a Go

Now that you know you possess the right characteristics to be a masseur, and you've spent time (but not too much money) getting the basic equipment and creating the right ambience, you've reached the point of no return – you are actually going to do a massage! In this chapter, I'll take you very quickly through the basic moves and show you a swift massage sequence. The real nitty-gritty of massage – where I go into great detail about every move and part of the body – is dealt with in Parts Two and Three. This is simply a taster, or sampler, to whet your appetite and to give you confidence to tackle what's to follow.

In this chapter...

✓ A simple example
✓ Making it up as you go along
✓ Relief at your fingertips
✓ Variations on a theme
✓ When to say no

A simple example

ALTHOUGH I'VE SAID MANY TIMES that every massage is individual, you will find there is often a pattern to the sequence of movements. After a gentle hold to introduce your touch, your massage will start with light, soothing strokes. Deeper movements, such as kneading and pressures, are then gradually introduced. Use stroking as a link action, and finish off the massage with it if you want a relaxing end. If your partner needs to be alert, finish with percussion.

I think it's best to start by massaging your partner's back: it's a large area, which makes it easier, and most of the massage techniques can be used on it. Almost everyone loves having their backs massaged so if you start on this area, you'll get favourable comments, which is very encouraging.

A basic massage sequence

Every massage is different, but there is often a pattern to the sequence of movements. A sample massage sequence might proceed as follows:

1 Holds: use a simple, positive hold to begin your massage. This makes initial contact with your partner, and says hello with your hands.

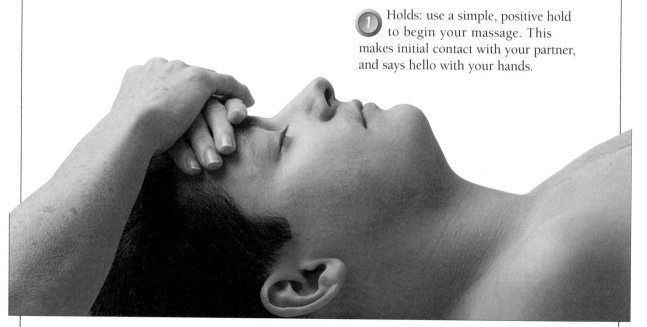

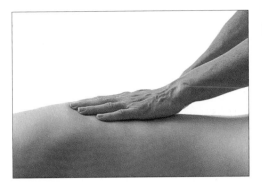

2 Applying the oil: use light strokes to apply the oil. Keep your hands relaxed. When you need more oil, ensure that contact with the body is not lost.

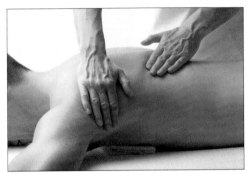

3 Deeper strokes: gradually increase the depth of your strokes. Mould your hands around the contours of the body, both to soothe and to feel for any tension.

4 Kneading: knead the area to warm it up. This deeper movement will also stretch the tissue, and relieve muscle tightness and congestion.

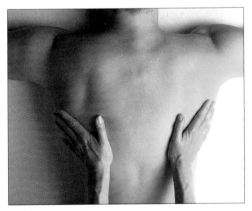

5 Linking strokes: stroke the body again, both as a linking movement and to relax the area and encourage the elimination of waste products.

6 Stronger movements: now that the area is relaxed, introduce deeper movements such as raking, knuckle strokes, circular pressures, or skin rolling.

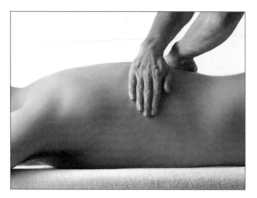

7 Strokes: relax the body after deep massage work by rhythmically stroking your hands over the whole area. Use the strokes to connect different parts of the body with each other.

8 Feather stroking: use very light, superficial feather strokes with your fingertips. These will lift away the last vestiges of tension, and let your partner know that the massage is nearly over.

9 Percussion: say goodbye, either by using brisk, stimulating percussion movements to wake up your partner, or by finishing the massage as you started, and using calm, positive holds.

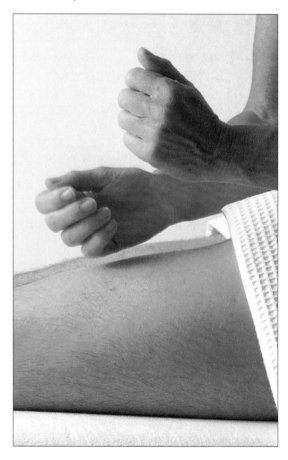

If your hands and arms feel really tired or sore after doing a massage, soak them in cold water for a few minutes. It really works.

Making it up as you go along

THE SECRET OF A GOOD MASSAGE *is not to be bound by rules; in fact there are very few rules, simply guidelines (see tips below). Massage is about communication without words – in fact your hands are doing the talking. Use them to say hello, to listen to the needs of your partner's body, and to say goodbye. I tell my students that whenever they are not using one of their hands in active massage, it should be placed on the client just to "listen".*

Tips for the perfect massage

Whether you rigorously follow a sequence or use your own initiative, the following do's and don'ts will help make your massage a good experience:

(a) The most important element of a massage is rhythm. A rhythmic massage will send waves of relaxation through your partner's body

(b) Massage should be pleasurable. Ask your partner to tell you if anything you do is unpleasant or painful

(c) Mould your hands to the contours of your partner's body; imagine you are sculpting the body into its perfect shape

(d) Practise the movements on yourself to see how they feel

(e) Vary your pressure from very light to very strong. It should be lighter over bony areas and firmer over large muscles. Don't be afraid to apply deep pressure – it can feel really good

(f) Never use force during your massage; simply use the weight of your body to apply pressure

(g) Concentrate on the massage and restrict talking to the necessary minimum. Your massage will be more successful if both you and your partner focus on touch sensations

■ **Not all men are blessed** *with a physique with the anatomical and physiological perfection of Michelangelo's David, but that shouldn't stop you from trying to sculpt your partner's body into the ideal form.*

8   Don't worry if your first movements seem clumsy. All touch feels good, and if you keep practising, your massage will become flowing and confident

9   It's easier to learn and practise on a partner: try the techniques out on each other and make sure you give and receive feedback about what feels good and what doesn't

10 You need to be totally relaxed, so don't try too hard. If in doubt about what to do next, just stroke

NO-GO MOVES AND AREAS

There are various moves and parts of the body that should be avoided when doing massage on a perfectly healthy person. While most of these might be common sense, I thought it worthwhile to outline them briefly.

Moves

If ever you feel any resistance to a move you are making, stop immediately. Never make sudden, jerky movements, and do not do the following:

- Twist or pull the neck (it's alright to gently stroke the head to the side so the chin moves sideways and down towards the shoulder)
- Crack a joint
- Press heavily on bones
- Overstretch a joint

Areas

Be very gentle if massaging in any of the following areas because they may be tender as the nerves are near the surface:

- Throat and the front of the neck
- Side of the neck
- Top of the jawbone just below the ear
- Eyeball
- Armpit
- Groin
- Back of the knee

One of my clients coined the phrase "grateful" pain and I was so taken with its aptness that it has become one of my pet phrases. It perfectly illustrates the difference between acceptable and non-acceptable pain (the "ouch, that really hurts" variety).

A TICKLISH PROBLEM

Many people, particularly children, are incredibly ticklish and this can have serious consequences for the masseur. The problem is usually caused by nervous tension and it often helps to increase your pressure in that area and persevere. Fast finger movements can tickle, so flatten your hand, reduce the tempo, and increase the depth. If this doesn't help, massage the surrounding

■ **Don't be put off** *if children giggle and wriggle about – small adjustments may help the problem.*

area first and when this is relaxed you can return to the ticklish area, which should now be less sensitive. Alternatively, ask your partner to start massaging the area – as you can seldom tickle yourself – and then you take over. Massaging under water often relieves the problem, but this is not usually a practical solution. If all else fails, you will simply have to avoid the area.

Be adaptable

It is important to be flexible – mentally as well as physically – so that you can respond to your partner's needs. If you find areas that feel stiff or taut, you need to give them extra attention. If your partner seems stressed or anxious, you should concentrate more on relaxing, soothing strokes. The next time you give a massage, your partner's problems may be different or in different places, so you will have to improvise.

I always tell my students that the person having the massage is in charge. Ask the receiver to tell you if there is anything that he or she doesn't like or that hurts; conversely, ask what is particularly good and you can do more of that.

Your technique and repertoire of strokes will increase dramatically the more people you try them out on. It will boost your confidence in your ability if you massage a range of people of different ages, with different body types and personalities, and with different problems. As with most things in life, variety is all important.

Go out and seek as many willing massage guinea pigs as possible. Your massage skills will improve immeasurably with practice.

Relief at your fingertips

TO SHOW YOU THAT MASSAGE *can be done anywhere, at any time, try this quick, refreshing massage. You don't need a massage table or any other special equipment – just grab a partner and a chair and get to it!*

Ten minutes to happiness

Allow about 1 minute for each step that follows, and in no more than 10 minutes your partner will be feeling thoroughly relaxed and energized.

1 Rest your forearms on the fleshy area on the top of the shoulders. Lean forwards so that your weight gently eases the shoulders down. This helps to break down some of the tension that makes the shoulders hunch up.

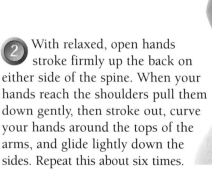

It is important that you press down on the muscles and not on the bone, which can be painful.

2 With relaxed, open hands stroke firmly up the back on either side of the spine. When your hands reach the shoulders pull them down gently, then stroke out, curve your hands around the tops of the arms, and glide lightly down the sides. Repeat this about six times.

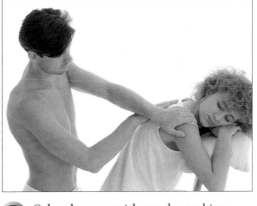

3 Knead the muscle across the top of the shoulders. Use both your hands on one side, alternately squeezing and releasing the flesh. Work on both shoulders and out across the tops of the arms. It is a warming movement that helps to relax taut muscles.

4 Calm the area with gentle stroking. Repeat the initial T-stroke (step 2), then do extra work around the shoulders. Stroke in a circle over the top of one shoulder and around the top of the arm, with one hand following the other. Then work on the opposite shoulder.

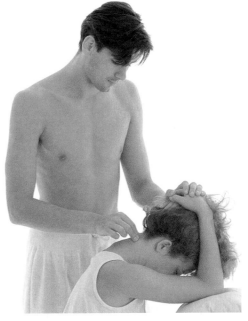

5 Place your thumbs on either side of the spine and lean onto them. Hold the pressure for a few seconds, then glide up about a little and repeat, working upwards from the lower back. When you reach the top, work out across the shoulders and around the shoulder blades.

6 Support the head with one hand and massage the back of the neck with the other. Stroke up the neck, then apply circular pressures. Work thoroughly on the neck and around the base of the skull.

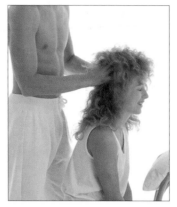

7 Now use both hands to make circular pressures all over the head. Do not pull the hair, but try to move the scalp around. Massage all over the head, around the ears, and on the temples and forehead.

8 Rub briskly back and forth all over the head with your fingertips. This stimulating movement relieves tension and leaves your partner feeling alert and refreshed.

9 With open, very relaxed hands hack across the shoulders and upper back. This is an upward springy movement, with your hands rhythmically bouncing up and down. The effect is lively and simulating.

Avoid the kidney area, and don't strike the spine when hacking the shoulders and upper back.

10 Soothe the whole of the back by repeating the initial stroking, then flow into the cat stroke. Stroke down the back with one hand following the other in a lazy, monotonous rhythm. Finish with the feather stroke, using just your fingertips to stroke very lightly down the back.

Variations on a theme

SO, YOU NOW HAVE A MINI-MASSAGE sequence under your belt. You will learn more about individual strokes and how to combine them together in Parts 2 and 3 of the book. However, in addition to the endless combinations and routines you will find there, I would briefly like to touch on other ways of achieving infinite variety.

You can make two sequences that use the same strokes feel completely different to your partner simply by altering the speed of your touch: fast, brisk movements are invigorating, whereas slow, gentle movements are relaxing. The strength of your strokes can also produce different effects: use deep pressing moves where you feel tightness or tension in fleshy, muscular parts of the body and use a less firm touch in bony areas and parts of the body that are less fleshy.

Trivia...

A few years ago a prototype of a mechanical massage machine was built, designed to deliver a soothing massage to the back and legs without human intervention. A robot arm travelled up and down the body, gently lowering the massaging "head" to pummel the flesh. The pressure and type of massage were programmable, and safety systems ensured that the robot didn't become too rough!

Outside assistance

Another way to vary your massage is to incorporate one of the hundreds of massage gadgets that are available. You might question why you should spend money on devices when your beautifully engineered hands come free, but these items do have a place in the massage kit. They are fun to use and you can use them on yourself, so if there's no-one else around when you're in desperate need of a massage they are the perfect solution. They can help if your hands are tired. They can change the rhythm of the massage. Most of all – they feel good (although never as good as a pair of hands).

■ **Massage gadgets can come in handy** *when you want a different type of touch, or when there's no-one else around to reach those hard to get at places.*

When to say no

ALTHOUGH FOR 99 PER CENT *of the time massage is of enormous benefit, there are occasions when it is simply not advisable – technically, known as* **contraindications** *(see chart opposite). While most of these conditions will be obvious, you may have to ask your partner about others, for example infectious diseases or tumours.*

DEFINITION

The medical term for a condition that precludes a particular procedure or treatment is **contraindication**. *The literal translation is "indicated against".*

If you are ever in doubt, don't massage – even if your partner's symptoms don't fall into the list opposite.

The most obvious contraindication to massage is aversion to touch. Some people really do not like being touched and even the thought of being given a massage will make them anxious.

What about ill-health?

Ill-health in itself is not a contraindication to massage; in fact, massage is enormously beneficial for people who are seriously ill, even those with a terminal illness. However, certain types of massage are not suitable in these circumstances, so get the doctor's consent and adapt your routine if necessary.

Cancer patients can benefit from massage but you must consult their doctor first, as some areas may need to be avoided. The massage recommended for these patients is usually very gentle.

INTERNET

www.miami.edu/ touch-research

Touch Research Institute's web site is a fascinating mine of information about past, present, and future research, that will persuade anyone who has doubts about the therapeutic benefits of massage otherwise after just a few minutes scouring the site.

■ **Massage can have beneficial effects** *under almost all circumstances (but be sure to check for contraindications first).*

When not to massage

Generally speaking, you should never massage someone with the following contraindications without first obtaining the advice of their doctor:

- Any serious medical condition
- A high temperature

- An infection or contagious disease
- A bleeding or clotting disorder, or the taking of anticlotting medication

Take care if someone has any of the following conditions. Avoid the "local" areas, and massage an unaffected area instead:

- Oedema (swelling), acute inflammation, or bruising
- An open wound, recent scar tissue, skin infection, weeping skin condition, broken skin, or rash
- Broken bones
- Acute back pain, especially if pain shoots down the legs or arms when you massage the back or neck
- Undiagnosed lumps
- Breathlessness

- Hernia
- Varicose veins, phlebitis, or thrombosis (as thrombosis is difficult to recognize, show caution if there is vague aching in one leg and tell your partner to see a doctor)
- Pregnancy – massage very gently in the first 3 months
- Chronic fatigue syndrome – keep your movements gentle

A simple summary

✓ Every massage is unique and different.

✓ Massage can be simplicity itself using only stroking movements, or you can incorporate many different techniques.

✓ You, the giver, need to be guided by the receiver so the right type of massage is achieved.

✓ Gadgets can occasionally be used if you want the massage to feel different.

✓ Certain medical conditions preclude the use of massage.

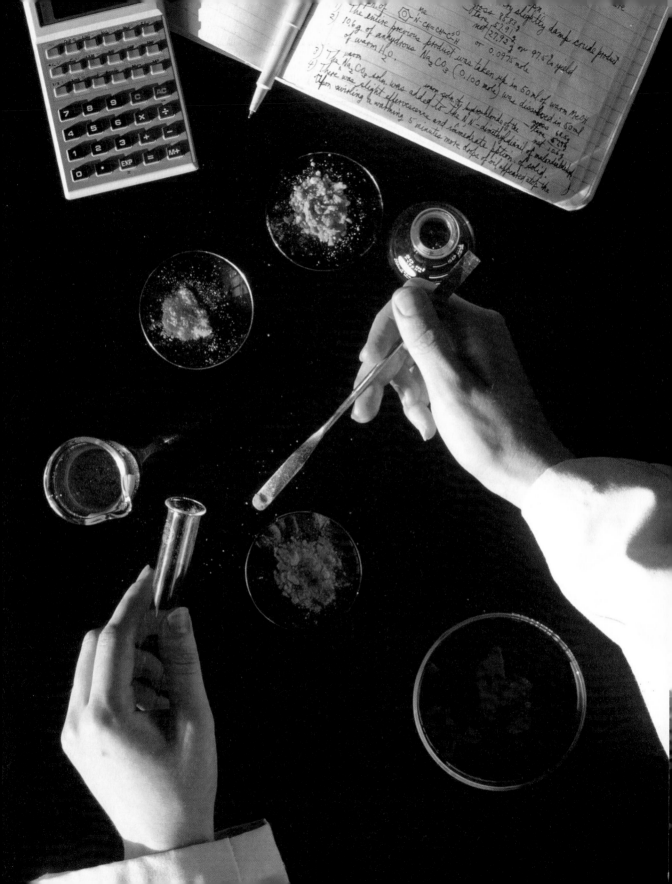

Chapter 4

Aromatherapy

AROMA IS DERIVED FROM THE GREEK WORD FOR SPICE (scent) and "therapy" means treatment, so aromatherapy literally means curative treatment using scent. There are many essential oils, derived from the flowers, leaves, and other parts of plants, each with a different scent and with different beneficial effects. When combined with massage, the benefits are increased. The best way to find out about the benefits of aromatherapy massage is to give it a go. Read through the effects of different oils, smell a few samples, and get massaging.

In this chapter...

✓ The essence of life
✓ A catalogue of scents
✓ Using and looking after oils
✓ Perfumed massage
✓ Scenting trouble

THANKFULLY, ESSENTIAL OILS CAN NOW BE BOUGHT READY-MADE – ALL YOU HAVE TO DO IS MASSAGE THEM IN!

The essence of life

AROMATIC PLANTS *and oils have been valued throughout history for their therapeutic properties. Many powers have been attributed to fragrant plants and their extracts, and they have been used in the pursuit of happiness and health in medicine, religion, magic, and cosmetics for centuries. In ancient Egypt, herbal oils were used to embalm the dead, and there are references to oils such as myrrh and frankincense in the Bible. In India, literature dating back to around 2000 BC lists and recommends around 700 different plants, and*

■ **This lithograph** *shows the Hindu deity Lakshmi performing a scented massage on her counterpart Vishnu.*

they are used to this day in some forms of traditional Indian systems of medicine.

Throughout history there are references to scents being used to improve or maintain good health. For example, incense was used to ward off evil spirits; herbs were strewn on floors to perfume the house and prevent disease; burning herbs and spices were used to fumigate streets and homes to fight infection; the Greeks are even said to have scented pigeons' wings so that when they flew around a room the perfume would be dispensed!

Healing powers

The term "aromatherapy" was coined by a French chemist, Gattefosse, in the 1920s. Several years earlier he had badly burned his hand while working in his laboratory. Absent-mindedly, he put his burnt hand into the nearest liquid, a bowl of lavender oil. To his amazement, the pain diminished and the burn healed much faster than he expected, leaving no scar. Gattefosse was prompted to study the therapeutic effects of plant oils, and his work on the subject was published in 1936.

During World Wars I and II, an army surgeon named Jean Valnet used essential oils to treat battle wounds, burns, and psychiatric problems. In the 1960s, he published his first book, *Aromatherapie*, which became a classic. From the 1960s onwards, doctors in France began to use essential oils alongside conventional medicine. Other parts of the Western world were not so enlightened, and it is only very recently that aromatherapy has gained any degree of respect from the medical profession as a healing treatment. An Austrian biochemist, Marguerite Maury, was responsible for bringing aromatherapy to the UK, and she rekindled the ancient link between aromatherapy and massage.

The power of scent

Of all the senses, smell has the most sensitive receptors, and smell is the most memorable and evocative of sensations. A whiff of a particular aroma, pleasant or unpleasant, is all it takes to rekindle all types of memories. This is because when you smell an aroma, an impulse travels immediately down the *olfactory nerve* to the limbic system – a tiny part of the brain where emotion, hunger, memory, and other responses are evoked.

We all use aromatherapy without realizing it. We use smells to revitalize ourselves and enrich our lives: we give bunches of flowers as gifts; we pamper ourselves with a favourite cologne or soak in a scented bath; and we are invigorated by the fresh smell of the sea.

> **DEFINITION**
>
> The nerve that conveys smell sensations from the nose to the brain is called the **olfactory nerve**. *It is one of a pair.*

■ **Inhaling the smell of the sea** *is one of life's simple pleasures, and unbeknown to many, is actually a rudimentary form of aromatherapy.*

Testing, testing

Perception of scent varies – our reaction to scent is emotionally loaded and highly subjective. In aromatherapy, the aim is to discover an aroma that you like and will enjoy using. If you don't like the smell of a certain oil, try mixing (blending) different oils to create an aroma you do like. I find that the easiest way to learn about a new essential oil is to put a drop on a strip of blotting paper, then smell it, and write down your impressions. Is the aroma light and fresh, or heavy and warm? Is it flowery, powdery, woody, medicinal, or spicy? Do you like it or dislike it? Does the aroma hit you or is it subtle and difficult to distinguish? Smell it again every few hours and you will see how the scent changes as the oils evaporate. (Be careful not to expose your smelling strips to extreme heat or flame when disposing of them, as essential oils are highly flammable.)

As you will discover from smelling the oils individually, some are very strong and the general rule when blending is that a little is best. In aromatherapy massage, a lighter blend will often smell better, and therefore be more effective, than a stronger blend.

In many ways essential oil is a misnomer, as there is usually nothing oily about it. Most essential oils have the consistency of alcohol and evaporate (e.g., lavender and rosemary), but some are thicker and stickier (e.g., sandalwood and myrrh). Some people call essential oils ethered oils, which is a good name as when left in the open air most will evaporate and leave no trace.

A catalogue of scents

ALTHOUGH THERE ARE HUNDREDS of essential oils available, most people tend to stick to a select few. The important thing is to choose an aroma that is appropriate for the situation and, if you are looking for a therapeutic end, select a suitable combination of oils. Most importantly, you should use oils that both you and your partner like the smell of, as any benefits will be lost if you end up with a headache or feeling queasy. Some of the "heavier" scents, such as frankincense and jasmine, should be used in small quantities.

Trivia...

The cost of an essential oil is a reflection of the amount of raw material required and its availability. For example, it takes about 200 kg (440 lb) of rose petals to produce 1 litre (2.1 pt) of rose oil, whereas 200 kg of lavender flowers yield about 6 litres (12.6 pt) of lavender oil. So, lavender oil is much cheaper to buy.

INTERNET

www.the-ispa.org

The International Society of Professional Aromatherapists (ISPA) is one of the largest and longest standing associations for professional aromatherapists with a worldwide membership. The ISPA publishes a quarterly journal, Aromatherapy World, and organizes events and conferences. The web site also contains a directory of accredited training schools.

The chart opposite shows some of the most commonly used essential oils, along with information about their aroma and therapeutic properties.

When buying essential oils, make sure that you are getting the real thing and not some synthetic approximation. Check the labelling. Some expensive oils, such as jasmine and rose, are sometimes diluted with another oil to make them cheaper.

OILS AND THEIR PROPERTIES

This list provides an overview of some of the most frequently used essential oils, along with their scent and some of their potential uses. Many oils share some of the same therapeutic qualities, so you can often choose an oil with a smell you like.

Essential oil	Scent	Therapeutic properties
Bergamot	Fresh, lively, citrus	Calming; antidepressant; antiseptic
Clary sage	Warm, nutty, herbaceous	Antidepressant; euphoric; antispasmodic; analgesic; anti-inflammatory
Eucalyptus	Camphor-like, sweet, woody	Expectorant; antiseptic; antibacterial; antiviral; analgesic; anti-inflammatory; fever reducing
Frankincense	Balsamic, rich, sweet, warm	Rejuvenating; calming, induces deep breathing; anti-inflammatory and antiseptic; healing to skin and respiratory tract
Geranium	Sweet, floral, herbaceous	Antidepressant; relaxing; antibacterial; insecticidal
Jasmine	Sweet, heady, rich, floral	Uplifting and stimulating; antidepressant; aphrodisiac
Juniper	Woody, fresh, sweet	Purifying; diuretic; stimulating; analgesic; antiseptic; antiviral
Lavender	Sweet, floral, herbaceous	Sedative and calming; analgesic; antispasmodic; antiseptic
Marjoram	Camphor-like, sweet, warm	Sedative; comforting; warming; restoring; soothing; decongestant; antiseptic; antispasmodic; antifungal
Melissa	Soft, lemony, herby	Calming and uplifting; antidepressant; stress relieving; antiseptic; antiviral; antifungal
Neroli	Intensely sweet, rich, floral	Sedative; soothing for mature and sensitive skins
Peppermint	Minty, grass-like, balsamic, fresh	Stimulating; antispasmodic; decongestant
Pettigrain	Floral, citrus, woody	Relaxing; stress relieving; soothing
Roman chamomile	Pungent, herbaceous, fruity	Calming and soothing; antispasmodic; antiseptic
Rose	Intense, lingering, floral	Antidepressant; stimulating; antihistamine; antiseptic
Rosemary	Piercing, fresh, herbaceous	Stimulating; decongestant; antifungal; antibacterial
Sandalwood	Sweet, woody, balsamic	Calming; antidepressant; decongestant; antiseptic; diuretic; anti-inflammatory
Tea tree	Medicinal, spicy, fresh	Antibacterial; antiviral; antifungal; antiseptic

Using and looking after oils

NOW YOU KNOW A BIT ABOUT THE SMELLS and effects of the most commonly used essential oils, you need to supplement this knowledge with some practical bits and pieces. In this section, I will explain how to combine essential oils with carrier oils so that they are in the right form for massage. I will touch on other ways in which essential oils can be used other than for massage, and discuss storage and safety. It is important that you read this section so that you can make the best use of your oils and maximize their shelf life. Essential oils are expensive but will last a long time if given the right care and attention.

Carrier oils

Like carrier pigeons, these oils are used as a means of delivering a message – the message is transmitted through a massage. As essential oils should never be put directly onto the skin, carrier oils are used to dilute the potency of the concentrated essential oils; their beneficial effects can then be spread all over the body. The carrier oils contain vitamins, proteins, and minerals, which makes them highly effective moisturizers. Examples of commonly used carrier oils include apricot kernel oil, soya oil, and sweet almond oil.

■ **Just as carrier pigeons** *transport messages, carrier oils transport massages.*

Blending oils

One of the great treats about blending oils is that you can create your own mixture according to the scents you prefer. It is very important that both you and your partner like the smell of the oil you are using; if you use something too heavy or cloying it could leave you or your partner with a headache, and the benefits of the massage will be reduced. Create what Marguerite Maury called an "individual prescription". First decide what effect you are hoping to achieve: do you want the aroma to sedate or revive, to energize or to calm? Do you want to use oils for their therapeutic properties or simply to pamper? Once you have decided, refer to the chart of oils on page 69 and make a list that is suited to your requirements. Select two or three from your list and make a light blend (see chart opposite). A weak blend usually smells better and is more effective than a stronger one.

SIMPLE BLENDING GUIDE

Use this guide to achieve the safest dilution of essential oils for a balanced fragrance and maximum therapeutic benefit. Aromatherapists refer to normal and low dilutions in percentage terms and this chart shows you how to work out how much essential oil you need to add to the carrier oil.

Normal dilution of 2 per cent
This dilution is suitable for most skin types and most people. For every 10 ml of carrier oil add up to four drops of essential oil; if you are making up 20 ml, you add up to eight drops of essential oil.

Low dilution of 1 per cent
Use this dilution for sensitive skin, and during pregnancy.
For every 10 ml of carrier oil add up to two drops essential oil; if you are making up 20 ml, you need four drops essential oil.

Extremely low dilution
Use for very sensitive skin, children, and babies. Mix just one drop of essential oil to 10 ml carrier oil, or just use a plain carrier oil by itself.

I usually use a 2 per cent dilution on my clients – eight drops of essential oil to 20 ml carrier oil – as I prefer to use a lighter fragrance rather than an overpowering one.

When you come to make your blend, pour the amount of carrier oil you need into a small, dark bottle using a funnel. With your chosen essential oils work out the number of drops required and carefully add this number to the carrier oil. Close the bottle and label clearly. Shake well before using.

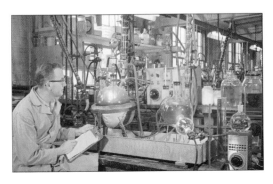

You can make enough of your blend for just one massage or you can make a larger quantity and store it. For a full body massage, you will need about 20 ml of oil; if you are just doing a face massage, 10 ml of oil is enough. It is probably not worth mixing quantities of less than 10 ml.

■ **Blending oils** *needn't be as difficult as this: all you need is a funnel, a dropper, and a bottle.*

Storing oils

Essential oils are highly volatile and therefore evaporate easily. As heat, air, and light can affect them, they should be kept in dark glass bottles in normal to cool temperatures (about 18°C/64°F). Although some wood oils can improve with age, most oils deteriorate and should be used within 2 years. They can be stored in the bottom of the fridge to prolong life. (Don't worry if your oils solidify in the fridge – they will return to liquid form when back at room temperature.) Citrus oils should be used within a year. However, once essential oils have been diluted in a carrier, their shelf life is reduced to only a few months.

STORAGE GUIDELINES

1 Store oils in dark glass bottles in a cool, dark place with the tops tightly secured to prevent evaporation

2 Label bottles with the name of the oils, dilution, and date

3 Store bottles out of reach of children

4 Keep essential oils away from naked flames – they are highly flammable

5 Do not store bottles on polished surfaces, as the oils can leave marks

6 Wipe up spills immediately

Allergies

Some people are allergic to essential oils. If you think you might have an allergy, it's worth trying this simple patch test. Place a drop of normal diluted essential oil on the inside of your wrist or the crease of your elbow. Cover with a plaster and examine after 12 hours.

If an oil causes any redness or itching, do not use it.

Occasionally, an allergy to a particular oil develops suddenly after using the oil quite happily for some time. If this happens to you, you should stop using it and switch to another blend. If ever you have an adverse reaction to an oil, apply a carrier oil to the area, then wash with cold water. Some people can even be allergic to carrier oils. I have had a couple of students who thought that they must be getting sensitive to the essential oils when it was the carrier oil that was the culprit.

Perfumed massage

THE WHOLE POINT of all these descriptions of different oils, how to blend them, and how to look after them is how you are going to incorporate them into your massage routines. As you can imagine, this is purely an individual choice and there are no rules and regulations about the oils, or the combination of oils, that you use for any particular type of massage.

The important thing to remember is to choose scents that both you and your partner like. If you are going purely for a pampering, relaxing experience, the aromas of the oils are possibly more important than their therapeutic effects; however, if you are trying to alleviate mental or physical symptoms, it is important that you select oils primarily for their therapeutic benefits. You should experiment and not just stick to one particular blend; no two massages are the same and you can ring the changes further by varying the aroma. As they say, variety is the spice of life!

Apart from massage, there are other ways of using essential oils, which will release their benefits. These include compresses, inhalations, bath drops, air fresheners, and vaporizers.

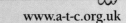

INTERNET

www.a-t-c.org.uk

This is the site of the Aromatherapy Trade Council (ATC), the authoritative body of the UK aromatherapy essential oils trade. Its mission is to promote responsible marketing and consumer safety. The ATC provides lists of approved essential oils suppliers.

Scenting trouble

ESSENTIAL OILS CAN BE USED to treat a range of minor ailments, and massage is usually the best way of delivering the healing oils. The combination of the therapeutic properties of the oils with the healing effects of massage can be profound. The chart on the following page shows the oils that are the best to use for a range of common complaints. You can select just one or choose up to three of the recommended oils by deciding which scents appeal to you most. Before beginning your massage, dilute the essential oils with a carrier oil.

COMBATING COMMON COMPLAINTS

Used in conjunction with massage, you may find that the oils mentioned below are helpful in alleviating some of the symptoms of these common ailments.

Problem	Useful essential oils
Insomnia	Chamomile, Lavender, Marjoram, Neroli, Orange, Petitgrain
Stress	Chamomile, Frankincense, Juniper, Lavender, Lemon-grass, Marjoram, Neroli
Headache	Chamomile, Geranium, Lavender, Marjoram, Peppermint, Petitgrain, Rose, Rosemary
Muscular aches and pains	Eucalyptus, German chamomile, Juniper, Lavender, Marjoram, Rosemary
Sprains, strains, swollen joints	German Chamomile, Cypress, Frankincense, Juniper, Lavender, Marjoram, Rosemary
Coughs and colds	Bergamot, Cypress, Eucalyptus, Frankincense, Lavender, Marjoram, Peppermint, Rosemary, Sandalwood, Tea tree
Sore throat	Clary sage, Cypress, Lavender, Peppermint, Sandalwood, Tea tree
Indigestion	Juniper, Lavender, Orange, Peppermint, Roman Chamomile, Rosemary
Constipation	Lemon-grass, Marjoram, Orange, Rosemary
Colic and wind in babies	Peppermint, Roman Chamomile
PMS and period pain	Chamomile, Clary sage, Geranium, Jasmine, Marjoram, Melissa, Rose
Acne	Bergamot, German chamomile, Geranium, Juniper, Lavender, Lemon-grass, Petitgrain, Tea tree
Superficial capillaries	Chamomile, Cypress, Frankincense, Geranium Rose
Eczema and psoariasis	Chamomile, Cypress, Frankincense, Geranium, Juniper, Lavender, Sandalwood

If a condition does not improve within a couple of days or if it is a persistently recurring complaint, visit a doctor.

Topping it off

For a really good, perfectly natural treatment to get rid of head lice, add to 10 ml jojoba ten drops of each of your choice from the following essential oils: geranium, lavender, rosemary, and tea tree. Work through the hair with a fine-toothed comb and then rinse out. The mix can be left on overnight if prolonged treatment is necessary.

Did you know?

In a 1998 experiment, 40 adults were given 3 minutes of aromatherapy using either lavender oil or rosemary oil. The lavender group showed increased relaxation and were less depressed, and they were able to perform simple maths tasks faster and with fewer errors following treatment. The rosemary group showed increased alertness, lower anxiety scores, and were faster, but not more accurate, at completing the maths test.

■ **Essential oils can be useful** *without massage, too. Head lice can be treated by applying the oil mix with a comb and then rinsing the mixture out.*

A simple summary

✔ Aromatherapy is literally healing with scents. It is an ancient art that has regained popularity in recent years with the rise in interest in all types of complementary therapies.

✔ Essential oils should always be diluted with a carrier oil before use.

✔ Most essential oils have multiple benefits; always use the oil, or combination of oils, best suited for your needs.

✔ Using essential oils in combination with massage enhances both the beneficial effects of the massage and the healing effects of the oils.

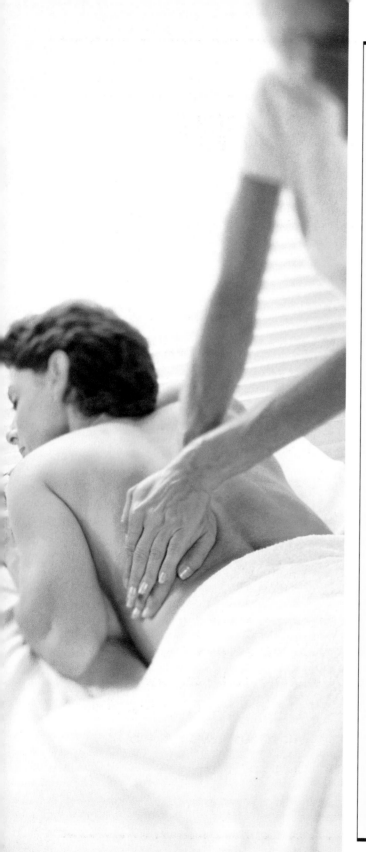

PART TWO

LEARN TO REDUCE TENSION WITH A LITTLE PRESSURE

LEARNING THE STROKES

MASSAGE MOVEMENTS CAN BE extraordinarily *precise*, ranging from the lightest brush in the air above the skin to deeply modulated pressures and sweeps; from movements that *rock the body* to those that roll the

 muscles. These individual strokes form the basic components of a massage that can be varied almost infinitely and blended to make your own unique style.

In Part Two, I'll be teaching you the different types of stroke you can carry out on a partner. I'll start with the simplest of strokes, *fanning*, before embarking on the more technical ones like percussion movements and *vibration*. Finally, you get to practise on yourself and discover not only how your hands feel on others but also how to *soothe* away your own tensions or pain.

Chapter 5

The Simple Strokes

NOW YOU ARE READY to start practising. I will start at the very beginning with the simplest and easiest move – stroking. If this is the only move you ever learn, you will still be able to do a full body massage; to add variety and interest simply change the speed and pressure of the strokes. Slow, light movements are calming and hypnotic, while brisk, deeper ones are stimulating. When you progress to more advanced moves, stroking provides an excellent link between the different types of movement.

In this chapter...

✓ Stroking

✓ Round and round a circle

✓ Side by side

✓ Criss-cross strokes

✓ Deep, deeper, deepest

✓ Light as a feather

Stroking

STROKING IS PERFECT *for the beginner and is the most versatile of all massage techniques. For example, if you ever get stuck for the next move in a massage, just stroke your partner's body until another move comes to you. As stroking allows you to cover a lot of ground, you can get a good feel for your partner's body at the start of a massage. You also get to know which parts of the body need extra attention.* Effleurage *is a good way to warm up the skin and muscles and also to spread the oil of your choice.*

DEFINITION

Stroking is often known by the term **effleurage***, from the French verb meaning to brush against or touch upon.*

Fan stroking

This type of simple stroking – fanning – is most suitable for large areas, such as the back and abdomen. The secret of the movement is to mould your hands to the curves of the body without dragging the skin and to maintain a steady rhythm. The lengths of the strokes can vary, but your hands should never lose contact with your partner's skin. This stroke is easier to perfect if you visualize your hands in the shape of an opened-out fan or butterfly as you move up the body.

The spine

As it's best to start with the back, some anatomy might be helpful. The spine, also known as the vertebral column, holds the body upright, supports the head and surrounds the spinal cord. It is made up of 33 bones called vertebrae. The flexible neck area is known as the cervical spine, and here the vertebrae are small. The middle region, or thoracic spine, is less flexible and each vertebra has a rib attached to either side. The lower back vertebrae make up the lumbar spine and each vertebra is large and strong, creating great flexibility. Between each vertebra is a protective spongy pad, known as a disk. The spinal cord runs through the central cavity of the vertebrae.

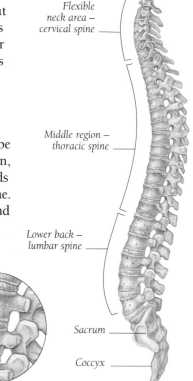

Flexible neck area – cervical spine

Middle region – thoracic spine

Lower back – lumbar spine

Vertebra

Intervertebral disk

Sacrum

Coccyx

ANATOMY OF THE SPINE

Doing it on the back

Have a go at your first basic massage strokes by following the steps below.

1. Place the palms of your hands face down next to each other on either side of the spine in the lower back region. Stroke up the back, applying a firm pressure with your palms.

2. When you reach the top of the back, open your fingers and fan your hands out away from the spine, reducing the pressure on your partner's skin.

3. Now glide your hands down the sides of the body moulding your palms and fingers to its contours. You should apply less pressure on the skin when you are using this downward stroke.

4. Pull up slightly at the waist and return your hands to the starting position. Repeat steps 1–3 several times to achieve a fluid movement. Vary the length of the upward stroke so you have covered the whole back after several cycles.

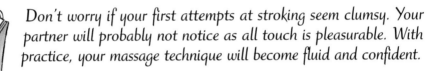

Don't worry if your first attempts at stroking seem clumsy. Your partner will probably not notice as all touch is pleasurable. With practice, your massage technique will become fluid and confident.

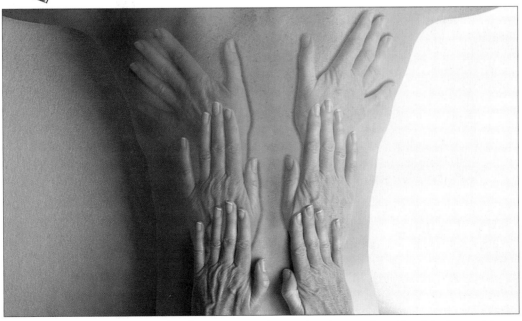

■ **When fan stroking the back,** *always start with your hands on either side of the base of the spine. Keep your fingers together as you move up the back, fanning out your hands as you reach the top.*

Doing it on the abdomen

Ask your partner to turn over onto his or her back and you can try out the same moves on the abdomen.

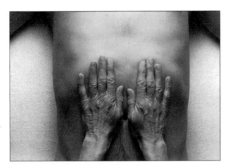

1 Place your hands side by side on the lower abdomen with your fingers pointing towards the head. Stroke gently and carefully upwards until the tips of your fingers just touch the lower edge of the ribcage.

2 Move your hands further up the ribcage, angling your fingers outwards and stroking across the ribs. Keep the pressure on the body as even as possible. Once you have reached the top of the ribcage, slide your hands gently down the sides of the body, moulding your fingers to its curves. Use a steady, careful pressure as you stroke up and decrease the pressure as you glide back to the beginning.

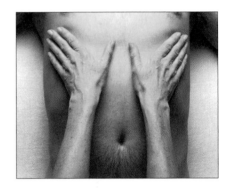

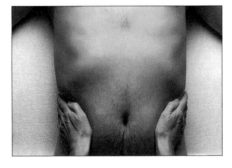

3 Pull the body up at the waist. Repeat steps 1–3 several times. Vary the length of your strokes each time so that you have touched the whole of the abdomen after several cycles.

Alternate fan stroking

In this variation on a fan theme, instead of synchronizing your hand movements you alternate them. Begin by placing your hands side by side as if you were doing a simple fan stroke. Stroke your right hand up the right-hand side of the body, keeping the pressure firm and even. When you reach the top of the area you want to cover, fan out your fingers towards the right side, moulding them around the body's contours. Glide your right hand down the side of the body as your left hand starts the movement from the beginning. This time your left hand mirrors the previous right-handed movements working up and down the left side of the body. Repeat the sequence so that as one hand strokes up the body, the other glides down. Try to keep the strokes flowing as freely as possible. With practice this should become a wonderfully smooth and rhythmic stroke.

Researchers have found that stroking a pet can actually lower your blood pressure. I maintain that stroking another person has the same relaxing effect for both the giver and the receiver.

Using your thumbs on your hands and feet

The same fan movements can be used to great effect on smaller areas of skin by simply using your thumbs. This technique is ideal for relieving tension in the hands (see the example below) and feet.

1 For fan stroking the hands, support the right hand with your fingers. Using a deep, steady pressure, stroke both thumbs up the right palm as far as you can go.

2 When your thumbs reach the base of the fingers, reduce the pressure and move your thumbs out to the sides. Glide lightly back in a circle to your starting position and repeat the two steps several times for full effect and then repeat on the left hand.

Fan stroking the feet

To fan stroke the soles of the feet, first support the right foot with the fingers of both your hands. Stroke the thumb of your left hand firmly upwards and out to the edge of the foot. As you reach the top of the area you are covering, do the same movement with the thumb of your right hand on the right side of the foot. Take your left-hand thumb back to the starting position. Repeat the movements several times, stroking higher up the foot until you get to the base of the toes so that you cover as much of the sole as possible.

Round and round a circle

CIRCLE STROKING IS A FLOWING movement that is perfect for
spreading oil around your partner's body. It is ideal as a linking stroke when
you want to glide smoothly from one move to another during a complete body
massage. The direction in which you stroke is up to you, whichever feels more
comfortable, but when stroking the abdomen it is best to use a clockwise stroke
to follow the direction in which the intestines work.

Light circle stroking

Light circular strokes with your hands gliding over the skin create a soft, soothing
effect. These soothing movements can be used on the shoulders, abdomen, and hips.

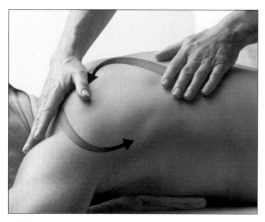

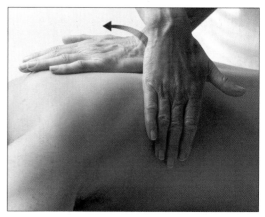

1 Place your hands apart on the body,
with your fingers pointing forwards.
Start to stroke your left hand gently in a
large circle, either in a clockwise or
anticlockwise direction. Stroke the right
hand in the same way.

2 As one hand meets the other wrist,
lift it over, and place it lightly on the
other side to complete the circle, as the
other hand continues stroking. Repeat the
sequence, applying slightly more pressure
on the upwards and outwards stroke, and
reducing the pressure as you glide down
and in. Try to build up a steady rhythm.

Deep circle stroking

Deep circular stroking, in which you use your whole body weight, moulds the flesh and can be used on the back, shoulders, and backs of the thighs. Deep circle stroking is a good way to help stretch tight muscles.

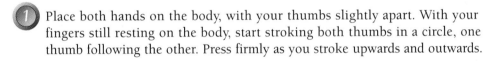

Massage should be pleasurable so ask your partner to tell you if anything you do is unpleasant or painful, particularly if you are making deeper movements in areas of tension.

The movements of this stroke follow the same sequence as for light circle stroking, but you need to use your body weight to lean into each stroke. As you stroke, use the fingers and heels of your hands to mould and sculpt the flesh.

Never press on the spine whenever you are using deep massage strokes on the back. Arrange your movements so that you work on either side of the spine and use only a gentle stroking action when your hands pass over the spinal area.

Circular thumb stroking

Using the thumbs is an effective method to ease tension in small, tight areas.

1 Place both hands on the body, with your thumbs slightly apart. With your fingers still resting on the body, start stroking both thumbs in a circle, one thumb following the other. Press firmly as you stroke upwards and outwards.

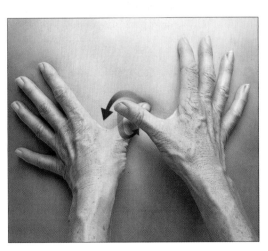

2 When one thumb meets the other, lift it over and continue the circle on the other side, releasing the pressure on the downwards stroke. One thumb completes a circle while the other one does a half circle. Keep the movements precise.

Side-by-side

SIDE STROKING IS ONE OF THE SIMPLEST massage techniques to master and it is one of the most soothing both to give and to receive. Its repetitiveness is hypnotic, and as your partner relaxes, you can apply deeper pressure. The movement is used to best effect on the back, abdomen, and thighs.

Light side stroking

Using very relaxed hands, light side stroking is a deeply relaxing, flowing movement. It should be performed in a smooth sequence and is a good way to ease tension in your hands following deeper work such as kneading.

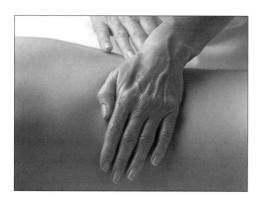

1 Facing sideways onto your partner, place both hands on the far side of the body, fingers pointing downwards. Stroke your right hand lightly and slowly up the side of the body towards you, and follow with your left hand in the same way.

2 Lift your right hand away as you reach the top of the body and repeat with your left hand. Continue, so that one hand follows the other in a relaxed, continuous movement. If you are working on the side closest to you, push up with your hands or swivel yourself around so you can pull up instead. If you find it easier you can move to the other side of your partner's body so that you can pull up. Remember, always try to keep your back straight.

Deep side stroking

The more vigorous version of side stroking uses the whole hand and forearm to provide a really deep motion that reaches the muscles. It is ideal for stretching muscular tissue in the back, abdomen, and thighs, thus releasing muscle tension. Start by facing your partner's side and placing both your hands on the opposite side, with your fingers pointing away from you. Stroke one hand firmly up the side and use your body weight to make the movement deep, pulling in and up towards you, and moulding the flesh with the heel and fingers of your hand. When your hand reaches the top of the body, lift it off as you start the movement with your other hand. Repeat several times, gradually working more slowly and deeply.

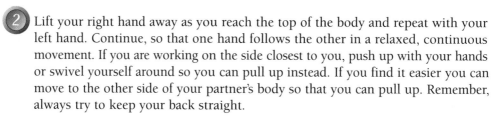

Criss-cross strokes

STROKES THAT CRISS-CROSS THE BODY combine smooth, gliding movements with gentle squeezes. Both hands work simultaneously to create a fluid rhythm that is wonderfully relaxing for the recipient. Simple criss-crosses are very easy to learn and you will be able to use them in your routine straight away, but figures of eight is a more complicated manoeuvre that requires practising. You need to achieve a smooth and seamless movement without any interruptions, such as your hands crashing into each other.

Simple criss-crosses

This is a very simple technique to learn and your partner will find it soothing and comforting. It can be used all over the body but you must take care to avoid pressing down on the spine. If you are working on the legs, take care not to pinch the flesh.

If your partner has varicose veins on their legs, don't use criss-cross movements or any strong movements over the affected areas.

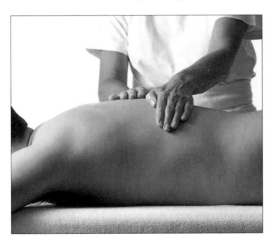

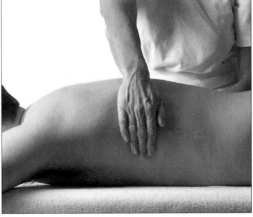

1 Facing your partner side on, place one hand on each side of the area, with your fingers facing away from you. Pull one hand and push the other firmly up each side and glide them smoothly across the body.

2 Slide your hands past each other and down towards the other side of the body. Make a distinction between firmly pulling up at the sides and then very gently gliding across the skin. Repeat the stroke, working along the whole area systematically.

FIGURES OF EIGHT

This is a more difficult technique that may require practice. It is best used on the back and thighs, and can induce a feeling of deep relaxation.

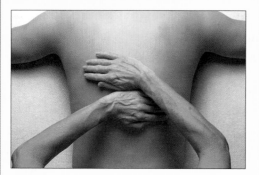

1 **Position your hands**

Place your hands side by side on the skin so that the fingers of one hand face the opposite way to the fingers of the other hand. Gently glide your hands out to the sides of the area.

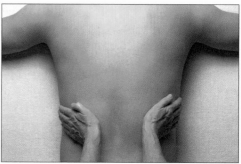

2 **Squeeze the sides of the back**

As you reach the edges of the area, swivel your fingers around as smoothly as possible, then pull them upwards so that you gently squeeze the sides of the body.

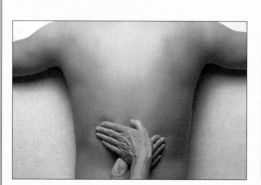

3 **Slide your hands across**

Reduce the pressure and glide your hands across the body again, a little further down from the point where you started. Keep the movement fluid as one hand passes the other.

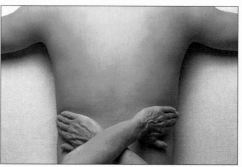

4 **Cross your arms and pull**

Swivel your fingers around so that your arms cross, and pull up at the sides again. Then continue with these figures of eight down the area, working as rhythmically as you can.

Deep, deeper, deepest

REALLY DEEP STROKES *can compress muscle tissue against the bone. They should only be used once an area has been sufficiently relaxed with gently stroking. This move is very effective when applied to large muscle groups such as those found on the back and thighs. Deep strokes broaden and stretch the muscle tissue and should generally follow the direction of the muscle fibres. On the back, work up or down with deep strokes on the muscles, taking care to avoid the spine; on the limbs, stroke towards the torso, following the circulation.*

Forearm strokes

Face your partner's side and rest one hand or forearm on the body as a support. With your other forearm, stroke firmly up the area, slowly rotating your arm to give a deep pressure that lengthens and compresses the muscular tissue. Make sure that your hand is relaxed so that the pressure comes from the arm. You can also stroke both your forearms in opposite directions to create more of a stretch.

Did you know?

In a Hawaiian form of massage known as Lomi Lomi, *deep forearm stroking is aptly described as ironing. Try to imagine yourself at the ironing board as you practise this stroke – ironing away the tension in your partner's body as you would iron away creases in your washing.*

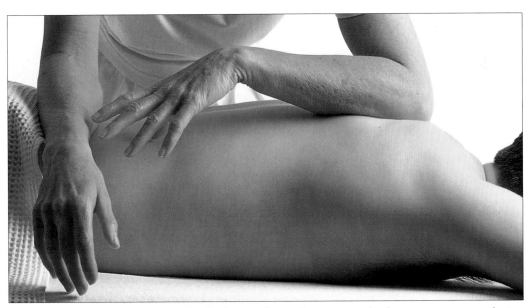

■ **By applying firm pressure to the back muscles with one arm,** *the forearm massage stroke is a great way of relieving tension and ironing out any stress.*

Knuckle strokes

This technique is used to ease taut muscles on either side of the spine or on the arms.

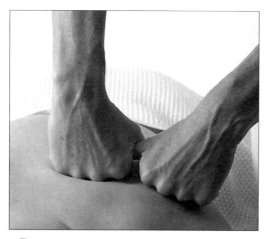

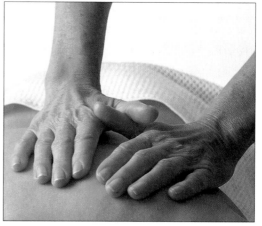

1 Loosely clench your fists, putting the thumb of one hand into the palm of the other for support, and stroke your knuckles firmly up the area, using your body weight to apply a deep pressure.

2 Roll your fingers out from under your palms and gently stroke your hands back down the area. Then make your hands into fists again and repeat the whole movement, aiming for a wave-like motion. This is a very relaxing stroke for the giver.

Raking

Raking is a deeply relaxing movement that is best used on the back either parallel or at right angles to the spine. Flex the fingers of both hands so that they are quite rigid and rake-like, and stroke them towards you, either together or alternately. When you reach the end of the area, return your hands to the start and repeat.

V-strokes

Used on bulky, muscular areas, such as the thighs, this action results in warmth and relaxation. Using the V-shape between your thumb and fingers, stroke one hand after the other up the area in a firm motion, shaping your hands around the body. Keep your hands relaxed, with the depth coming from your body.

INTERNET

www.mtwc.com

Massage Therapy Web Central is a comprehensive resource centre with a regular newsletter and interesting articles. You'll also find a global directory of massage organizations and schools.

Light as a feather

TO FINISH THE MASSAGE *try using the lightest, gentlest strokes you can manage using your whole hand or just your fingertips. Feather stroking has a calming influence that permeates the whole body. Gentle stroking movements vary from sweeping your hands softly and rhythmically over the skin's surface to aura stroking where you don't touch the body at all.*

Cat stroking

As you would expect, this movement is just like stroking a cat so try to imagine this is what you are doing as you practise the steps. If you are not a cat lover, visualize another furry animal. This step is best suited for the back. Place one hand at the top of the area you are massaging and stroke gently down the body, moulding your palm and fingers to its contours. Lift your hand off at the bottom of the area and return it to the start while your other hand begins the downwards stroke. Continue stroking one hand after the other and make the return movement as smooth and rhythmic as the stroke itself. Repeat for as long as you like but take care that the relaxing effect doesn't send you to sleep!

INTERNET

www.amtamassage.org

The web site of the American Massage Therapy Association provides lots of general massage information plus more specific details about massage therapists in the 30 countries that the body represents. It even includes a virtual massage room with soothing music and sequences of relaxing pictures!

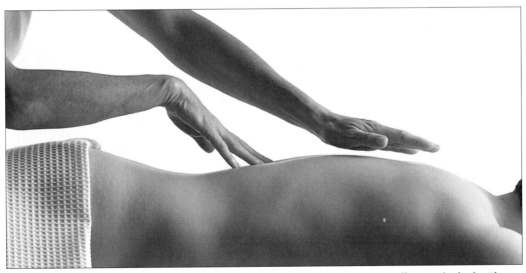

■ **Light, superficial massage strokes** *have a highly soothing and calming effect on the body. These gentle cat strokes, as they are known, are usually used at the beginning or end of a deep massage.*

Cat stroking is the perfect movement to send someone to sleep. Just repeat it over and over again and he or she will soon be snoring.

I sometimes have bets with myself to see how quickly I can send a client to sleep. My students also tell me that it is the best way of getting hyperactive children to sleep.

■ **Like stroking a real cat,** *cat stroking in massage can be so relaxing that you may have to stop yourself from falling asleep. At the same time, it may be a useful sedative for getting others to sleep.*

Feather stroking

This movement can induce deep relaxation and for this reason is sometimes known as nerve stroking. Any part of the body responds to the soothing and seductive feel of this motion. Stroke the fingertips of both your hands very lightly down the body. Repeat this movement, and as you continue, stroke more and more gently until your hands barely touch the skin. Most people love this stroke but if your partner is particularly sensitive and ticklish you may have to put this movement on hold.

HANDS NOT TOUCHING THE SKIN IN AURA STROKING

Aura stroking

Place your hands side by side just above the surface of the skin and slowly move them together over the area. Take great care to avoid actually touching your partner's skin. As your hands begin to generate heat, your partner may feel a warm, tingling sensation. Use this technique wherever there is tension.

When in doubt about what to do next, just stroke. This is particularly important when you are learning how to massage and can't remember the next step; don't worry, just stroke and you won't disrupt the flow and your partner will be in blissful ignorance.

A simple summary

✔ Stroking is the simplest and most versatile of all massage techniques. It is ideal for starting off a massage, for finishing a massage, or for linking more complex massage strokes. You can even do a complete body massage using just this one movement!

✔ Gentle stroking can be extremely relaxing and soporific while deeper strokes will invigorate and stimulate your partner's body and relieve tension.

✔ You can use stroking movements in any direction, but if you are working on the abdomen, it is best to follow a clockwise motion as this is the way the intestines work.

✔ If you are massaging the back, it is important to avoid pressing on the spine; work on either side of the vertebral column instead.

✔ Stroking can be as beneficial to the giver as to the recipient.

Chapter 6

The Need to Knead

I T WILL COME AS NO SURPRISE that kneading as a massage technique is just like kneading dough. Imagine that you are baking bread and your hands are wrist-deep in a soft and yielding mixture of flour and water; you must squeeze, lift, and roll with all your might to get the dough full of air and just the right consistency for the perfect loaf of bread. As a massage technique, kneading is one of the most pleasurable to receive and for maximum benefit it should never be approached tentatively: you should use your whole body to make the movement. Kneading is especially useful on the shoulders and fleshy areas such as the hips and thighs.

In this chapter...
✓ *The first steps*
✓ *Wring that body*

SQUEEZE, LIFT, ROLL, AND REALLY FEEL THE DIFFERENCE

The first steps

THE SUCCESS OF KNEADING relies on an even rhythm, which can vary in depth and speed. Fast kneading can be used for a stimulating effect and slow kneading for a more soporific result. Kneading stretches and relaxes tense muscles making them more pliable; it improves the circulation bringing blood and nutrients to the area; and it helps the absorption and elimination of waste products. You may find that the muscles in your partner's body are so tense that it is difficult to lift the skin; in this case, you should knead the area with flat hands and the rhythm of the movement should relax the area enough for you to get in deeper at a later stage.

The most basic type of kneading, or *petrissage*, is best used on fleshy areas such as the back, thighs, hips, and buttocks. It relaxes and stretches tight muscles. Use enough oil to allow your hands to move freely without sliding around uncontrollably.

DEFINITION

The original word for kneading, from the French verb petrir, *was* **petrissage** *– it remains a term often used today.*

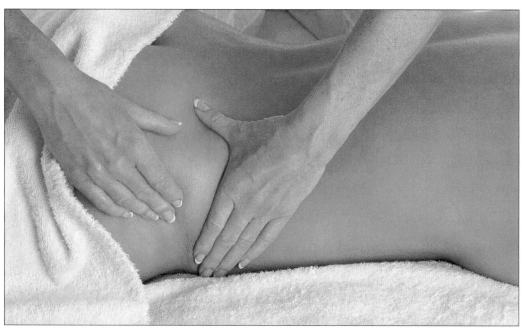

■ **Firmly kneading the fleshier parts of the body** *is a great way of improving blood circulation to the area, which in turn helps increase the elimination of waste products.*

PRACTICE MOVES

A great way of practising kneading is to make some bread dough, and cut off bits of varying sizes to represent different parts of the body. You'll find that you need to use your whole hand to knead large areas (equivalent to the back), and with little pieces you will only be able to use your fingers and thumbs.

GETTING TO GRIPS WITH KNEADING

Putting petrissage into practice

When kneading, I imagine that my hands are describing a circle. I put the pressure on the upward part of the circle with whichever part of my hand is in contact with the body. My hands want to fit the contours of the body. Follow the two steps below and try to imagine this circle yourself as you perform the strokes.

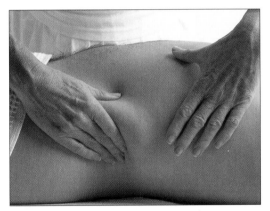

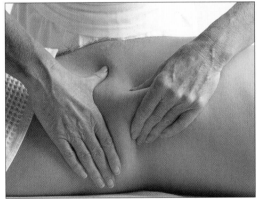

1 Place your hands flat on your partner's body with your elbows out to each side and fingers pointing towards each other. With your right hand, gently grasp and squeeze some flesh, using as much of your hand as possible so you don't pinch the skin. Then release your grip and push the flesh towards your left hand. If there is not much flesh to pick up, make the pushing movement on the surface of the skin.

2 Grasp the flesh with your left hand in the same way as in step 1, then release it into your right hand again. Repeat this several times, pushing the flesh from side to side. Count in your head to keep your strokes even and rhythmic.

Trivia...

I was recently given a badge that says: "I need to be kneaded!"

The twister

Wringing is a deeper movement and is great for loosening and stimulating tense muscles. The action is basic kneading with a twist – a bit like wringing out a towel. Pull up the flesh with one hand, then twist it into your other hand, pressing deeply into it with your thumbs. Imagine you have a wet towel between your fingers as you twist the flesh from one hand to the other.

PULLING AND TWISTING THE FLESH

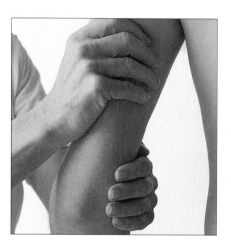

SQUEEZING THE ARM ONE HANDED

Doing it one handed

One-handed kneading is a useful stroke for areas of the body where there is not enough room for two hands to work effectively, such as the tops of the shoulders, the arms, and the calves. Support the area you are working on with one hand and squeeze and release the flesh with the other hand. If you are working on an arm or calf, you can use alternate hands on either side to squeeze and release.

Fingers only

Fingertip kneading is a very small and precise movement that is ideal for areas without much flesh, such as the neck and face. Lift and squeeze the flesh with the thumb and fingers of one hand, then glide it towards the other hand. Repeat the movement with the thumb and fingers of the other hand.

When fingertip kneading, beware of pinching your partner's skin. You can prevent this by keeping your elbows sticking out and using as much of your hand as possible.

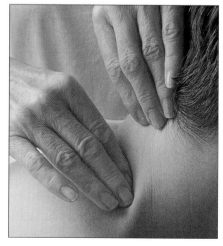

GENTLE FINGERTIP KNEADING

Wring that body

SKIN ROLLING IS USED ON AREAS *that feel tight and as though they are stuck together, for example the tops of the shoulders and either side of the spine. This movement differs from basic kneading in that instead of lifting the muscle, you lift the skin away from the underlying muscle. It has a warming and softening effect.*

Simple rolling massage

Follow steps 1 and 2 below for effective relief of tightness. Remember rhythm, rhythm, rhythm. It's this undulating rhythm that makes the strokes so relaxing.

1 Place your hands on your partner's skin in such a way that you create a triangle between your fingers and thumbs. Then, without sliding your fingers on the skin, pull the flesh towards your thumbs.

2 Push your thumbs firmly towards your fingers, rolling the flesh as you do so, and taking care not to pinch the skin as your thumbs meet your fingers. Then, reach forwards with your fingers again and repeat the movement as rhythmically as possible.

Kneading can be ticklish on some people, particularly if you are using only your fingers. Try using your palms, which makes the movement flatter and, therefore, less irritating.

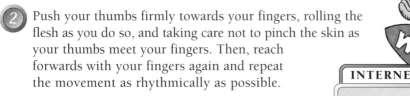

INTERNET

www.cmhmassage.co.uk

The web site of the Clare Maxwell-Hudson school of Massage has information on the school, the teachers, courses, and publications.

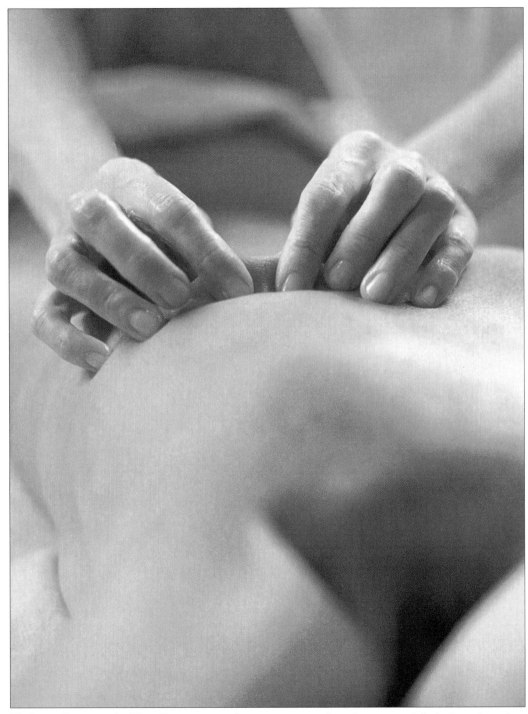

■ **Skin rolling is a highly effective way** *of easing tension in the tighter areas of the body, such as the back and shoulders.*

Alternative skin rolling

In another form of skin rolling, you slide your thumbs towards your forefingers so that they squeeze the flesh, and then walk your fingers forwards as your thumbs push the flesh behind. I call this movement "inchworming".

Like all other types of kneading, you can practise skin rolling on a cushion. Then if you are like most of us with a little bit of extra flesh on the thighs, you can try practising there; this has the added benefit of letting you know exactly how it feels.

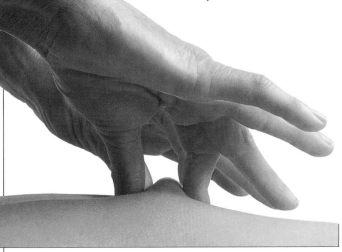

"INCHWORMING" THE SKIN

Did you know?

In June 1900 an article on general massage was published in the Journal of the American Medical Association, which highlighted the benefits of kneading. It stated that this particular form of massage could result in " ... a fall in arterial pressure, both mean and maximum ... "

A simple summary

✔ Kneading produces one of the most pleasant sensations of all massage movements.

✔ Kneading is used to best effect on large fleshy parts of the body, but the movement can be adapted to suit smaller areas containing less fat and muscle.

✔ Successful kneading relies on a steady rhythm and strong confident movements.

✔ As with other strokes, you can vary the depth and speed of kneading to produce different effects – fast kneading can be extremely stimulating while slow kneading tends to be soporific.

Chapter 7

Shake, Rattle, and Roll

NOW IT'S TIME TO TRY SOME INVIGORATING MOVEMENTS – like playing a drum kit. Don't worry, you don't actually need a drum: I learned percussion on a table. I couldn't hurt the table but it did hurt me if I was too heavy handed! Percussion boosts the circulation, stimulates, and invigorates – perfect for waking up your partner. Plucking and finger tapping are smaller strokes that also rely on a steady, even rhythm. Vibrations can release tension at the start or end of a massage. They include energetic shaking of the limbs; comforting, rocking movements; and trembling superficial vibrations along the surface of the skin.

In this chapter...
✔ Beat the drum
✔ Chop, chop
✔ Turn down the volume
✔ Shaking and rocking
✔ Good vibrations

LEARN THE RHYTHM AND FEEL THE BEAT

Beat the drum

PUMMELLING *is one of the easiest types of percussion, or* **tapotement***, movements, and works best on the back, hips, and thighs. The secret of perfect percussion is to keep the movements light and springy and move around an area rather than sticking to one place for too long. You do not need to use oil with percussion strokes as there are no gliding movements over the skin.*

> ### DEFINITION
>
> *Percussion movements are also known as* **tapotement** *from the French verb* tapoter, *meaning to "tap" or "drum".*

Practising percussion

Make your hands into loose fists and, with relaxed wrists, bounce the sides of your fists alternately against your partner's skin. Flick your hands away as soon as you touch the skin, so that the movement is light and bouncy rather than heavy and thumping. Move all around the area for about 30 seconds. Fast pummelling is stimulating and slow strokes are relaxing.

■ **Like beating a drum,** *pummelling strokes need to be controlled and rhythmical.*

The secret of carrying out good percussion movements is to keep your wrists really loose. Practise first on a pillow, then as you get better try it on yourself, and finally use a table; you will certainly feel the pain if you haven't got the technique right.

Never use percussion movements on bony areas, superficial veins, or bruises, and avoid the spine and the areas over the kidneys.

■ **Pummelling is a light, springy** *movement that requires loose wrists, both for a stimulating as well as a relaxing effect.*

Chop, chop

KNOWN AS HACKING, *this stroke is used on the back and fleshy areas such as the hips and thighs. Like pummelling, it is stimulating if done at speed and relaxing at a slower pace.*

INTERNET

www.massagemag.com

An online version of one of the best-selling massage magazines, this site contains research articles, massage-related news, expert advice, and course information.

A little light hacking

Use the sides of alternate hands to strike your partner's body lightly and briskly. Concentrate on the upward movement, flicking your hands away as soon as they touch the skin, and keeping both hands relaxed so that can hear your fingers knocking together. Continue this action for about 30 seconds, moving your hands quickly from one spot to the next and never remaining in the same spot for too long.

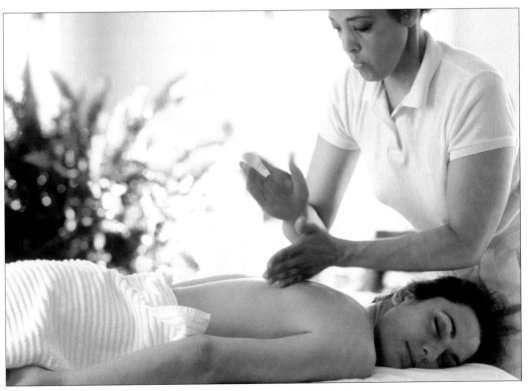

THE HACKING STROKE

Turn down the volume

AFTER THE STRONGLY INVIGORATING *strokes we've just tried, it's time to try some movements that are almost as energizing but softer in tone. These techniques are ideal for smaller areas of the body, but can be used on the larger expanses as well. Like the other movements, getting a good rhythm is crucial, and it's a good idea to practise on a pillow or your thighs before trying the moves on your partner. Notice the different sounds made by the different techniques.*

Simply plucking

Plucking is a very light stroke that can be used on any part of the body. Use the thumb and fingertips of alternate hands to pluck and pinch the skin briskly. This stimulates the nerve endings in the skin and can be surprisingly relaxing. In some traditional forms of massage, for example in Tunisia, this plucking movement is used for a complete body massage.

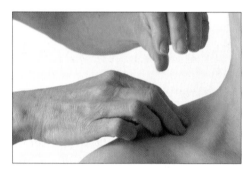

PLUCKING AND PINCHING

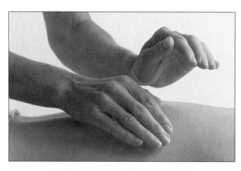

PATTING WITH CUPPED HANDS

A cup in the hand …

Cupping is a stimulating action that helps relieve congested areas, and is used particularly on the back and buttocks. Cup your hands with your fingers pointing downwards, and pat the area with alternate hands.
This movement is softer than pummelling and children, in particular, enjoy its lovely hollow sound.

Cupping can be used over the upper back area to relieve congestion in people with respiratory problems. It helps stimulate the respiratory system and loosen mucus.

Tap that rhythm

An energizing stroke, finger tapping is best used on the face and scalp. Rhythmically tap the fingertips of both hands on the body using an energetic, galloping motion. The movement can be superficial or deep, but it should never be heavy. Try using flat fingers to vary the effect. If you are working on your partner's face, keep the movements very gentle around the eyes.

FINGER TAPPING WITH FLAT FINGERS

Shaking and rocking

THESE TWO TECHNIQUES, which are easy to learn, help to release physical and emotional tension at the start or end of a massage sequence. As the name suggests, shaking is an energetic movement and you should not worry about jostling your partner around. Shaking is used to best effect on the back, legs, and arms. Rocking is a more gentle, calming motion covering the whole body, and it is one of the most effective ways to relax your partner.

Shaking

Shaking is used either to relax muscle groups or a whole limb. This movement should be used when the muscles feel very tight – the shaking loosens and warms the area. For instance, use this on the shoulder area to release the excessive tension that accumulates in this area. The secret of good shaking is to have really relaxed hands.

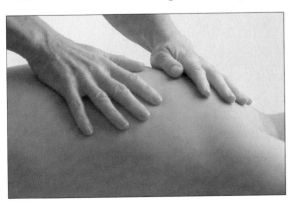

1 To shake the back, stabilize your partner's body with one hand and use your other hand to shake the flesh from side to side. You can make this movement either superficial or quite strong.

2 To shake an arm or leg, hold the wrist or ankle firmly, taking care not to drag the skin. Then shake the limb up and down and from side to side. Start by shaking slowly and gradually increase the speed. Imagine you are sending waves of relaxation through the body.

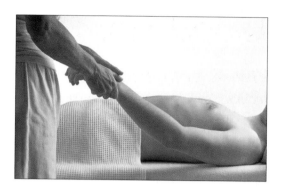

Rocking

Rock the whole body by placing one of your hands on the back, with one hand on the sacrum and the other beside the spine. You can also rock with one hand beside the spine and the other at the top of the thigh. Press into the muscles, then gently pull and push, back and forth, building up a steady rocking motion. If you want to rock an arm or leg, stabilize the area with one hand and rock the limb with your other hand, so that only one of your hands is creating the movement. Keep the rocking flowing smoothly and rhythmically, just like the waves of the sea.

To perfect the rocking movement, rock your partner's body as far as it will go and then let it roll back to its position naturally. Try to pick up your partner's rhythm and work with it to create a lovely, flowing, wave-like movement.

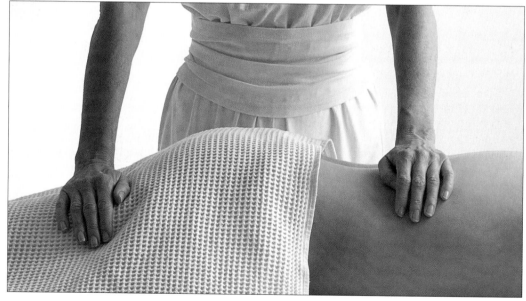

POSITION OF HANDS FOR MOVING THE BODY BACK AND FORTH

Good vibrations

VIBRATION CAN BE A DIFFICULT

technique to learn. It's a knack, so don't worry if it takes you a while to master. However, it has such a dramatic effect on the body that it is well worth the effort of persevering. Vibration is good for stimulating the nerves, and is used on the back and around the joints. It is a profoundly soothing movement that, while only skin deep, has an effect that is felt throughout the whole body. You do not need to use oil with vibration strokes.

■ **Picture a pneumatic drill**
breaking up concrete as you break down tension with vibration strokes.

When I first tried to practise vibrations on a client, I was mortified when she asked me if I was alright because I was trembling. This put me off the movements for ages but then someone used them on me and I realized how good they could feel. So I persevered and eventually got the knack, and now I find them easy to do.

I like to imagine that my hands are on a pneumatic drill but instead of breaking up concrete they are stimulating nerve endings and breaking down tension.

Putting vibrations into practice

To start, place one palm across the other and try to create a subtle vibration in your lower hand. Use the palm on top to apply a gentle, trembling pressure. Alternately contract and relax your forearm while keeping your lower hand relaxed.

You can perform this movement either on the spot or by slowly pulling your hands towards you. You can also use your fingers to make stationary vibrations. You need to keep your shoulder and upper arm relaxed as you contract and relax your forearm.

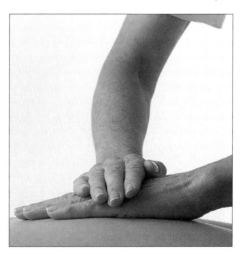

APPLYING GENTLE VIBRATION

Alternative method

Pull the fingers of one of your hands back with the other and alternately contract and relax the muscles of your lower forearm to create a subtle vibration. Gradually pull your hands towards you in a gentle, tremulous motion.

■ **It may seem** *like the vibrating stroke is almost too subtle to affect more than the area immediately below the skin, but, if you get it right, you can induce a profoundly soothing sensation through the whole of the body.*

Did you know?

In the early 1980s, an experiment was carried out on 36 patients who were suffering from intractable tooth pain of over 2 days duration, either due to infection or following removal of impacted wisdom teeth. Mechanical vibration was applied to various points on the face or skull. Over 90 per cent of the patients experienced a reduction in the pain, and of these 12 patients reported complete relief from pain.

Hot practice tips

To practise vibration movements, fill a hot water bottle or a strong balloon with cold water and oscillate up and down. Use the whole of your hand first and then just your fingers. This technique can also be used to practise shaking movements. For this, you need to move sideways making a backwards and forwards motion.

■ **A hot water bottle** *is perfect for practising your vibration technique.*

Over the years, I have found that vibration is a movement that people either love or hate; either they find it extraordinarily effective and relaxing, or this stroke does absolutely nothing for them at all.

A simple summary

✔ Percussion strokes boost the circulation, stimulate, and invigorate.

✔ Percussion movements are ideal for waking up your partner at the end of a massage.

✔ When using percussion actions make sure you always use light, springy movements and move around an area so there is no danger of hurting your partner.

✔ Shaking and rocking actions help to release tension at the beginning or end of a massage.

✔ Vibrations are difficult to perform but are ultimately very rewarding because of the profoundly soothing effect on the receiver.

✔ There is no need to use oil with percussion and vibration strokes.

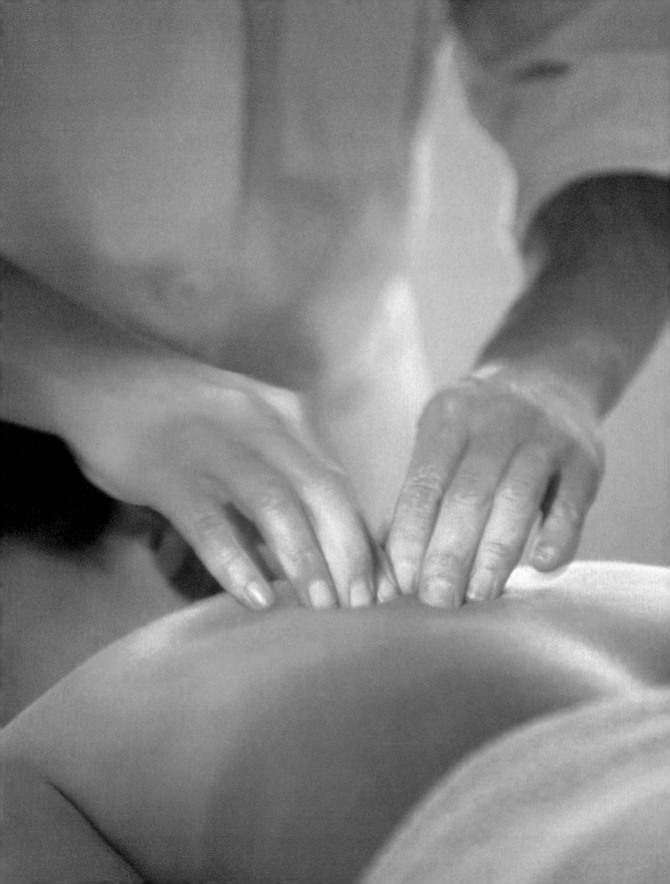

Chapter 8

Pressure-sensitive

THIS CHAPTER IS ABOUT RELIEVING PRESSURE through a surprisingly relaxing stroke that can be directed at a very precise spot of tension. It also covers holds – movements that provide wonderful moments of stillness at the beginning and end of a massage.

In this chapter...

✓ Static pressure

✓ Circular pressure

✓ Fingers only

✓ Hands on

✓ The full force

✓ Holds: taking the pressure off

✓ Comforting holds

✓ And finally

Static pressure

STATIC PRESSURES, OR PRESSING,
*can vary from deep, focused movements using the
thumbs or fingers to broader compressions using the
heel of your hand or your elbow. Pressure is ideal
for use on the muscles on either side of the spine
and around the shoulders – areas notorious for
being tightly knotted with tension – but they should
only be applied once these areas have already been warmed or massaged. These
movements help prevent and break up local adhesions in the connective tissue.*

> **DEFINITION**
>
> *The medical term for the
> abnormal union of parts of
> the body due to inflammation
> or a band of tissue joining
> such parts is* **adhesion**.
> *Scar tissue is an example
> of an adhesion.*

Slow, steady pressure

Static pressures should be applied slowly
and steadily and you should never poke
sharply. Make sure you don't accidentally
gouge the flesh with your thumb nails.
Use very little or no oil as your hands do
not need to glide around your partner's
skin. Place the pads of your thumbs, or
the palms, fingers, or heels of your hands
on your partner's skin and gradually lean
onto them with all your body weight.

Hold and press for a few seconds, then
gradually release your touch and glide
onto the next area. As the skin tissue
relaxes and stretches, deeper pressure
can be applied, which helps to release
muscular tension.

*It's essential that you use
your relaxed body weight
to achieve depth of pressure,
without poking or prodding
your partner or straining your
fingers or thumbs.*

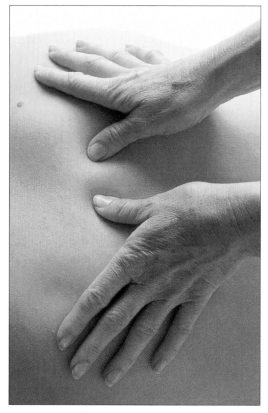

APPLYING STATIC PRESSURE TO THE BACK

Circular pressure

CIRCULAR PRESSURES *are sometimes known as "friction". To perform these movements, press your thumbs or fingers against your partner's skin as for static pressures then make small, circular movements. Your hands and your partner's skin should work together as one so that you move the superficial layer of flesh against the deeper tissue in a circular motion.*

When practising circular pressures, experiment with soft, superficial circles and slow, deep ones. You can also make a half circle so that you go back and forth over a more precise area. After using deep circular pressures, always gently stroke and soothe the area.

Causing "grateful" pain

When applying circular pressures, you want to exert enough pressure so that your partner experiences "grateful" pain but not "ouch" pain. If you work too deeply, or go in too fast, the muscles will tense up in discomfort. Get feedback from your partner, and go in slowly and sensitively.

Always work within your partner's comfort zone, gradually increasing the pressure.

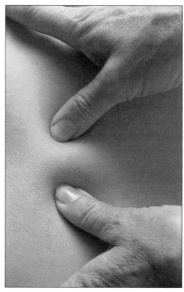

■ **Make circular** *or semi-circular motions with your thumbs so that pressure is applied to a wide area.*

Fingers only

OVERLEAF, YOU'LL FIND A FEW EXAMPLES *of pressure movements in which you use only your fingers or thumbs. With the general rule that the smaller the point the deeper the pressure – the stiletto effect – finger pressures can be very effective where deep pressure is needed. These movements are generally used to release muscle tension over a tiny, specific area, and so are ideal for use on the shoulders and on either side of the spine. They are also particularly effective on some areas of the face, the hands, and feet.*

Finger pressing

This movement can be static or circular. Use three or four fingers of one hand to apply even pressure to the skin while using your other hand to support the area. The supporting hand should aim to keep the area in a relaxed position to enable the fingers of the other hand to get in and apply deep pressure.

If applying a pressure hurts, stop! This applies both to you and your partner. Sometimes, however, you can just use another part of your hand to apply the pressure, for example if your thumbs begin to hurt.

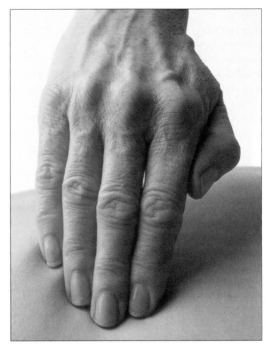

FOUR-FINGERED PRESSURE

EXERTING DEEPER PRESSURE

Double finger pressing

To exert a deeper static pressure on a tight point, try crossing your index finger over your middle finger and then slowly press down, hold the pressure, and then release equally slowly. Alternatively, you can apply the pressure and then make small, deep, back-and-forth movements.

These little movements are frequently made across the muscles and are known as cross-fibre work. Cross-fibre work – as the name implies – involves working across the muscle fibres, rather than in the same direction. It is usually done with the fingertips or thumbs, and it helps to break down adhesions and increase pliability and flexibility. It is a technique used extensively in sports massage.

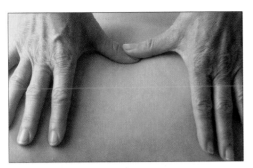

POSITION OF THUMBS FOR CROSS-FIBRE WORK

Using thumbs

Place one thumb on top of the other to produce a very deep pressure. First, find the area of tension and slowly apply the pressure; hold for a few seconds and slowly release the pressure. You can also use your thumbs in this position to do deep cross-fibre work.

All deep movements, and especially the most penetrating pressures of the fingers and thumbs, should only be used after the knotted area has first been soothed with lighter, less penetrating massage movements.

Hands on

BY USING YOUR WHOLE HAND or just the heel of your hand you can produce a much stronger effect than by using fingers alone. These techniques give a broad, deep pressure that compresses tight muscle bands and relieves very tense areas. You can create different types and strengths of pressure by using different parts of your hands in combination, for example the heel of one hand with the palm of the other, or the thumb of one hand with the heel of the other. When your body weight is exerted on top it can produce quite different results.

■ **Like untangling** *a ball of wool, ridding the body of knots of tension requires patience and care.*

I find it helps to think of a knot of tension like the knot in a ball of string or wool. It has to be undone slowly and carefully.

If you start pulling, you tend to make the tangled ball worse, whereas if you work slowly starting from the outside and gradually working towards the centre you eventually succeed in untangling it.

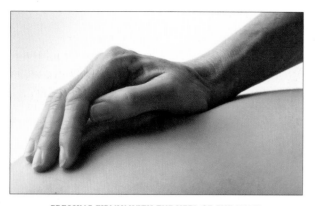

PRESSING FIRMLY WITH THE HEEL OF THE HAND

Heel first

The heel of your hand can create a broad pressure that can be either static or circular. Press firmly with one hand deep down into your partner's skin using the full weight of your body to emphasize the action. Make sure your fingers are totally relaxed when you make this movement. You can try the same action with your other hand to avoid getting tired.

Two-handed

For even deeper pressures, put one hand on top of the other with the heel of the bottom hand over the area of tension in your partner's body. Lean right over your hands so that the power of the movement comes from your body.

Don't overwork a tense area all in one go; it has probably taken years for it to get so tense, so you can't expect to get rid of it in one session.

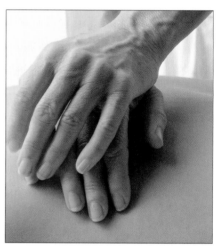

DEEP DOUBLE-HANDED PRESSURE

A helping hand

Place the thumb of your left hand on the point of the body that you are trying to relax. Put the heel of your right hand on top of your left-hand thumb and press down with the weight of your body. Make sure you keep your thumb flat so that the pressure is both deep and diffused. After a few presses, you can swap hands.

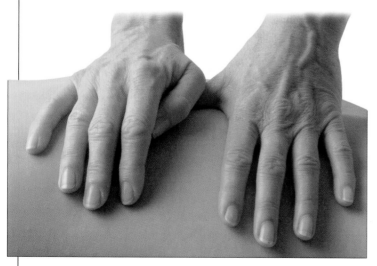

HEEL AND THUMB PRESSING

The full force

IF YOU GET TIRED, or if you feel like a change, you can use other parts of your hands and arms to create deep pressures. Some of these moves are slightly more difficult to achieve well, but with practice you will be able to incorporate them into your massage routines. As before, you need to apply your body weight for the pressure to have an impact on deep, tense muscles. My favourite combinations are the elbows, knuckles, and interlocking the fingers of both hands.

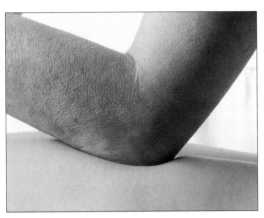

ELBOW PRESSURE

Elbow grease

Although it probably looks somewhat ungainly, you can use your elbow to create a really deep and penetrating pressure. As elbow pressure can feel incredibly deep, you need to go in carefully. The flatter you have your elbow, the broader and less painful the pressure will feel; the more pointed your elbow, the more penetrating your touch will be. Make sure that your arm and hand are relaxed, and that you use your body to apply the pressure

As your elbows don't have the same sensitivity as your hands, first find the correct spot using your fingers, and then go in slowly and sensitively with your elbow.

Knuckle roll

Using the knuckles of your four fingers, make a rolling motion deep into the flesh. The action should be firm, slow, and circular. If you use your thumb as a support your hand won't tire so quickly. This is a really useful movement for relieving stiff muscles and I use it all around the shoulders, the shoulder blade, on either side of the spine, and at the base of the spine.

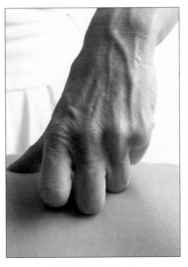

ROLLING KNUCKLES

CLASPED FINGERS IN A VICE-LIKE GRIP

Interlocking pieces

For some reason, interlocking fingers seem to be much more than the sum of their parts. Used in this way, your hands can produce a vice-like grip. Don't slide, but just press your palms over the muscle. Hold for a minute and slowly release. This is very good on the shoulders, neck, thighs, and calves. This movement is also called "compression", and you should take care not to squeeze your partner too hard as it could be painful.

After deep pressure work, the massaged area may feel a little tender the following day, a little like the muscle soreness you experience after an exercise session at the gym. This is nothing to worry about, and it will soon go.

Holds: taking the pressure off

HOLDS ARE SIMPLE MOVES requiring no oil and very little expertise; they are really just an extension of one's instinct to touch and to empathize. At the start of a massage, it is vital to impart confidence and put your partner at ease.

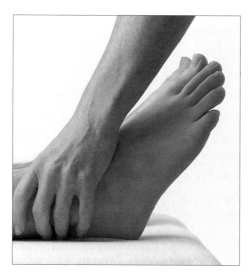

AN INITIAL HOLD ON THE ANKLE

The first hold

To accustom your partner to your touch, lay your hands on the area you wish to start on and hold your position for about 10 seconds. Relax your hold, focusing your attention on your partner, then gradually lift your hands away. Use the time when you do the initial holds to centre yourself and to tune into your partner.

Don't be heavy handed when applying holds. The hand should feel confident and definite, but not heavy.

Comforting holds

HOLDING EACH HAND on a different area of your partner's body for a few seconds during a massage can be very comforting. You can also make this move if you are changing the focus of your massage from one part of the body to another without disrupting the flow. Try holding your hands on the forehead and stomach, the base of the neck and **sacrum**, or the hip and ankle.

DEFINITION

The triangular bone at the base of the spine is called the **sacrum**; it is made up of five fused vertebrae.

When I'm working in hospitals, I am occasionally asked to see patients who are too ill to take much massage. Instead, I simply apply positive holds as the effect can feel very reassuring and comforting.

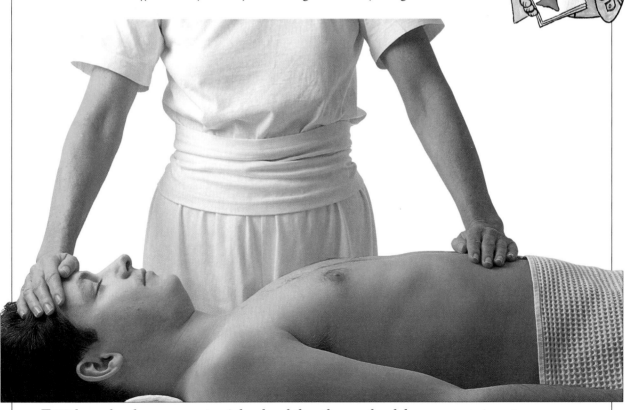

■ **With one hand on your partner's head and the other on the abdomen** *you can impart a wonderful feeling of well-being and comfort at the beginning or end of a massage.*

And finally

AT THE END of a massage, say goodbye with your hands by holding them on the area of your partner's body on which you have just been working.

Holding hands

To complete a hand massage, for example, sandwich your partner's hand between your palms. Slowly press your hands together for a few seconds, then release them and gradually slide your hands off the tips of the fingers. This will leave the hand completely relaxed.

Alternative method

You may not always wish to end a massage holding your partner's hand. An equally comforting alternative is to cup your hands over the forehead, stomach, or back.

1 Place one of your hands over the other in a cupped position and lay them gently on the forehead. Feel the heat gather beneath your palms, then gently flatten them to ease the heat into the body.

A RELAXING HAND HOLD

2 Now lift your hands away as slowly as possible, so that your partner does not know when your hands have left the body. This produces an incredible feeling of lightness.

STEP 1

INTERNET

www.bmtc.co.uk

Click here for the web site of the British Massage Therapy Council.

A touch of confidence

Although holds are deceptively simple, they are incredibly effective. It is very important that you perform them with confidence. Your partner will subconsciously pick up on an unsure touch and if this happens at the outset of your massage sequence, he or she will not reap the full rewards of your efforts.

When practising, ask your partner for feedback about the feel of your holds so that you can gauge your success or otherwise.

A simple summary

✔ Pressures range from deep, precise movements using fingers or thumbs to broader penetration using the heel or palm of the hand or the flattened elbow.

✔ The smaller the point you use, the deeper the penetration – the stiletto effect.

✔ Light pressures are soothing and allow you to feel for tense muscles; deeper pressures compress tight muscles and in time can relieve areas of tension.

✔ Deep pressures should only be applied to areas that have been massaged and warmed previously.

✔ You do not need to use oil with pressures as the movements are fairly restricted and the hands do not have to glide across the skin; this makes these movements ideal for when you are massaging through clothes.

✔ Holding your partner is a simple way to impart confidence and trust.

✔ Holds may be used at the beginning or end or a massage or as a linking move during the massage.

✔ The aim of a hold is to communicate feelings of empathy and support to your partner.

Chapter 9

Do it Yourself

NOW THAT YOU HAVE BEEN INTRODUCED to all the basic strokes, I am sure you can hardly wait to put the moves together into a complete sequence. Don't worry if you don't have a willing partner close at hand, because doing a massage on yourself is the perfect alternative! By practising on yourself, you can discover how your hands might feel on others.

In this chapter...
- ✓ Face and scalp
- ✓ Neck and shoulders
- ✓ Legs and feet
- ✓ Abdomen
- ✓ Lower back
- ✓ Arms and hands
- ✓ Final touches

LEARN TO MASSAGE YOUR OWN WAY OUT OF TENSION

Face and scalp

SELF-MASSAGE is often just as therapeutic as being given a massage by someone else and you should try to do it on a regular basis; it can boost energy levels when you are feeling exhausted, ease away aches and pains, banish the tensions of the day, and, most importantly, provide you with the opportunity to spend time on yourself.

Feeling your way to a full facial

The face and scalp are especially well suited to self-massage; we instinctively stroke our foreheads when we have a headache and hold our foreheads when concentrating. The face contains a huge number of nerve receptors and, therefore, a face massage can have profound effects all through the body, changing our mood, enhancing relaxation, and controlling pain. The scalp, too, can store a surprising amount of tension – the skin will feel taut and difficult to move if it is not relaxed.

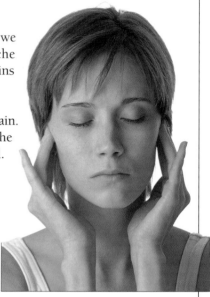

1 Stroke your whole face with soft, moulding hands. Then, with the fingers of both hands, stroke slowly and firmly from the centre of your forehead out to your temples. Stroke under your cheekbones, from your nose to your ears; this can help if you suffer from sinus congestion. Then stroke from your mouth out towards the edges of your jaw.

2 Explore your face with circular finger pressures, moving your skin against the underlying muscles. Vary the size, depth, and direction of the circles; try flat, shallow circles and deep, penetrating spirals. Feel for any taut, over-used muscles and pay particular attention to your jaw, as tension is often stored there.

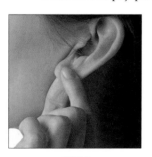

STEP 3

3 Gently squeeze and pull your ears with your thumb and forefinger, working around all the nooks and crannies.

4 Place a palm over each ear, then slowly and gently move your ears up and down in a circular motion, easing pressure on the upward movement. The noise you will hear sounds like the sea and I am sure you will find it very soothing.

(5) Gently stroke around your right eye with your right hand and your left eye with your left hand at the same time. Then squeeze along each eyebrow from the bridge of your nose to your temples using your index fingers and thumbs. If you find a particularly tight spot, keep holding this point until the tension eases.

(6) Use the pads of your fingers to tap lightly under your eyes and over your eyelids. The sensation should resemble lightly falling rain. This movement helps to disperse congestion in the area and reduce puffiness around the eyes that can be caused by tiredness.

STEP 6

(7) Place your palms on your temples, with your fingers resting on your head, and slowly circle your palms ten times in one direction and ten times in the other. Then make circular palm pressures all over your scalp.

(8) In each of your hands, clasp some strands of hair at the root, twist them around your fingers, and gently pull. Imagine you are pulling out tension. Hold the hair for a few seconds longer and then release it. Repeat the sequence using hair from all over the scalp. You can use both hands together or one hand after the other.

(9) Comb the fingers of one hand through the hair from the roots to the ends, then follow the movement with the other hand. Repeat this sequence all over your head, trying to achieve a smooth, fluid rhythm. Try not to hurry these movements as they can be surprisingly relaxing.

(10) Use percussion movements on your head to wake yourself up. Use the fingers and thumbs of alternate hands to pluck the scalp, or pummel the area with relaxed fists. Vary the lightness and speed for different effects.

STEP 9

Neck and shoulders

MOST PEOPLE *suffer from tension in their necks and shoulders at some time in their lives, which is hardly surprising if you consider the job the neck has to do! Poor posture, bad working positions, and carrying heavy bags all conspire to make the problem worse. However, you can ease the pain with a remedy literally at your fingertips.*

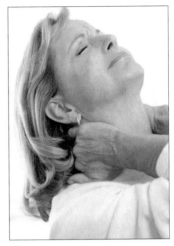

■ **By the end of the day,** *many people need to find some form of relief from the tension that has built up in their neck and shoulders.*

Getting to the core of tension

This simple self-massage exercise gets right to the core of the tension and eases it gently and effortlessly; you can try it almost anywhere and at any time. Try to focus on the areas that feel most tense, and work slowly, deeply, and methodically.

1. Tilt your head back, and with the palms and fingers of each hand, squeeze the flesh at the base of your neck on either side of your spine. Then, slowly roll your head forwards, still squeezing your skin. Hold the stretch for 10 seconds, then return your head to an upright position. The amount of flesh you can squeeze depends on your state of relaxation.

2. Stroke your hands up and down the back of your neck to warm the area. Then use the fingers of both your hands to make deep, circular pressures all around the neck area, making sure that you do not apply pressure to the spine itself.

3. Place your left hand on your right shoulder and squeeze the muscle. Hold the squeeze and slowly rotate your shoulder backwards. A grinding noise indicates that the muscles are tense and should be freed up. Repeat with the right hand on the left shoulder.

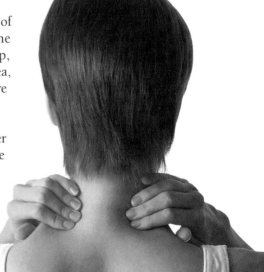

STEP 2

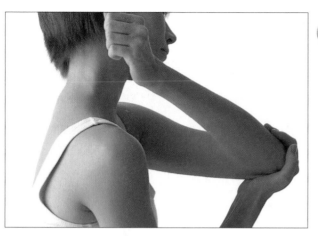

4 Pummel your right shoulder with your left hand to bring fresh blood to the area. Support your left elbow with your right hand for comfort, and keep your wrist loose and floppy as you swiftly strike the flesh. Repeat on your left shoulder.

5 With your fingers, stroke firmly from the centre of your chest outwards, applying deep pressure between your ribs. When your fingers reach the outer edges of your ribcage, return to the centre and repeat the movement. Feel for tense spots and concentrate on these as you work over the chest.

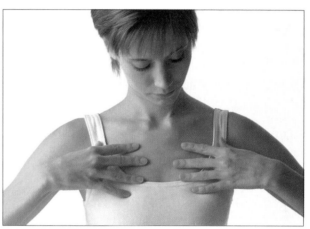

Trivia...

I know a professor at Oxford University, UK, who has a heavy schedule lecturing in all corners of the world. He told me recently that he always travels with a bottle of oil so he can give himself a daily massage. He is convinced that his self-massage not only keeps him healthy but also that it is the best antidote to jet lag.

Never attempt to massage any part of your body if you are in a situation that requires your full concentration.

For example, do not massage your neck and shoulders as you are driving along a motorway; if you can't wait till you get home, just pull in at the nearest opportunity and stop the car before doing the massage.

Legs and feet

OUR LEGS AND FEET *have to support all our weight so it's not surprising that they often ache and feel tired. A good massage can relieve this tension and leave them feeling light and energetic. Knowing how to massage your legs is useful whether you lead an active or a sedentary life, and regular massage of your thighs can even improve their appearance.*

Few things are more exhausting and aging than sore feet. By massaging your feet daily, you can relieve tiredness and really relax; in fact, some practitioners, notably reflexologists, believe that foot massage can stimulate your whole body.

Soothing aching legs

With massage, you can relieve aching legs after standing for too long, and you can help tired muscles recover after exercise. As in other parts of the body, light strokes stimulate the *lymphatic system* and deeper strokes help circulation. Always use firmer strokes as you work up the legs towards the body, and use oil to keep the movements fluid.

> ### DEFINITION
>
> *The **lymphatic system** is a complex network of vessels and glands (lymph nodes) that carry fluid (lymph) from body tissues and return it to the blood system to maintain a constant balance of fluid within the body. As well as draining excess fluid into the blood stream, the lymph glands produce lymphocytes that help fight infection.*

1. Start the massage by stroking the whole of your left leg up towards your body, applying a firm pressure as you do so. You can either stroke one hand after the other, or place one hand on either side of the leg and stroke both hands together.

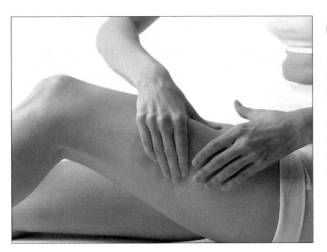

2. Next, knead your left leg. Using alternate hands, squeeze and release the flesh at the top of your thigh, working rhythmically and methodically. Work all over the top of your thigh, down to your knee, and continue along the back of your thigh. Then knead your calf muscles in the same leg.

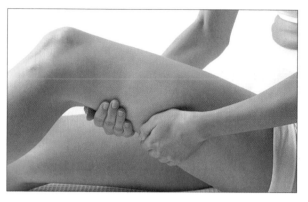

3 Soothe your leg with criss-cross strokes. Place one hand on each side of your thigh at the knee, and pull your hands upwards, squeezing your leg. Release your grip, cross your hands over, and glide them down the other side of your thigh. Then pull up your hands to repeat the action. Continue, working all the way up your thigh.

4 To soothe and relax your knee, apply circular pressures with your fingertips all around your left kneecap. Next, stroke softly behind your knee, stroking up towards your body

5 When you have completed the massage on your left leg, repeat the whole sequence (steps 1–4) on your right leg.

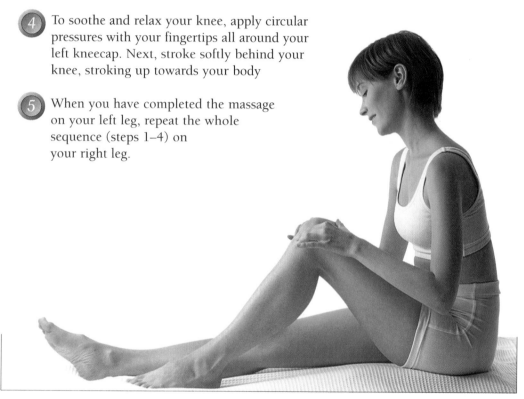

STEP 4

I always encourage my students to give themselves a self-massage once a week. They are often surprised at how good it feels. Try to choose a quiet area where you will not be disturbed, and sit in a chair or on the floor, or lie down. Then close your eyes and massage all your cares away.

Easy relief for feet

Your feet are among the easiest parts of your body to self-massage, and it's something you can do wherever you happen to be. If you are sitting, simply rest one foot on the opposite thigh. If you prefer to lie down, keep one leg bent up, and rest your other foot on your raised thigh. Give one foot a complete massage first, then transfer to the other one.

A great way to start a foot massage is to soak your feet in a bowl of warm, scented water.

Fill a large bowl with warm water and add a couple of drops of your favourite essential oil (lavender and peppermint are my favourites). Put your feet in and luxuriate for as long as you like before starting the foot massage below.

1 Rest the sole of your right foot on your left knee and sandwich your foot between your hands, with your fingers facing forwards. Rub your hands backwards and forwards along your foot to warm the whole area.

2 Support the heel of your right foot with your left hand and clasp the toes with your right hand. Energetically squeeze, extend, and flex your toes to increase their flexibility.

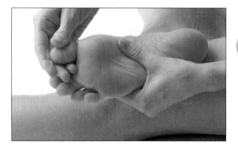

3 Still supporting your right foot with your left hand, massage your toes with your right hand by squeezing, twisting, and rolling each one in turn with your fingers.

4 Place one thumb on top of the other, using your fingers to support your foot, and make deep, circular thumb pressures over the sole of your foot. Stroke the area. Repeat the whole sequence (steps 1–4) on your left foot.

Abdomen

IT'S NATURAL to rub your abdomen when you have a stomach ache, and any form of abdominal massage, however basic, is extremely comforting. Although you can massage your abdomen while sitting up, it is much more relaxing if you lie down. Lie somewhere comfortable, with a small pillow under your knees so that both your back and abdomen are relaxed. Always use a clockwise motion when massaging the abdomen as this follows the workings of the intestine; this can help to relax the abdomen, which, in turn, can aid digestion.

1 Stroke one hand after the other around your abdomen in a clockwise direction, lifting one hand over the other in a continuous flow. Increase the size of the circle to cover the whole area, then gradually make it smaller again.

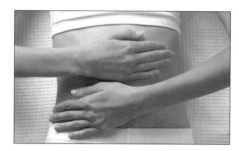

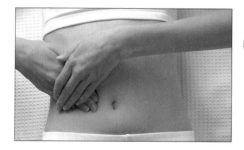

2 Apply static and circular pressures all around the abdomen, following the outline that you traced with your strokes in step 1. Use one hand on top of the other, or the palm of just one hand, depending on how much pressure you want to apply.

3 Bend your knees over to your left and knead the right side of your abdomen with the fingers and thumbs of alternate hands. Rhythmically pick up and release the flesh wherever you can, then bend your knees to the right and knead the left side.

You don't have to be in the perfect surroundings to do a self-massage — you can massage your feet while watching tv, or your hands while talking to a friend.

Lower back

YOU CAN MASSAGE your lower back by sitting cross-legged, as shown here, or by lying down on your side with your top knee bent in front of you. The movements outlined below are designed to release muscular tension and aid relaxation.

Relieving muscular tension

Start by vigorously rubbing the palms of both your hands up and down the small of your back, and from side to side, to warm the area and release any muscular tension.

1 For a stronger, deeper movement, make your hands into fists and press the thumb side of your hand into your sacrum, the lower part of your spine. Then stroke your fists firmly up and down the area.

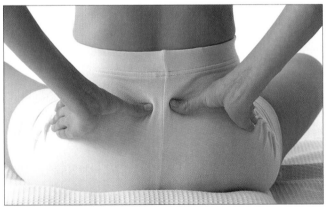

2 Make deliberate, circular pressures with your fingertips or thumbs all around your sacrum.

3 Now, pummel the area with floppy, relaxed fists, taking care to avoid your kidneys. Finish with some gentle stroking.

Arms and hands

FOR MOST PEOPLE, *the arms and hands are the most used parts of their bodies, whether from spending long periods of time at a computer for work, playing a racket sport for pleasure, or just carrying out the day-to-day chores. Everyone, therefore, will benefit from a massage of their arms and hands. Not surprisingly, tension in your arms can create aches and pains in your shoulders and neck; strong movements are required to unlock tightness in the upper arms and forearms.*

One-handed kneading

This one-handed massage can be done fully clothed, so you can do it wherever you happen to be when the need arises.

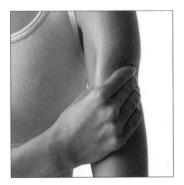

STEP 2

STEP 3

STEP 4

1. Begin by stroking the whole of your left arm from the wrist to the shoulder, working firmly as you move up the arm and then gliding gently back down again.

2. Squeeze and roll the muscles of your left arm between the fingers and heel of your right hand. Start kneading on your upper arm, and work down from the shoulder to the wrist.

3. Use your knuckles to make rotary pressures all along your arm, working as deeply and rhythmically as you can.

4. Stroke one forearm with the other, slowly rotating the top forearm as you stroke from the elbow to the wrist of your other arm. This stroke massages both arms simultaneously, and is very effective.

Hands

Our hands are in constant use and, as a result, they can harbour a lot of tension. Most of our hand movements are holding, clutching actions, so it is very relaxing to counteract these by opening your palm and pulling your fingers. There are very many nerve endings on the palms of your hands, and massage here can benefit the whole body. In fact, in reflexology (see Chapter 24) each part of the body is reflected in a map of the hand (or foot) and massaging a particular area of the hand will have an effect on the equivalent part of the body.

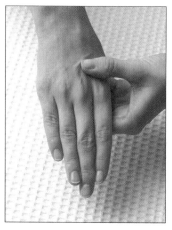

STEP 1

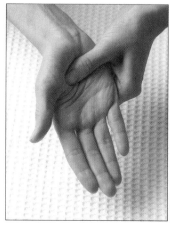

STEP 2

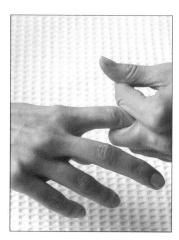

STEP 3

1. First, rub your palms together to warm them. Then use your thumb to stroke deeply between each tendon of your right hand, from your knuckles to your wrist.

2. Stroke your left thumb firmly down the palm of your right hand and out towards the side several times in a fanning motion. Then make deep, circular thumb pressures all over your right palm.

3. Pull and twist each finger of your right hand with the knuckles of your left hand. Work right up to the fingertips.

4. Repeat the whole sequence (steps 1–3) on your left hand.

Self-massage can be particularly useful if you suffer from chronic or short-term pain. It helps to stimulate the release of endorphins and diverts your attention away from the pain. Above all, self-massage gives you a sense of control over your situation.

Final touches

JUST AS A MASSAGE given by someone else has a defined ending phase, a self-massage needs to close on a relaxed note.

Feather stroking

Use light, feather strokes starting at your forehead and then stroke the fingertips of both your hands over your face and neck, down both arms, and leave your body at the tips of your fingers. Then stroke the front of your body, down your legs, and withdraw your touch at your feet. This movement should leave you feeling refreshed, calm, and as light as a feather.

GENTLE STROKES

A simple summary

✔ Self-massage can be done wherever you happen to be whenever the need arises; you don't even need to undress.

✔ Giving yourself a massage is a great way to feel how your touch feels on others and allows you to experiment and improve your technique. You don't have to worry about making mistakes and can try out ambitious new moves.

✔ Giving yourself a massage can be as therapeutic as being given one by someone else. You can really pinpoint areas of tension and focus on them.

✔ Self-massage can be used to energize yourself for a new day, to soothe away your pain or tensions, or to calm yourself before sleep.

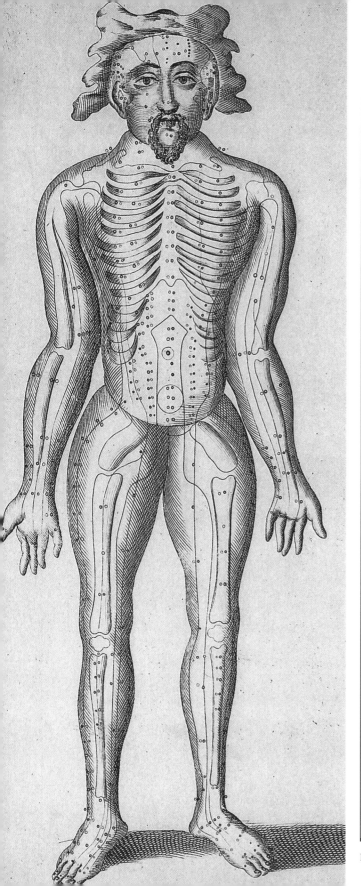

PART THREE

Chapter 10
Back Strokes

Chapter 11
Chest and Neck

Chapter 12
Feet and Legs

Chapter 13
Hands and Arms

Chapter 14
Abdomen

Chapter 15
Face and Head

EVERY PART OF THE BODY CAN BENEFIT FROM MASSAGE

MASSAGE AROUND THE BODY

NOW THAT YOU'VE BEEN INTRODUCED to the strokes, you can put them into ordered practice. In Part Three, I will outline a tour of the *human form*, working the *restorative* magic of massage from head to toe. If you want to relieve tension in one particular area, dip in and follow the instructions in a single chapter, or alternatively treat your partner to a full body massage.

I will begin with one of life's luxuries: a back massage. From here, I will take the whole body into consideration one part at a time: concentrate on the chest and neck to improve posture, the abdomen for stomach complaints, feet for weary walkers, hands to soothe, and head to disperse a tension headache.

Chapter 10

Back Strokes

THIS CHAPTER TELLS YOU ALL ABOUT one of the greatest delights in life – a good back massage. It is one of the easiest types of massage to do, and therefore a great place to start on our voyage around the body. It can have a profoundly relaxing effect, lowering stress levels, easing pain, and inducing a blissful state of repose. After all, most of us get the occasional backache, which is not surprising as we slouch over our desks, carry heavy loads, hunch up our shoulders, and stand badly. Massage can help to relax the back muscles and alleviate accompanying aches and pains.

In this chapter...

✓ Simply the back

✓ Move on up:
  neck and shoulders

✓ Down to the buttocks

✓ And back to back

THE BACK IS ONE OF THE BEST AREAS TO MASSAGE FOR COMPLETE RELAXATION

Simply the back

THE BENEFITS OF A BACK MASSAGE

go well beyond simply relaxing the back muscles – it can enhance the wellbeing of the whole body. If you are among the many people who suffer from back pain, you will know just how debilitating it can be. The spine is a tower of discs and bones, and the muscles, ligaments, and tendons that support it are easily strained by everyday life. A back massage can help soothe and heal.

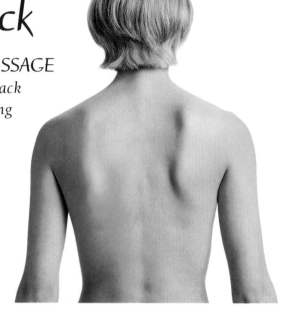

THE BACK: A CENTRAL SUPPORTING PILLAR

To help set the tone for your massage, cover your partner's back with a towel and place your hands on top of it, one on the nape of the neck, and the other on the waist. Breathe deeply and evenly, and your partner will pick up your breathing rhythm and will start to relax. After about 30 seconds, put the oil on your hands and pull back the towel. Stand or kneel by your partner's waist, facing his or her head, and begin the massage by stroking to spread the oil.

The T-stroke

I call this basic, simple massage stroke the T-stroke, because this is the shape you are making with your partner's back.

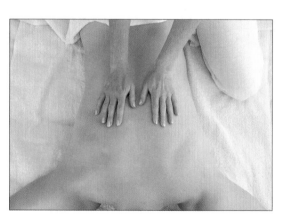

1 Start with your hands on the lower back, your thumbs on either side of the spine and your fingers pointing towards the head. With relaxed hands, stroke firmly up the back. Lean onto your hands, using your body weight to apply pressure.

② Pull back down on the muscles at the base of the neck, then stroke out across the shoulders and the tops of the arms, moulding your hands to the curve of the shoulders. Sweep your hands around the tops of the arms and then down the sides.

③ Glide your hands lightly down the sides of your partner's body, keeping them relaxed and taking care not to drag the skin. When you reach the waist, pull inwards and upwards. This gives the lovely feeling of having a tiny waist. Repeat up to ten times.

Stroking variations

For a slightly different movement, try fan stroking. Start with your hands on your partner's lower back, as above, and stroke firmly up the back pressing on the muscles on either side of the spine. Fan your hands out over the lower ribs, moulding them to the contours of your partner's body, and glide them lightly down the sides. Repeat the stroke, fanning your hands out a little higher on the back each time, until you reach the shoulders.

Take this variation a step further by continuing to stroke the back, but use your hands alternately. One hand strokes firmly upwards as the other glides down the side. Practise this stroke until the move is smooth and rhythmic, and when you have perfected it, your partner will benefit from its wonderful relaxing flow.

During a back massage, ask your partner at regular intervals to change the direction in which the head is turned. You will be able to reach all parts of the neck, shoulders, and upper back, and your partner won't get a stiff neck.

Did you know?

In a study by Touch Research International in Miami, USA, a 30-minute back massage was given daily for 5 days to 52 children and adolescents who were being treated for psychiatric problems. When compared to a control group who had not been massaged but who had been allowed to watch relaxing videos, the massaged children were less anxious and agitated, were able to sleep better, and were more co-operative.

Kneading

After the gentle stroking movements with which you started your back massage, a slight change of tempo feels good for your partner. Kneading is an extremely versatile movement; it can be done slowly and deeply, or fast and stimulating depending on your partner's needs.

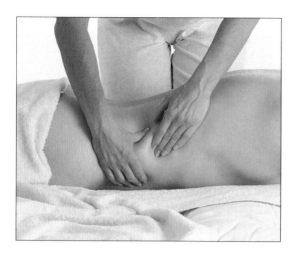

1 Turn to face across your partner's body, with your hands facing each other and your elbows sticking out, and grasp and squeeze handfuls of flesh with alternate hands. Imagine you are rhythmically kneading dough, but with a smooth, flowing movement. Grasp the flesh with one hand, squeeze it but do not pinch, and push it towards your other hand. Release the first hand, then pick up and squeeze the flesh with the second hand. Start at the hips and work up the sides of the body.

2 Continue kneading at the base of the neck, over the shoulders, and out across the upper arms. The deltoid muscle at the top of the arm is often very tense, and since it lifts the shoulder working with the large muscle across the upper back, you need to include this area in the massage in order to relax the back thoroughly. Then work on the side nearest you – either lean down so that you can push up with your thumbs, or move to the other side of the body and reach across again. Work your way around the back twice.

The deltoid muscle is named after the Greek letter delta, which is the fourth letter in the Greek alphabet. The capital version of the letter is shaped like a triangle, just like the shape of the muscle.

Sides stroking

To relax your hands after these kneading strokes, I like to use side stroking. With loose, relaxed hands, vertically stroke up the sides of the body pulling inwards towards the spine. Work all around the back, with one hand following the other in a smooth, flowing rhythm. This is an easy stroke that is relaxing for both giver and receiver.

Circle stroking

This is a wonderful linking movement. It is a circular, flowing action that can be done in either direction on the back. It's a great move for spreading more oil over the back, and to help make the massage feel continuous and flowing.

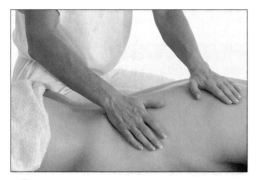

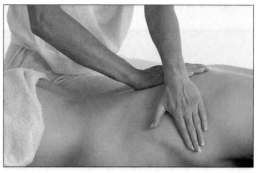

1 Place both hands on the right-hand side of your partner's back, one hand slightly higher than the other. Slide the top hand down the side in a large curve, and at the same time slide your lower hand up to the spine.

2 Continue stroking round in these wide curves. Imagine a circle on the back, and stroke around it in a clockwise direction, one hand following the other. You must always work up and away from the spine.

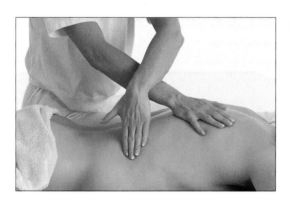

3 Lift your left hand over your right arm while your right hand continues stroking in a circular motion. Your right hand does a complete circle but your left hand does only a half circle.

4 Complete the circle with your right hand and place your left hand down gently. Work up the back on this side, then slide your hands down and work on the left-hand side. This time you are working anticlockwise as you are stroking away from the spine, with your left hand doing the complete circle, and your right hand working just a half circle. This continuous, flowing stroke can induce a dream-like state in some people.

Circle thumb stroking

This is similar to circle stroking (see above), but the movement is concentrated in much smaller circles. These are very useful on either side of the spine and all around the *scapula*.

DEFINITION

The shoulder blade is known medically as the **scapula**

 Start with both thumbs on one side of the spine and stroke around in a circle.

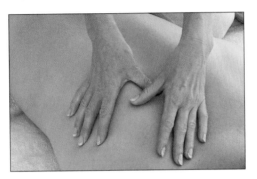

 One thumb follows the other as you stroke up and out, pushing the muscle away from the spine. The movement is precise, working about 3 cm (1 inch) from the spine.

3 Lift one thumb over the other hand and continue circling. As in circle stroking, one thumb makes a complete circle, and the other just does a half circle.

Additional moves

You can then relax the small muscles on either side of your partner's spine with a series of firm pressures. Start on the lower back with your thumbs on either side of the spine. Lean your weight onto the pads of your thumbs, keeping your elbows straight – you need to apply a relaxed pressure, not a sharp poke. Press firmly, then release, and repeat a little further up the back. Do extra work on the shoulders and the base of the neck as these are the areas where most tension is stored. Then glide back to the base of the spine, and start again. Vary the movement by making small, penetrating circles over these muscles.

Continue with some finger drumming. Although this movement can be tiring to give – as you cannot use your full body weight, just the strength of your hands – it is very useful for relieving tension pressure in the shoulder muscles. Drum your fingers down individually, pressing heavily on the muscle. Keep your hands close together and, if you're like me, and one of your hands is stronger than the other, cross your thumbs to equalize the pressure. This heavy drumming movement brings blood to the area and helps to ease away pain.

Did you know?

According to researchers at the University of Cologne, Germany, finger drumming and hand exercises boost the circulation, and this helps keep the brain fit and enhances memory. Remember this as you drum away on your partner's back – you are stimulating your own brain cells at the same time as soothing away aches and pains.

Move on up: neck and shoulders

NEARLY EVERYONE EXPERIENCES *stiffness and tension in their neck and shoulders, and when giving a massage, special attention should be given to these areas. The neck muscles have to work continuously to support the weight of the head so it is hardly surprising that these muscles are often painful. Many people habitually hunch their shoulders, which makes the muscles at the sides of the neck as well as the shoulder muscles, very tense.*

Stroking

Gently stroking the neck and shoulders is a wonderful way of easing tension. Keep the movements smooth and slow – any jerky or heavy movements may increase tension in the area. To avoid becoming stiff yourself, move further up towards the neck so that you can reach the area more easily. If you are working with your partner lying on the floor, put one of your knees up with your foot resting on the floor so you have more control and can keep your movements steady and smooth.

If your partner is not comfortable with his or her head turned to one side, they can rest their head on their hands, a cushion, or rolled-up towel.

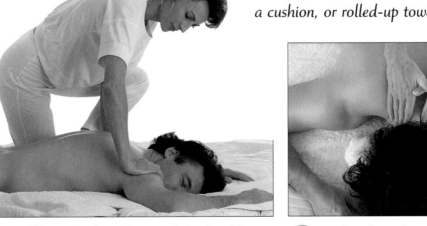

1 Stroke from the top of the shoulders up the sides of the neck, moulding your hands to the body's shape.

2 Reach right to the top of the neck, then glide your hands down, keeping the pressure smooth and even. Repeat four times.

Additional moves

Ask your partner to lie face down and knead the neck muscles gently. Work on both the shoulders and up the neck to the base of the skull.

Circular pressures

Follow this with circular pressures applied up the neck on either side of the spine. Use only one of your hands, with your thumb on one side of the spine and your index and middle fingers on the other side. Put your other hand on top of the head to convey reassurance. Press into the muscle and make small circular movements. Continue to make these movements up into the hair around the base of the skull.

CIRCULAR PRESSURES

So that you don't disturb your partner when you need to apply more oil, put a few drops on your forearm and top of the hand. You can wipe it off with your other hand while continuing the massage.

Down to the buttocks

WHEN YOU HAVE FINISHED WORKING *on your partner's neck, make some long stroking movements over the whole of the back to warm up the area, and then move down to start working on the buttocks. Keep your hands on your partner's back as you move down to stand or kneel by his or her hips. Face towards the head as you massage the buttocks.*

The buttock muscles are among the most powerful in the body, and a good massage in this area really helps to release tension.

Fan stroking

Remind yourself of this gentle stroking movement before you start (see Chapter 5).

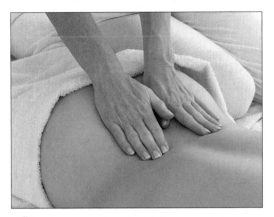
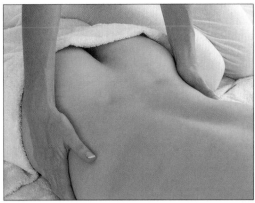

1 Place your hands at the top of the buttocks, and stroke smoothly up towards the waist and then out towards the side.

2 Keeping your hands relaxed, mould them gently round the sides of the waist, and then down and in towards the top of the buttocks.

3 Pull firmly up at the sides of the buttocks, then swing your hands round to the starting position and repeat steps 1–3.

Circle stroking

This movement feels wonderful on the buttocks if you keep it flowing and rhythmic. Work on each buttock separately, circling clockwise on the right side and anticlockwise on the left side.

1 With both hands on one buttock, stroke round in a circle, with one hand following the other.

2 Stroke gently as you glide down the sides, and pull firmly up at the buttocks.

3 Lift one hand over the other arm to complete the circle, and continue. Repeat steps 1–3 on the other buttock.

Additional moves

Kneading actions are great for fleshy areas and the buttocks can take a lot of this movement. Put a twist into the massage for a really stimulating response. Circular pressures also work well on the buttocks. Apply around the sacrum using the thumbs of both hands simultaneously.

And back to back

TO COMPLETE THE BACK MASSAGE, you need to return to the broad expanse of your partner's back so that you can calm the whole area down. Turn so that you are facing sideways across the back in a standing or kneeling position. Depending on time and how tired you are, you can use all or just some of the following techniques.

INTERNET

www.portable practitioner.com

This site is an international resource and networking forum for all healing arts professionals, including massage therapists.

Cradling

This is a warm, comforting movement that makes a gentle start to this final phase of the back massage.

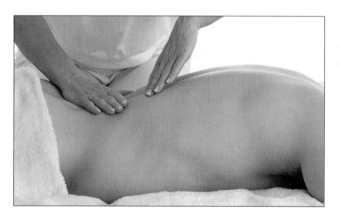

1 With relaxed hands facing each other, do some open-handed kneading on the lower back.

2 Simply sway your hands back and forth across your partner's flesh in a deep and penetrating stroke. Do not grasp or squeeze the flesh.

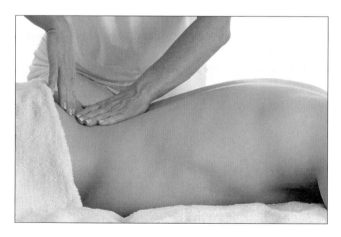

Criss-cross strokes

The combination of gliding movements and the gentlest of squeezes creates a wonderfully relaxing sensation in your partner.

 Put one hand on each side of your partner's waist, with the fingers of both your hands facing away from you. Pull your hands firmly up the sides of the body, gently pulling in at the waist, and glide them across the back.

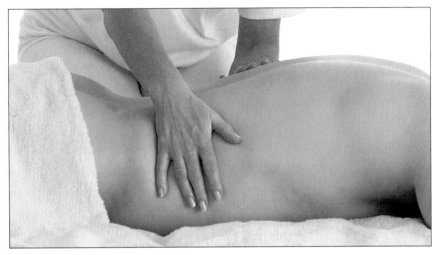

2. Slide your hands past each other and down the other side of the body. Make a definite contrast between firmly pulling up at the sides of the body, and lightly gliding across the back. Work up and down your partner's back a couple of times.

Finishing moves

You can proceed to the end of the back massage with a combination of some of the next moves or, if you have time, you can try them all. They are not in any particular order and you can experiment to find out which ones your partner prefers. I vary the ending depending on whether my client wants to be woken up – in which case pummelling is invigorating – or wishes to stay in a relaxed state – when I would use cat strokes.

Pummelling is the easiest percussion movement, and is therefore ideal for beginners. It should be really rhythmic – I always imagine I'm playing the maracas in a steel band!

Pummelling

Pummelling is an ideal pounding movement for the back. Make loose fists with your hands and pummel all over your partner's back. Your wrists should be very flexible so that the movement is light and stimulating, not heavy and painful.

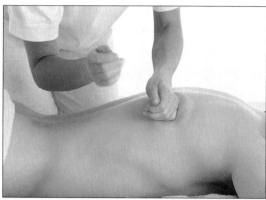

PUMMELLING

While you are learning the technique, put a towel over the back and pummel through this to avoid stinging the skin or striking the flesh too hard.

Start at the buttocks and move up the back towards the neck. Vary the speed for different effects: slow for relaxation and vigorous for stimulation.

Work gently over bony areas, and never strike the spine. Also, steer clear of the kidney area, as pressure here can be painful.

Cat stroking

Cat stroking is perfect for ending the back massage as it imparts a wonderfully hypnotic and soporific effect. Start at the neck and stroke gently down the spine with one hand, and as it reaches the buttocks, follow it with your other hand. Lift off your hand at the small of the back and return it to the neck. The return movement is as important as the stroke itself, so move rhythmically. Gradually, stroke more and more slowly and lightly.

When the cat stroke is as light as you can make it, move on to the feather touch. Stroke very, very lightly down either side of the spine with both hands together, using just your fingertips. When you reach the small of the back, lift your hands off and return them to the neck. Flick your hands gently between each stroke to keep them feeling light and to get rid of the feeling of electricity that tends to gather. The movement should feel that it has no beginning or end, and you can carry on with it for as long as you like.

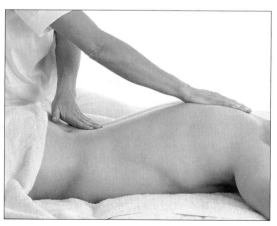

CAT STROKING

Additional moves

There are also extra movements and positions that you can include to extend your back massage or to ring the changes if you are massaging regularly. Get feedback from your partner to see which he or she prefers.

Raking down the spine

Start at your partner's neck with your index and middle fingers on either side of the spine. Make small, firm strokes down the back, one hand after the other.

Stretching

A good way to begin or end a back massage is to give your partner's back a gentle stretch. Cross your arms and place one hand on the sacrum and the other half way up the spine, with your hands facing away from each other. Lean forwards, keeping your arms rigid and do not let your hands slip up or down the back. As you lean, the pressure of your arms being pushed apart gently stretches the lower back. You can give a diagonal stretch to the back by placing one hand on your partner's shoulder and the other on the opposite hip, with your hands facing away from each other. Again, lean forwards, keeping your arms straight, to stretch the back. Repeat on the other shoulder and hip.

If you perform stretching over a towel, you need to make a pleat in the towel to allow for the stretch.

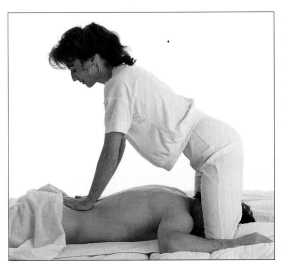

You can also massage your partner's back when kneeling by the head. Stroke firmly down the back, fan your hands out at the buttocks, and sweep them up the sides. Done very slowly and firmly, this gives a wonderful stretch to the lower back. Try it with both hands working together, and then alternately, one hand going down as the other glides up. This is also a very good position for working on the shoulders and neck.

■ **To stretch** *your partner's lower back following a massage, use both hands to stroke in opposite directions.*

QUICK CHECKLIST FOR A BASIC BACK MASSAGE

When I am teaching, I find a quick checklist can really help, particularly for beginners. It helps avoid having to wade through lots of text with every massage.

The back:

1. T-stroking
2. Fan stroking
3. Kneading
4. Circle stroking
5. Circle thumb stroking

Neck and shoulders:

1. Stroking the shoulders and neck
2. Kneading the neck
3. Circular pressures on the neck

The buttocks:

1. Fan stroking
2. Circle stroking
3. Kneading

Back to back:

1. Cradling
2. Criss-cross strokes
3. Pummelling
4. Cat stroking
5. Raking
6. Stretching

■ **Massage can help** *improve the condition and flexibility of the back.*

Final touch

A nice way to finish a back massage is by placing relaxed, slightly cupped hands over the small of the back. Hold them there and feel heat gathering underneath. Ease the heat into your partner's body by gently flattening your hands. Lift your hands away very, very slowly. The movement should be so gentle that your partner does not know when your hands leave. This can give such a feeling of lightness that a friend calls it her "magic carpet".

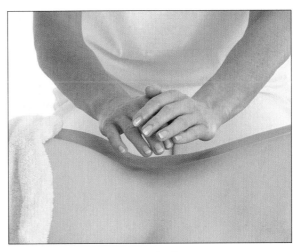

FINAL TOUCH

A simple summary

✓ Back massage is one of the simplest types of massage to do and yet it can give the greatest amount of pleasure.

✓ Although you can vary the actual moves, it is best to start with the broad expanse of the back, then move up to the neck and shoulders, then down to the buttocks, and finish by returning to the back.

✓ Always try to make your movements as continuous and flowing as possible so that your partner isn't aware that you are moving around from buttocks to shoulders.

✓ Use your body weight to put strength and pressure into the massage to make the actions more effective and also to reduce the strain on your hands, arms, and shoulders.

✓ Remember that stroking movements always feel good so use them whenever you tire of more strenuous moves, or to link different types of movement together.

Chapter 11

Chest and Neck

I AM ALWAYS SURPRISED at the number of people who carry tension in their chests. Bad posture; sitting cramped over a desk; hunching over a steering wheel; certain sports, such as golf; and illnesses such as asthma, can all cause strain and tension in chest muscles. The chest muscles shorten and contract, causing the muscles in the upper back to become overstretched. This results in rounded shoulders and tight, inflexible muscles in the neck and shoulders. Massage can really help to stretch and relax the chest muscles, and thus alleviate aching in the upper back and neck. Working on the muscles between the ribs can help to straighten out the shoulders.

In this chapter...
- ✔ *Get it off your chest*
- ✔ *Relieving tension in the neck*

ENCOURAGE GOOD POSTURE BY LOOSENING TENSE MUSCLES IN THE CHEST AND NECK

Get it off your chest

THE IDEAL TIME TO DO a chest massage is before you massage the face, but it also fits in naturally after a back or stomach massage, or after massaging one arm, and before the other. Your partner should lie on his or her back and you should stand or kneel behind the head. Some people like to put a small cushion or a thick book, such as a telephone directory (thick but not too hard), under the head to allow complete relaxation of the neck. As it is difficult to relax the chest and neck unless the shoulders are relaxed too, I always include them in a chest and neck massage.

Stretching the shoulders

Cup your hands around both shoulders and gently push them down towards the feet. Lean your weight onto the shoulders, keeping your arms straight. First push both arms down together, then alternately. Our shoulders tend to hunch up towards our ears as we become tense, and the gentle downwards pressure counteracts this habit, helping to stretch and loosen the chest muscles and release tension. Throughout the chest massage, whenever your hands stroke over the shoulders, give them a gentle push down towards the feet.

■ **To counteract** *the hunching instinct, push the shoulders firmly down towards the feet.*

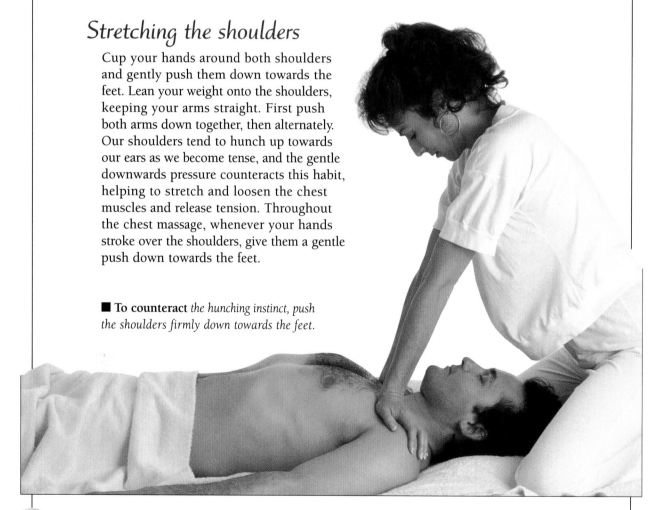

Stroking

Continue the chest and shoulder massage with gentle stroking movements. This will disperse the oil and soothe the area at the same time.

 Spread the oil by stroking the whole of your partner's chest and shoulder area. Try to make the movement feel firm and flowing. Start with your hands next to each other, just below the *clavicle* at the base of the neck.

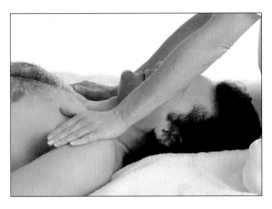

2 Stroke down the chest towards the breast or nipple, keeping the pressure smooth but firm. Then fan out your hands and, keeping them relaxed, glide out across the chest towards the shoulders.

3 Making sure your hands mould to the contours of your partner's body, stroke over the shoulders. Cup your hands over the shoulders and gently press the shoulders towards the feet or down onto the floor.

4 Swing your fingers around to the back of the shoulders. Stroke behind them, and bring your fingers slowly up the back of the neck. Then glide your hands very lightly down the sides of the neck to the collarbone. Repeat the sequence at least four times.

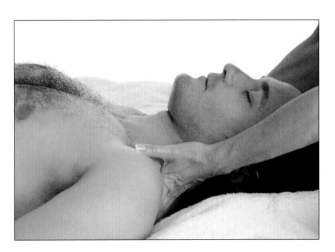

Additional chest touches

After stretching and stroking you can try any one, or a combination, of the following moves: knuckling, deep pressures, and kneading.

Knuckling

Make your hands into fists and ripple your fingers around to make small circular movements with your knuckles. Work gently all over your partner's chest, then move to behind the shoulders, and all around the base of the neck, where you can work more deeply.

Deep pressures

Make a series of thumb pressures on the muscles between the ribs. Start in the middle and work in lines out towards the shoulders. Pressures in this area can be painful, so be guided by your partner's reaction when deciding on depth.

Get feedback about what you are doing. Find out what feels good, what is not so pleasant, and what hurts. An involuntary flinch or a verbal expression will usually make it obvious. If you know your partner well, communication will not be a problem, but you may have to keep asking if you are massaging a stranger.

Kneading

You can use this technique to great advantage on the fleshy area in front of the armpits. Pick up and squeeze the muscle with alternate hands. Work with both hands together on one side of the body, and then move to the other side and repeat the action. This simple motion can release tension not only in the chest, but also in the arms and back.

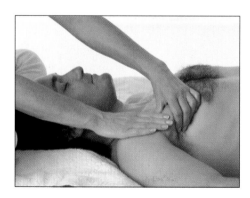

The muscle in front of the armpit is called the pectoralis, which is Latin for breast. This area is often affected by emotional stress, so massage the area with sensitivity.

■ **Work the pectoralis** *with both hands, kneading gently to relieve tension.*

Relieving tension in the neck

BEING ONE OF THE GREATEST sources of tension in the whole body, the neck can benefit hugely from a good massage. Bad posture, stress, draughts, and poor working conditions can all give rise to neck pain, but even the sheer weight of your head can often cause your neck to ache. As with chest and shoulder massage, work standing or kneeling behind your partner's head.

■ **You can** *administer a gentle neck massage while your partner is sitting or lying down.*

Side stroking

Your partner should be lying on his or her back. Using both of your hands together, stroke one side of the base of your partner's neck.

 Lean slightly towards the side you are working on, and stroke with one hand from the shoulder up the neck to the base of the skull. As your hand reaches the ear, follow the movement with your other hand.

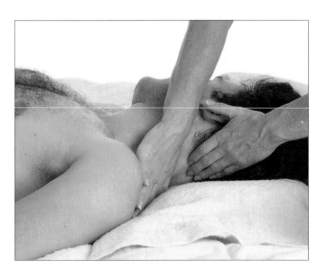

② Lift off your first hand and return it to the shoulder as your other hand strokes up your partner's neck. Try to keep the return movement smooth, so that the whole sequence feels flowing and your partner cannot tell when one stroke finishes and the next begins. Repeat the strokes several times on one side of the body, then copy the sequence on the other side.

Alternate stroking

This is a lovely flowing movement to follow side stroking.

1 With one hand on each side of your partner's neck, stroke with one hand first and then the other from the shoulders up to the base of the skull.

Your partner should not be lying on a pillow for alternate stroking; the head must be free to gently rock from side to side.

2 Sway from one side to the other as you make the movement so that the stroke is large and even as you gently ease the head from side to side. As your partner gradually relaxes, the movement becomes really rhythmic and fluid.

I use my forearms to help make alternate stroking a really big, smooth, flowing movement.

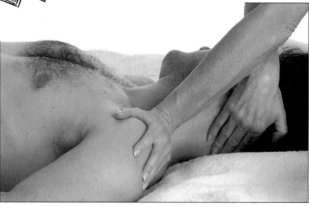

SIDE STRETCH

Side stretch

Cup one of your hands over one of your partner's shoulders, and your other hand around the base of the skull on the same side. Gently push the shoulder down while holding the head, without jerking the neck. This movement gives a gentle stetch to the neck muscles. Repeat on the other side of the body.

When giving a side stretch, on no account should you yank the neck. Pulling the head too sharply or roughly could leave your partner with more than just a small pain in the neck.

Pressures

Refresh your memory of making pressures (see Chapter 8) before starting.

 1 Slide your hands as far down as is comfortable to the base of the neck. With the two middle fingers of each of your hands, make small, firm, circular pressures on either side of the spine. Work slowly up to the neck, then press into the hollow at the top of the spine and the indentations on either side of the base of the skull.

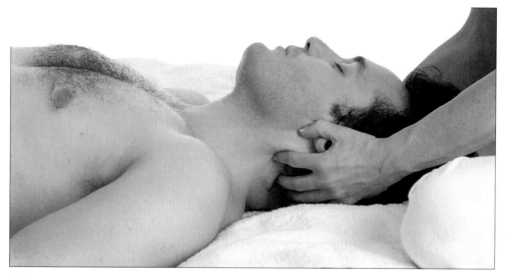

2 Make circular pressures all over the base of the skull. Press firmly, but with care. The muscles in this region are frequently taut and tense, and these pressures, which stimulate blood flow, can unknot the tension.

Extra movement

This is a lovely way of opening the chest, as well as relaxing the shoulders and the whole back. Ask your partner to lift up slightly, then slide your hands as far as you can reach under the back. Slowly glide up the back, taking your partner's weight in your hands. Use your own body weight to give a long stretch to the back.

If your partner is much bigger and heavier than you, take care when lifting them. You must position yourself so that you do not strain your own back; use your hips and stomach as you slowly pull back. If it causes you discomfort, don't do it. There is always another way of creating a similar effect (try the side stroking in Chapter 5).

Passive movements

As the term suggests, passive movements are actions performed by the masseur without any assistance from the person being massaged. When doing such movements, care should be taken not to force them but just to follow the client's natural range of movement.

Tension all down the back and up to the top of the head can be relieved by stretching the neck. Apply the stretch very gradually and smoothly, never jerk or pull suddenly.

1 Cup your hands around the base of your partner's skull and, without lifting the head up, lean back slowly, using your body weight to give a gentle stretch to the neck. Repeat two or three times.

2 Cup one of your hands around the back of the head and place your other hand on the forehead. Lift the head so that the chin drops forwards. Then gently lower the head, letting your hand take its weight. Repeat several times to encourage the head to move freely.

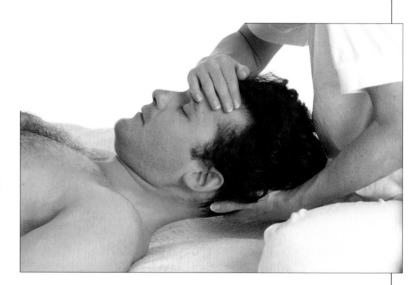

3 With both your hands in the same position as in step 2, slowly turn the head from side to side, making sure you support it all the time. Never force these movements – just encourage the head to move more freely.

QUICK CHECKLIST FOR CHEST MASSAGE

For a quick reminder, and to avoid going back over pages, use this list of the basic steps in a chest massage:

1. Stroking the chest

2. Knuckling, kneading, and circular pressures on the chest

3. Stroking the back of the neck and shoulders to stretch and relieve tension

4. Circular pressures at the base of the neck and on either side of the spine

5. Stroking the chest

6. Passive movements

INTERNET

www.rccm.org.uk

The web site of the Research Council for Complementary Medicine carries news, research, and a database of relevant articles on all types of complementary medicine, including massage.

A simple summary

✔ A lot of tension is carried in the neck, shoulders, and chest, and receiving a massage in each of these areas can be immensely therapeutic.

✔ Chest and neck massage is done from a standing or kneeling position behind the head facing towards the feet. Your partner should be lying on his or her back with a small cushion or book under the head.

✔ To alleviate pain and tension in the neck and shoulders, you need to open the chest and relax the shoulders and back by using stretching movements.

✔ For a really relaxing effect, repeat the neck exercises until the head moves completely freely.

✔ When stretching the neck, take care not to jerk or pull too hard, as this is a very delicate area.

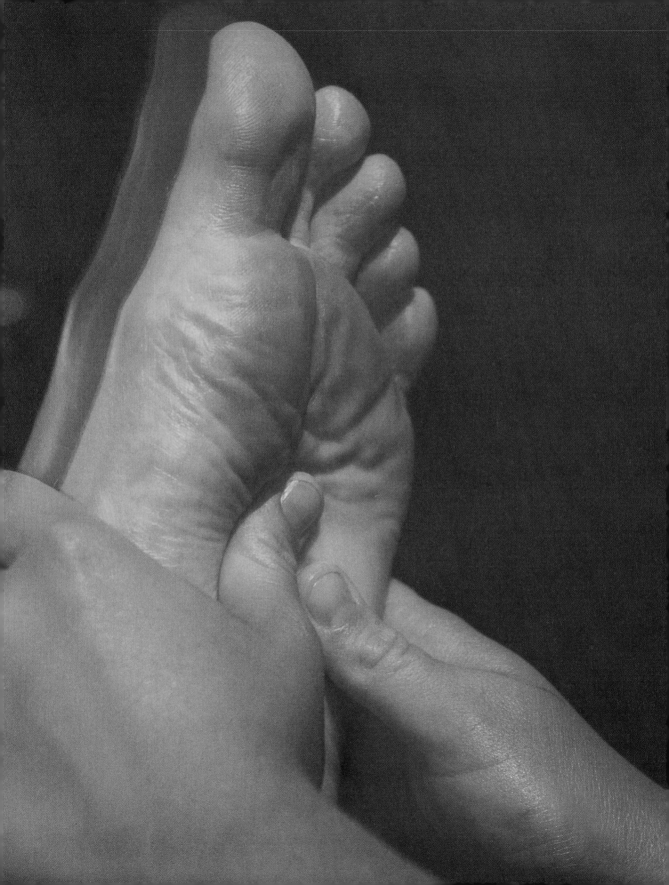

Chapter 12

Feet and Legs

F EW THINGS IN LIFE ARE MORE RELAXING than a good foot massage. Tired feet suddenly feel light again, and as the sole of the foot contains thousands of nerve endings, a foot massage can stimulate the whole body. Whether you lead an active or a more sedentary life, a leg massage can benefit anyone. And, as backache can be caused or aggravated by problems in the legs, a leg massage may actually help your back!

In this chapter...

✓ First the feet

✓ A leg start

✓ Calf and calf

✓ Don't knock knees

✓ Reach for the thigh

✓ Back of legs

✓ Finishing touches

KNEAD YOUR FEET BACK TO LIFE AND LIGHTEN THE LOAD

First the feet

I USUALLY START A LEG MASSAGE on the feet, as most people love to have them massaged, and it's a great way of relaxing the whole body. However, if your partner has slightly swollen ankles, I would recommend starting on the thighs with the aim of clearing the ankle swelling, by stimulating the circulation. The order of massage would then be thighs, knees, calves, and feet.

Did you know?

Post-operative foot massage has been shown to have surprising results.
In 1994, a study at The Middlesex Hospital, London, of patients recovering from heart surgery, revealed that a 20-minute foot massage lowered anxiety rates, decreased pain, and reduced tension.

Preparing the foot

Kneel at your partner's feet and work first on one foot, then on the other. You don't need to use much oil; if you have too much, your fingers will slide about, which can be very ticklish. If your partner has very ticklish feet, use very firm strokes for the massage; alternatively, if you massage the legs first, by the time you reach the feet they may be less sensitive. Ticklishness seems to be linked to tension, so if you can release some of the tension through massage, your partner may be more relaxed and better able to enjoy the foot massage. Work through the whole sequence of massage moves on one foot, and then go back to the beginning and start on the other foot.

The Foot

Leonardo da Vinci referred to the foot as "the greatest engineering device in the world". The feet contain almost a quarter of all the bones in the body, each having 28 bones. The bones are arranged in arches that help the foot support the weight of the body and provide leverage when walking. An intricate web of muscles, tendons, and ligaments surrounds and supports these bones.

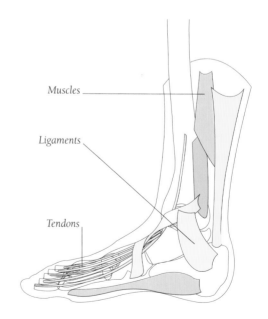

Muscles

Ligaments

Tendons

THE FOOT

Stroking

Start the massage by stroking one of your partner's feet to get it used to your touch.

1 Sandwich the foot between your hands and stroke firmly with both hands from the toes towards the body.

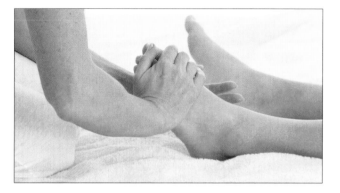

2 When you reach the ankles, swing your hands round and return them to the toes with a light stroke. This is a warming movement, and is ideal for anyone who suffers from cold feet. Repeat at least four times.

Thumb stroking

In this move, you will apply more localized pressure with your thumbs.

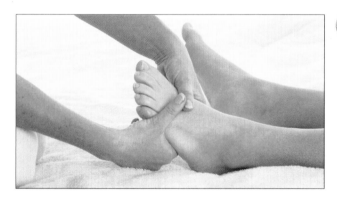

1 Support the foot with your fingers underneath it, and place your thumbs on top of the foot at the base of the toes. Stroke up the foot with your thumbs, fanning out to the sides and gliding back to the toes, ready to start again. Repeat three or four times.

2 Now stroke with your thumbs working alternately. Stroke up with one thumb as the other glides back down the side. The movement can go a little higher than before, reaching up to the ankle. Again, repeat several times.

Toe massage

Loosen and warm the whole area by wiggling the toes. Sandwich the foot just above the toes and rotate your hands.

Your toe massage will feel more effective if you press on the sides of the toes as well as on the tops.

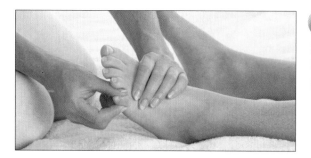

1 Massage your partner's toes individually. Squeeze and roll each one, rotate it in both directions, then pull it gently towards you.

2 Change hands when you reach the big toe, and massage it very thoroughly all over. Then squeeze all round the base of the toe.

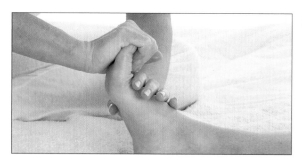

3 Clasp all the toes with one hand and then bend them gently backwards and forwards to encourage flexibility.

Stroking between the tendons

Support your partner's foot with both hands, placing your fingers on the sole of the foot and your thumbs on top of the foot. Stroke in each furrow between the tendons, with one thumb following the other. Run your thumbs up the foot towards the ankle, making about four strokes in each furrow.

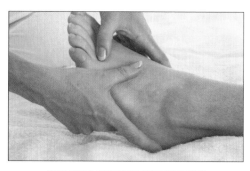

STROKING BETWEEN THE TENDONS

Pressures

Support the foot with your fingers on top and your thumbs underneath. Press firmly on the sole with one thumb on top of the other for 3–7 seconds, then move on about 2 cm (½ inch) and repeat the pressure. Work all over the ball of the foot and in a line down the centre to the heel. Follow with more pressures in lines on either side of this central line.

The sole has a thick layer of protective tissue. In some people this layer is extra tough, so use your body weight to make an impact and give extra depth.

Hacking

Hacking is a stimulating movement. If you try this on the top of the foot, you must be very gentle and flick your hands away as soon as they make contact.

1. Hold the foot firmly with one hand, and hack the sole with the side of your other hand. Keep your wrist very loose and flexible.

2. Now use both hands to hack the sole of the foot. This is wonderfully invigorating. Use it when you want to wake someone who is drowsy.

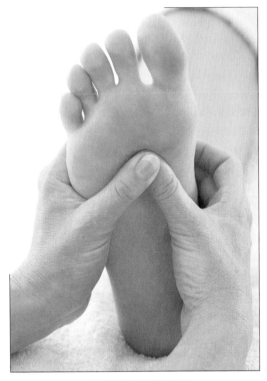

PRESSURES TO THE SOLE

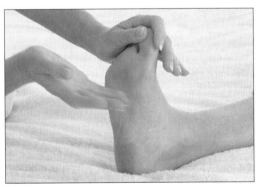

STEP 1

Although foot hacking sounds painful, it actually feels surprisingly good. I first experienced it in Morocco, and it had such a stimulating effect that it has been part of my repertoire ever since.

Additional touches

After all that stimulating work, you can soothe the foot with any or all of the following gentle moves to finish.

Stroking the arch

Rest one hand on top of the foot and stroke firmly into the main arch, using the heel of your other hand. Curve your hand back to fit the shape of the foot, and stroke from the ball to the heel. Return with a light stroke to start again. Repeat at least four times.

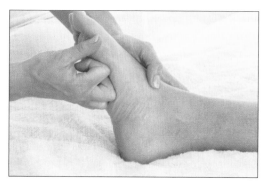

KNUCKLING THE SOLE

Knuckling

Keeping one hand on top of the foot, curl the fingers of your other hand into a loose fist so that you can massage the foot with your middle three fingers. Move your fingers round to make rippling rotary movements. Work firmly all over the sole.

Knuckling to the sole of the foot feels wonderful, and is also very good for your hands, keeping them supple and flexible.

Rotary pressures

Stroke the whole foot as you did at the start of the massage, then apply gentle circular pressures around the ankle with one hand on each side. Stroke firmly on the upwards sweep of the circle (towards the leg) and keep the pressure light on the return. Use your middle fingers on the sides and back of the ankle, and thumbs on the front.

Passive movements

Towards the end of the massage, use gentle, passive movements to loosen the whole foot and ankle. Support the ankle with one hand, while the other flexes the foot up and down. Hold at its furthest point from the floor for a count of four. Now turn the foot to each side, and finally rotate it about four times in each direction.

Did you know?

Native Americans practise foot treatment, including massage, as they hold a belief that the feet are our connection with the Earth and the Earth's energies.

The final touch

You are coming to the end of the foot massage, so you need to focus on calming movements. Stroke the foot with both hands, up towards the ankle as you did at the beginning, then glide lightly back down. Hold the foot for a few seconds, then slowly and gently slide your hands off the end of the toes.

1 To leave the foot feeling soothed and cared for, you must lift your hands away very slowly and gently. Clasp the back of the ankle with your right hand and rest your left hand on top of the foot. Gently pull the leg towards you without lifting it; just gently stretch it.

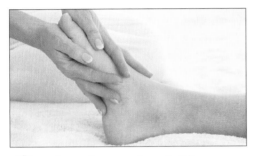

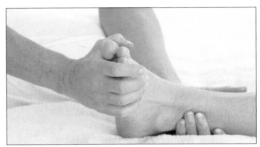

2 Release the stretch and slide your right hand under the foot. Hold the foot lightly between your hands for about 5 seconds.

3 Glide your hands towards the toes, moulding them to the shape of the foot. Slide them very, very slowly off the end of the toes. Repeat two or three times.

You can now repeat the whole foot massage sequence on your partner's other foot. If you want to incorporate a leg massage, it is better to carry on working on the same side of the body, and then return to massage the other foot, followed by the other leg.

QUICK CHECKLIST FOR FOOT MASSAGE

For a quick reminder of the steps in a foot massage, use this short list.

1 Stroke the feet with your whole hand, then just with the thumbs

2 Massage each toe

3 Massage the sole of the foot with pressures; then use hacking, stroking, and knuckling

4 Massage the ankles

A leg start

FOR A LEG MASSAGE, *your partner should be lying on his or her back on the floor, and you should kneel at the feet (or stand if using a massage table). Begin with gentle strokes, leaning into the movement as you stroke up the leg towards the body. Do the complete sequence of moves on one leg first, and then repeat on the other leg.*

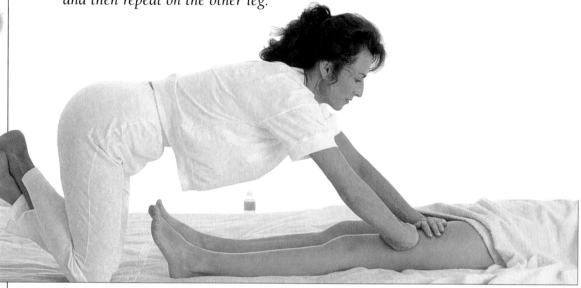

1 Cup your hands over your partner's ankle and stroke up the front of his or her leg, pressing on either side of the **tibia**. You should not press down on the knee as you stroke up the leg – so decrease the pressure as you stroke over the knee and increase it again on the thigh.

2 Fan out your hands at the top of the thigh and glide them down the sides. Repeat this move at least four times.

3 Stroke up the sides of the leg, pressing with the palms of your hands. Glide down to the ankle, and repeat the move about four times.

DEFINITION

*The larger bone of the lower leg – the shin bone – is known medically as the **tibia**. It can easily be felt beneath the skin at the front of the lower leg.*

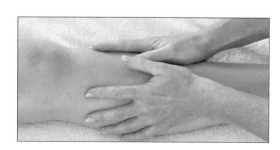

Calf and calf

ONCE YOU HAVE INTRODUCED *your hands to your partner's leg, proceed to work on the calf. You can remain in the starting position, kneeling with the foot of the leg you are working on by your knees. However, you will have to bend your partner's knee later in this sequence, so be prepared to move up a bit as you bend your partner's leg.*

Alternate stroking up the calf

Support the ankle and bend the knee so the foot rests on the towel. Working with alternate hands, stroke firmly up the calf, then glide one hand back as the other strokes upwards. Stroke firmly, pulling the muscle up and out to the side. While massaging, anchor the foot to help keep your partner's knee upright; if you are working on the floor, hold the foot between your knees; if your partner is on a massage table, sit gently on the foot.

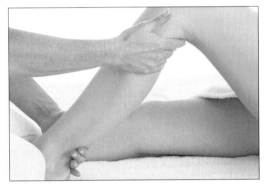

ALTERNATE STROKING

Criss-crossing the calf

Anyone who does a lot of sport or who stands for hours at a time is likely to appreciate this movement, as it relieves tension in the calf muscle. Place your hands round the leg, with your thumbs at the front of the leg and your fingers on the sides of the calf muscle. Slide your fingers round the calf, keeping your hands in contact with the skin. Release the pressure as your hands glide past each other. Work from the ankle to the knee, and then back again, taking care not to pinch the flesh.

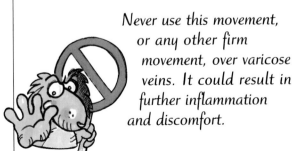

Never use this movement, or any other firm movement, over varicose veins. It could result in further inflammation and discomfort.

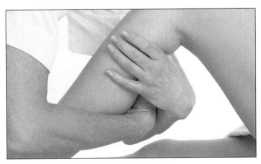

CRISS-CROSSING THE CALF

Don't knock knees

NOW IT IS THE KNEE'S TURN. *To work on your partner's knee you need to support it with your fingers cradling the back so it is slightly raised off the towel. As there is not much flesh on the knees, they are tender and sensitive and you must be very careful when you massage this area. You should stick to stroking and circular movements and exert only the gentlest pressure.*

Thumb circling

1 Start with your thumbs crossed resting just below the kneecap.

2 Stroke gently up the sides of the knee, with one thumb on either side until they meet at the top, and then let your thumbs pass each other.

3 Glide each thumb down the opposite side. Both thumbs do a complete circle passing each other at the top and bottom as they circle round and round the knee.

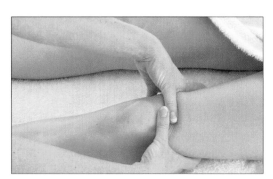

STEP 2

Rotary thumb pressures

Keeping your fingers behind the knee, make gentle rotary pressures with your thumbs around the knee. Again, start below the kneecap and work round it.

Stroking the knee

Stroke gently behind the knee using your fingers. Stroke up towards the body, and then make gentle rotary movements behind the knee. Your fingers should be flat and relaxed so that they don't poke into the knee.

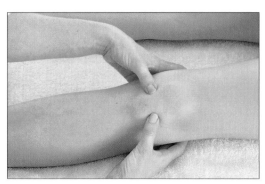

ROTARY THUMB PRESSURES

Reach for the thigh

NOW, MOVE UP TO YOUR partner's thigh. You begin this sequence with the leg still bent, and the foot between your knees; this position works for the initial stroking and criss-crossing. However, when you come to the next stage – kneading and pummelling – you will find it much easier to move up and kneel on the side you are working on. You must face in the direction of your movements.

Stroking

Lean forwards and stroke up the back of the thigh. Stroke firmly up towards the body and glide back down to the knee. Support the knee with the inner hand and stroke the outer thigh with your other hand.

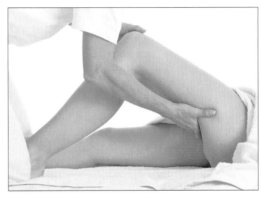

STROKING

The large thigh muscles that form the front of the thigh are called the quadriceps, and are each made up of four muscles; the muscles at the back are called the hamstrings, and they are each made up of three muscles.

Criss-crossing

Continue this sequence with some criss-cross strokes behind the thigh. Place your hands on top of the thigh, with your fingers curled round the sides. Squeeze the muscle at the back of the thigh by gliding your hands round under it. Work up and down the thigh, and then lower the leg down onto the towel, supporting it at the knee and ankle. Stroke around the knee a couple of times.

CRISS-CROSSING

Kneading

The thighs can take a lot of firm kneading. Work deeply and strongly on the outer thigh, where the muscles are large, and more gently on the inner thigh, which is more sensitive and has less to grab on to.

KNEADING

Pummelling

The thighs are the perfect place for pummelling and using other fast, stimulating movements. Most women love to have their thighs massaged, and kneading and pummelling in particular can help to improve the shape of the thighs by stimulating the circulation and smoothing down unsightly lumps and bumps.

Kneel alongside your partner's legs so your knees almost line up with his or hers. With flexible wrists and loose fists, pummel the outside of your partner's thighs. The movement should be light and bouncy and not painful or unpleasant.

Never, ever pummel on bruises or superficial capillaries on the thighs.

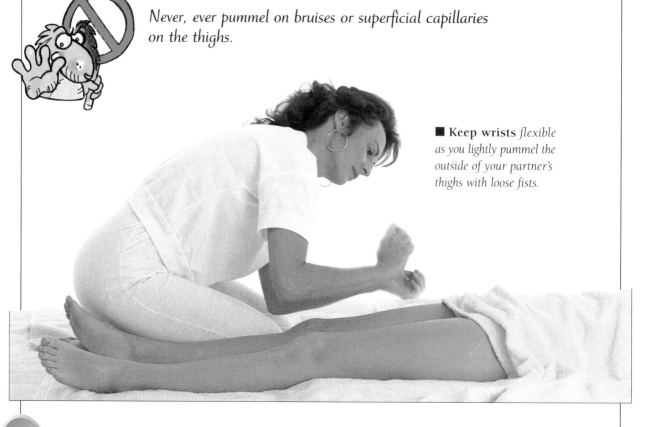

■ **Keep wrists** *flexible as you lightly pummel the outside of your partner's thighs with loose fists.*

Back of legs

IF YOU ARE GIVING A COMPLETE body massage, you can include the backs of your partner's legs immediately before or after the back massage as he or she will be in the correct position and you won't have to disrupt the flow by asking him or her to turn over.

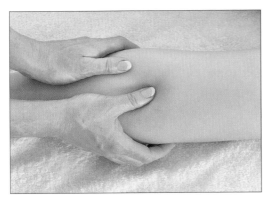

STEP 3

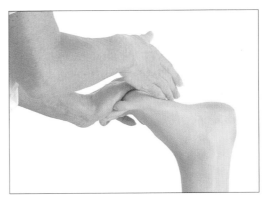

STEP 5

1. Stroke the leg from the ankle to the thigh, taking care not to press down on the knee as you pass over it.

2. Knead the calf muscles firmly, using both hands.

3. Stroke up the calf with your thumbs. Make small strokes upwards, using your thumbs alternately. Press firmly as you stroke upwards and outwards, and more gently as you glide back to the centre.

4. Gently stroke the back of the knee, with your fingers. Stroke up the thigh from the knee, then knead firmly and pummel the outer thigh.

5. Stroke the whole of the leg. Lift up the foot and, supporting it with one hand, hack the sole lightly with the edge of the other hand.

6. Lower the leg again then stroke it gently. Finish by gliding your hands off the foot, then repeat on the other leg.

Finishing touches

HERE ARE SOME MORE suggestions for moves that can be slotted in before you finish off the leg massage sequence, or at any other time during the course of the massage. Experiment to see what meets with approval.

Skin rolling

Rolling the skin is another good technique for releasing tension and for improving skin texture, so it is well suited for working on the thighs. Place both your hands on your partner's outer thigh, and make a triangle by putting your fingers and thumbs together. Push your thumbs towards your fingers, rolling your partner's flesh as you do so. Take great care not to pinch the skin as your thumbs meet your fingers.

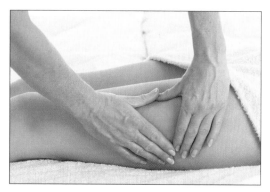

SKIN ROLLING

Passive movements

Gently flexing the knee and hip is a lovely way of relaxing your partner's leg towards the end of the massage. Kneel beside the hips and, holding the ankle and knee, bend the knee and lift up the leg. Make a large circle with the knee to rotate the hip joint. Circle three times in each direction, making as large a circle as possible, but never force the joint.

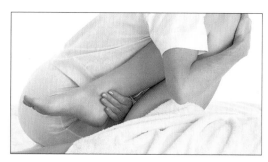

PASSIVE MOVEMENTS

The final movements

As with any massage sequence, when you come to the end use very gentle stroking actions. Kneel at the feet again and stroke the thigh as before. Place your hands across the ankle and stroke up the leg, pressing firmly on the sides and lightly over the bones. Fan out your hands at the top of the thigh, beginning with firm strokes and getting lighter, until you are barely touching the skin. Finish the leg massage in the same way as the foot massage. Hold the foot between your palms, then slide your hands off the end. Clasp the ankle and stretch the leg gently. Repeat the massage on the other leg.

QUICK CHECKLIST FOR LEG MASSAGE

This list will help to remind you of the steps in a leg massage.

1. Stroke the calf

2. Knead and criss-cross the calf

3. Massage the knee

4. Stroke the thigh

5. Knead, criss-cross, knuckle, and pummel the thigh

6. Finish by stroking all over the leg

INTERNET

www.reflexology.org

Take a foot massage one step further by visiting the Home of Reflexology's web site, which lists most of the reflexology organizations in the world.

A simple summary

✔ A foot massage is the perfect solution for tired, aching feet.

✔ As the foot is so well supplied with nerve endings, practically the whole body can be stimulated by a really good foot massage.

✔ Leg massage is particularly good for very active people, sports people, and people who spend a lot of time on their feet – that covers just about everyone. However, it is just as beneficial for individuals of a more sedentary inclination.

✔ The best time to incorporate a massage on the backs of your partner's legs is immediately before or after a back massage.

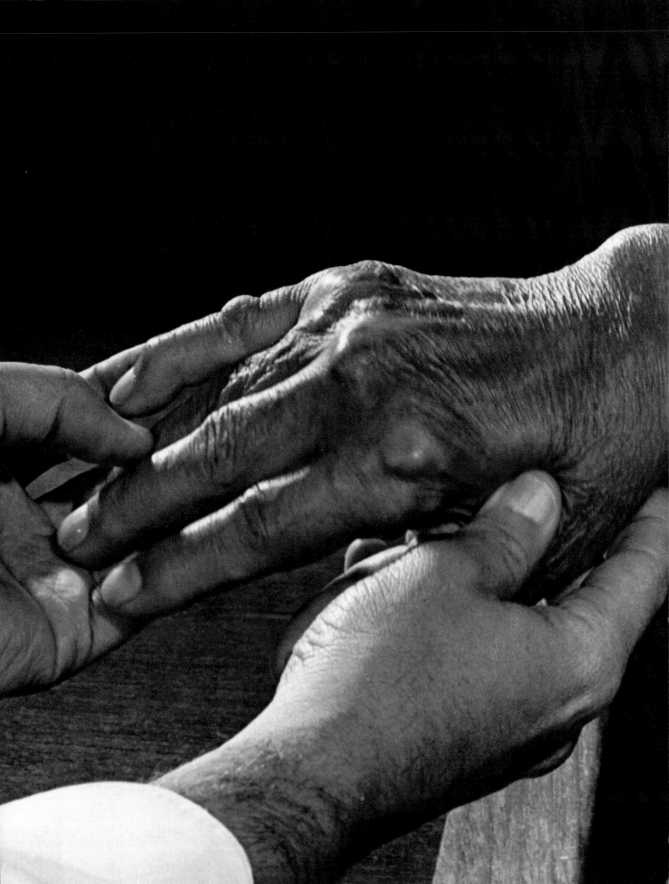

Chapter 13

Hands and Arms

I THINK THAT BEING ABLE TO GIVE a hand massage is one of the most useful skills in the world – you can always comfort or reassure someone, whatever their age or state of health. It often surprises people when they discover the delights of a hand massage. The hands are not normally considered an area of tension, but as we use them constantly, it's hardly surprising that they sometimes feel stiff and tired. By relieving tension in the arms, you can rejuvenate tired hands and ease headaches.

In this chapter...
✓ Simply hands
✓ Watching the wrists
✓ Forearmed
✓ Elbow grease
✓ Upper arm
✓ Passive movements

TAKE THE MATTER IN HAND ANY TIME, ANY PLACE

Simply hands

AS WELL AS BEING a marvellous way of relaxing or calming someone, hand massage is also a great way to keep hands soft, smooth, and supple. Sadly, because of their exposure to sun, cold, wind, and water, as well as to a huge range of chemicals, the hands tend to suffer and show neglect. They have very little fat, which, when combined with general wear and tear, leads to aging and wrinkling before other parts of the body. Massaging the hands with cream or oil moisturizes the skin and simulates the blood supply.

Did you know?

In a recent study, a group of smokers who were trying to give up their habit were taught to do a hand self-massage three times a day, when they had a craving, for a period of 1 month. The group reported lower anxiety, improved mood, and fewer withdrawal symptoms than the control group who were not doing massage. Also, the massage group was smoking fewer cigarettes by the end of the study.

If you know someone who is apprehensive about having a massage, suggest a hand massage. Most people are used to having their hands touched, and, as there is none of the inconvenience of getting undressed, you can do this anywhere.

Hand and wrist

The hand is the most versatile part of the body, capable of delicate manipulation as well as powerful gripping actions. It is made up of 27 small bones and 37 skeletal muscles, which are attached to the bones by tendons. The fingers are among the most sensitive parts of the body, having almost as many nerve endings as the tongue and lips.

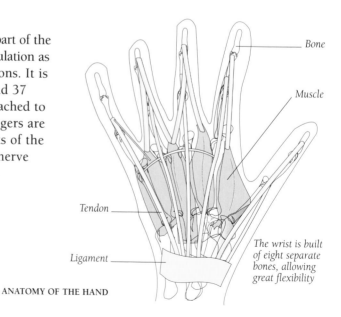

Bone

Muscle

Tendon

Ligament

The wrist is built of eight separate bones, allowing great flexibility

ANATOMY OF THE HAND

Stroking and stretching

To introduce yourself, hold your partner's hand palm up in one of your hands, and stroke the palm with the heel of your other hand. Push down towards your partner's wrist, then glide back up again.

1 Turn your partner's hand over, and support it with your fingers clasped gently behind and your thumbs resting on the back of the hand. Stroke with your thumbs, making fanning-out movements from the knuckles to the wrist.

2 Stroke towards the wrist with one of your hands, moving your fingers as well as your thumb up the hand. Instead of gliding back, pull back firmly to stretch one side of the hand as your other hand strokes up to the wrist.

Fingers

Although they are small and bony, fingers benefit greatly from a firm massage.

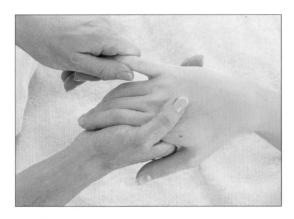

1 Hold your partner's hand palm down in one of your hands, and use your other hand to work on each of the fingers separately, starting with the little finger. Stroke firmly from the tip to the knuckle, then squeeze all over the finger.

2 Make circular pressures with your thumb around each joint, including the knuckle, then rotate the finger twice in each direction. Finally, make your hand into a fist and grip the finger between two of your fingers. Stretch the finger gently to ease the joints, but don't jerk it.

While stretching the finger, I like to imagine my fist is a corkscrew and I'm trying to open a superior bottle of claret – the cork is very tight fitting and I have to pull firmly but carefully.

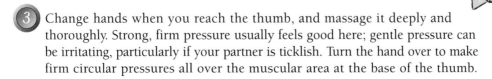

3 Change hands when you reach the thumb, and massage it deeply and thoroughly. Strong, firm pressure usually feels good here; gentle pressure can be irritating, particularly if your partner is ticklish. Turn the hand over to make firm circular pressures all over the muscular area at the base of the thumb.

Eliminating pain

You might be interested to know that there is a point on the web of skin between the thumb and index finger that in Eastern massage is called the *Great Eliminator*.

Pressing on the Great Eliminator can help to relieve pain, particularly headaches and toothache. In Canada, researchers applied ice to this point in people suffering from toothache; in over half the patients, the pain was relieved. Be aware: it is believed that pressing on this area in pregnant women could cause a miscarriage.

> **DEFINITION**
>
> *The acupressure point situated on the Large Intestine meridian is known as the* **Great Eliminator**. *It is used for the relief of pain.*

Between the tendons

Take your partner's hand palm down, and support it with your fingers. Stroke with your thumbs in the furrows between the tendons, starting between the knuckles and stroking towards the wrist, one thumb following the other. Do this a few times in each furrow, then turn the hand over and stroke the palm firmly with the heel of your hand, as you did at the beginning of the massage.

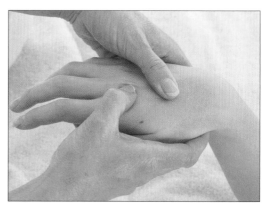

STROKING BETWEEN THE TENDONS

KNUCKLING THE PALM

Knuckling

Make a fist with one of your hands and support your partner's hand, palm up, with your other hand. Move your fist all over the palm, making small, rippling, circular movements with your knuckles. Vary the pressure from deep to gentle – both feel marvellous.

Knuckling your partner's palm is also really good for your own hands as it increases flexibility and co-ordination.

Stretching

By stretching your partner's hand you are counteracting the normal inclination for clutching movements, which helps to release tension from the hands.

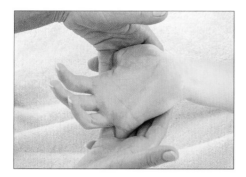

1 With your hands palm up, interlock your little fingers with your partner's hand; link one finger with your partner's little finger, and the other with their thumb. Bring your other fingers underneath to support the hand, then open it up to stretch the palm.

Never stretch arthritic hands as it would be very painful.

2 Keeping your little fingers interlocked with your partner's hand, continue to stretch the palm. Bring your thumbs round to stroke the palm all over with fanning-out movements. Then, using only one of your thumbs, make small circular pressures all over your partner's palm to relieve tension.

Watching the wrists

BEFORE MOVING ONTO THE ARM proper, be sure to make a little time for your partner's wrists. This joint can benefit greatly from gentle manipulation, which will help to keep it supple. To ensure that your partner has relaxed his or her wrists completely, always begin with stroking movements.

Passive movements

Support your partner's hand with your fingers and stroke all the way around the wrist with your thumbs. Start on the inside of the wrist and stroke upwards and outwards. Turn your partner's hand over and repeat.

Hold your partner's arm just above the wrist, and his or her hand with your other hand. Bend your partner's wrist gently backwards and forwards, then to each side. Rotate the wrist in each direction three times.

Never force passive movement. Go only as far as flexibility allows.

The final touch

As with all other massage, finish your hand massage with a few gentle moves.

(1) With your partner's palm facing up, stroke the whole of the hand, then turn it over and sandwich it between your palms. Press your hands together firmly.

(2) Release the pressure and slide your hands slowly off your partner's fingers. The hand should now be completely relaxed. Repeat this movement a couple of times.

Now, go back to the beginning and repeat the whole sequence on the other hand. If you are combining the hand massage with an arm massage, carry on working on the same side of the body and then return to work on the other hand when you have completed massaging the arm.

QUICK CHECKLIST FOR HAND MASSAGE

Here's a quick reminder of the steps to follow when giving a hand massage.

(1) Stroke the back of the hand with the thumbs working towards the wrist

(2) Massage each finger, ending with a gentle pull

(3) Stroke between the tendons on the back of the hand

(4) Massage your partner's palm with your knuckles

(5) Stretch your partner's hand

(6) Stroke a thumb stroke around the wrist with your thumbs, then rotate the wrist

(7) Clasp the whole hand between your palms, hold, stretch, and release, letting your fingers glide off the tips of your partner's fingers. Repeat several times

Forearmed

AT FIRST, YOU MAY FIND the arm a little difficult to massage as it is less fleshy than other parts of the body, and is also an awkward shape. However, do not be put off as the muscles are usually strong and your massage can be deep and firm. The techniques are almost the same as those used on the legs, and with a little practice you will find arm massage just as rewarding. Arm massage has beneficial effects not only for the arms, but also for the hands and shoulders. If you are working on the floor, kneel beside your partner to give the massage; if standing, make sure you are close to your partner and facing towards the head.

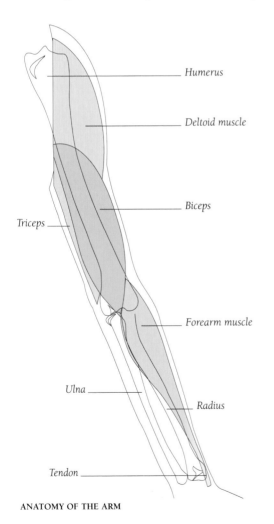

Humerus

Deltoid muscle

Biceps

Triceps

Forearm muscle

Ulna

Radius

Tendon

ANATOMY OF THE ARM

The arm

The bones of the arm have a similar arrangement those of the leg, although on a smaller scale. The upper arm bone, the humerus, is joined to the lower arm bones, the ulna and radius, by a joint at the elbow. The lower arm bones can be felt quite clearly through the skin as there is not much muscle overlying them. The upper arm is usually fleshier, especially at the shoulder end.

Trivia...

The benefits of massage to the giver should never be underestimated. I once received a letter from a lady who suffered from Raynaud's disease (poor circulation in the fingers causing numbness and lack of sensation). She found that after a year of massaging family and friends, her symptoms the following winter were greatly reduced.

Stroking

For a gentle, relaxing start to the massage, stroke your partner's arm, first with two hands, and then with just one.

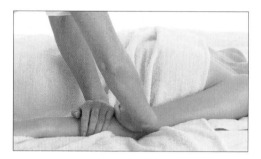

1 Rest your partner's arm, palm down, on the towel and place your hands across the wrist, with the little finger of one of your hands next to the thumb of your other hand. Stroke firmly up the arm with your hands slightly cupped so that the pressure is deep on the muscle, but light over the bones.

2 When you reach the top of the arm, open out your hands and stroke around the shoulder. Make sure that you reach right round the top of the shoulder with one hand, then glide your hands lightly down the sides of the arm to the wrist, ready to start again. Repeat this move about six times.

3 Now use only one hand for stroking. Support the forearm underneath with one of your hands, and stroke up the arm with the other. Stroke right around the shoulder and glide down the side; then change hands so that both sides of the arm are massaged. Repeat this action six times.

Draining the forearm

This is a great movement for releasing tension from the forearm.

1 Lift up your partner's forearm, supporting the wrist and leaving the elbow resting on the towel. Clasp your hands round the wrist with your thumbs on the inside.

2 Slide one hand down to the elbow, pressing with your thumb but not your fingers. When you reach the elbow, glide lightly back to the wrist. As your first hand returns to the wrist, stroke down with the other hand. Repeat three or four times.

3 With your hands in the same position, make fanning-out strokes with your thumbs on the inside of the wrist. Use your thumbs alternately, one stroking firmly down and out as the other glides back. Gradually lengthen the strokes until you have covered the whole forearm.

Kneading the forearm

The forearm is often tense and can be relaxed by the pumping movements of kneading. Support your partner's hand to make sure that the arm is totally relaxed.

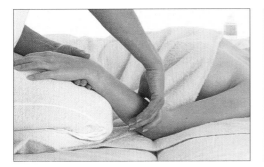

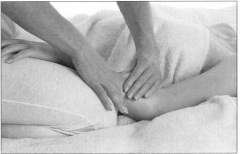

1 Place your partner's hand on your thigh or knee, and give further support with one of your hands. Knead the forearm gently with your other hand, starting at the wrist and working up to the elbow, then glide your hand back down. Repeat this movement a couple of times, then change hands to knead the other side of the forearm.

2 Either place your partner's arm on the towel, or leave it still resting on your thigh or knee, and release your supporting hand. Knead the forearm as in step 1 with both your hands.

The muscles of the forearms are responsible for moving the fingers. This is particularly important for sufferers of repetitive strain injury (RSI) and those at risk of getting it, because massaging the forearm can alleviate symptoms.

REPETITIVE STRAIN INJURY

Regular massage of the hand and arm (particularly the forearm) may help prevent the onset of repetitive strain injury (RSI). If you already suffer from it, massage can alleviate the symptoms. You can also massage yourself: either use your other hand, or squeeze a rubber ball. Stretching and strengthening the muscles is the key to prevention.

■ **Repetitive office work,** *such as typing, may cause RSI.*

Elbow grease

THE ELBOW IS ONE *of the most neglected parts of the body and massage here can feel surprisingly good. The elbow is well known for being ticklish – it is even commonly known as the funny bone, a pun on the medical name for the upper arm bone, the humerus. It tends to be ticklish because one of the main nerves supplying the arm is relatively exposed because of the lack of protective flesh at the elbow. If your partner has a particularly ticklish elbow, gradually introduce him or her to the feel of your hands in the area around the elbow before beginning the massage.*

Stroking the elbow

Use the palm of your hand and not your fingers to massage the ticklish area. Use plenty of oil as elbows are often very dry.

1 Bend your partner's arm so that the hand rests on the abdomen. Support the arm with one hand, and stroke the elbow with your other hand.

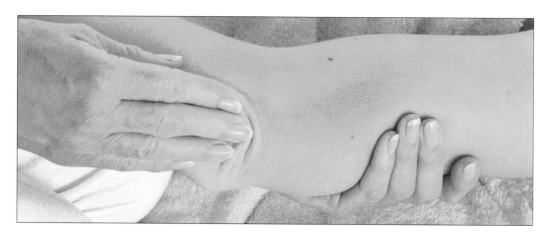

2 Stroke smoothly in a circle all round the elbow, using just the tips of your fingers and palm of your hand.

3 With your fingers on one side and your thumb on the other, make circular pressures all over the elbow. Be very thorough, working into all the nooks and crannies. Finish by stroking again to soothe the area, and the upper arm.

Upper arm

BEING THE FLESHIEST AREA of the arm, the upper part makes a nice contrast after the bony elbow and you can use some of the deeper massage movements here. The main muscles in the upper arm are the deltoid, which is attached to the collar bone at the top end and the humerus at the other, the biceps, which is on the front part of the upper arm, and the triceps at the back. These big muscles respond well to deep, firm massage, such as kneading.

Kneading the upper arm

You can use firmer kneading on the fleshier parts of the upper arm.

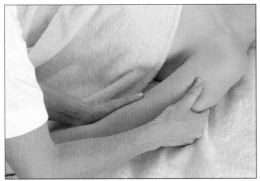
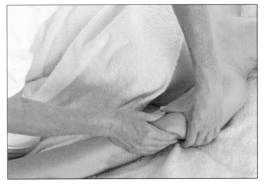

1 Support your partner's arm with one hand and knead the upper arm with your other hand. Work up both sides of the arm. Alternatively, rest the arm on the towel and knead either side of the arm with one of your hands.

2 If the arm is fleshy enough, you can work with both hands together on one side. Knead firmly up the arm from the elbow, wringing and squeezing the flesh without hurting or pinching.

The final touch

To finish the arm massage, you should make gentle and light moves. Stroke down the whole of the arm with both your hands together; make your touch gradually lighter and lighter until you are barely touching the skin. Then, clasp the wrist and lean back to stretch your partner's arm gently. Finish by holding the hand and then gliding your own hands very slowly off the very tips of the fingers.

Passive movements

AFTER THE MASSAGE, your partner's arm should be feeling really limp and relaxed. This is an excellent time to loosen the shoulder joints with some gentle passive movements. Kneel by your partner's shoulders so that you can stretch the arms as far as they will go. Make sure that you do not force the arms beyond their natural limits of flexibility.

Always remember that suppleness and flexibility are unique to every individual and that you must never extend your partner's boundaries when doing passive movements.

1 Rotate the shoulder to relax the whole area thoroughly. Place one of your hands on the shoulder and the other under the elbow. Lift up the arm and make a large circle with the upper arm to rotate the shoulder joint.

2 Hold the wrist with one of your hands and lift the arm up over the head. Stretch the arm as far as it will comfortably go, and slide your other hand down to the hip to give a lovely, long stretch. Then bring the arm down to the side again. Hold the hand in both of yours and, with the arm outstretched, shake the whole arm gently up and down. Finish with a gentle pull.

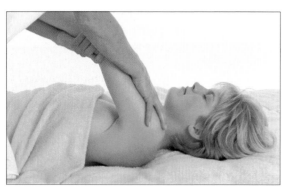

Now repeat the whole sequence on the other arm. If you are combining this with a hand massage, work on the other hand before doing the arm massage.

QUICK CHECKLIST FOR ARM MASSAGE

If you don't want to look back over the details of the routine, use this list as a "cheat" or reminder of the steps in arm massage.

1. Stroke the forearm

2. Knead the forearm

3. Stroke the elbow, and make gentle circle pressures all around it

4. Stroke and knead the upper arm

5. Stroke the whole arm and hand, slowly and rhythmically

6. Rotate the shoulder and stretch the arm to finish with passive movements

INTERNET

massagetherapy homepage.com

The Massage Therapy Homepage lists articles, professional organizations, and educational information for anyone interested in massage. It is also a marketplace for services and products.

A simple summary

✔ Hand massage is one of the most useful forms of massage as it can be done on anyone, anywhere, at almost any time.

✔ As the hands are practically the most used part of the body, a hand massage is universally beneficial.

✔ Massaging someone else's hands can also benefit the giver's hands.

✔ Arms can be less flexible and more awkward to massage than many other parts of the body, but it is worth persisting so your partner reaps the rewards.

✔ Tension carried in the arms can cause a range of physical symptoms, such as headaches and neck pain, which can be relieved by massage.

Chapter 14

Abdomen

SOME PEOPLE ARE APPREHENSIVE about having their abdomens massaged. I believe this is because they carry tension there, and exposing the abdomen makes them feel vulnerable. However, once the joys of a good abdominal massage have been experienced, most people will be converted. I teach a gentle, relaxing abdominal massage, which calms the nerves and stimulates the digestive system. If you suffer from stomach ache – caused by tension, indigestion, or period pain – an abdominal massage can soothe it away. The relaxing strokes can also relieve constipation. Abdominal massage is useful for weight-watchers – it makes them more aware of the area and helps them to keep to a diet more conscientiously.

In this chapter...

✓ Starting out

✓ Roundabout the navel

✓ Add to your repertoire

✓ Finishing off

THE ABDOMEN CAN CARRY A LOT OF TENSION

Starting out

IF YOUR PARTNER IS NERVOUS *about the idea of abdominal massage, begin by stroking over the towel. Just stroke round and round the navel area and your partner will gradually relax to your calming touch. When you massage the abdomen, all your movements should be gentle and sensitive.*

If your partner is pregnant, check with her doctor before massaging her abdomen. See the massage instructions in Chapter 17, as a slightly different technique is used for pregnant women.

Stroking

Kneel beside your partner and place a pillow under the knees to help relax the back and stomach muscles.

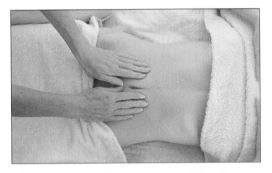

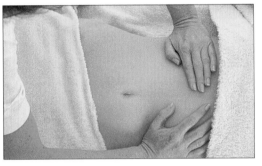

1 Face towards your partner's head and place your hands side by side on the lower abdomen, with your fingers pointing towards the head. Stroke slowly up to the ribs, keeping the pressure even.

2 When you reach the ribs, pull your hands out to the sides, and glide them down. Mould your hands to the curves of the body, making sure you don't leave any parts untouched.

3 Pull your hands firmly up and in at the sides of the waist, then swivel round to start again. Keep the movement flowing and continuous, and repeat at least six times.

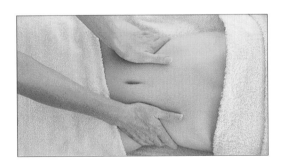

Roundabout the navel

THE FOCUS OF ABDOMINAL MASSAGE *is relaxation and most of the soothing movements involve circular stroking around the navel. Make soft, round movements using the palms of your hand and try to keep them as flat as possible. Return to this "home" move at any point during the massage. Movements that involve circling the navel are extremely comforting and can be repeated as often as you like during the massage, particularly if your partner is apprehensive. It is also a useful means of spreading oil so try it whenever you need extra oil.*

Simply circling

To encourage the elimination of waste products, and thus relieve constipation, start by massaging your partner's left side, then work up the right side, and finish in the centre of the abdomen just below the rib cage.

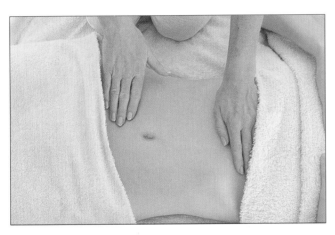

1 Turn to face across your partner's body, and put your left hand on the lower ribs. Start with your right hand below the navel. Flatten the palm, and stroke gently in a wide curve up towards your left hand, keeping the pressure smooth and light.

2 Continue stroking with your right hand in a circle around the navel, maintaining a clockwise direction when making circular moves over the colon (large intestine); this reflects the way the intestines work and encourages *peristalsis.*

DEFINITION

The rhythmic, wave-like contraction and relaxation of muscle that moves food and waste products through the intestines is called **peristalsis.**

The colon, or large intestine, is made up of three parts that roughly form the two sides and top of a square. The right-hand section is called the ascending colon, the top section is the transverse colon, and the left-hand section the descending colon.

Double circle stroking

This is a similar movement to the previous one, but this time you use both hands.

 Place your hands on the abdomen and begin stroking round in a circle, one hand following the other.

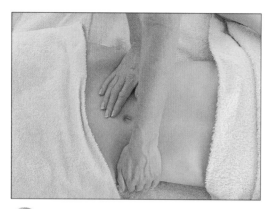 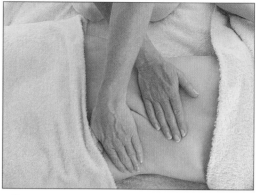

 Glide your left hand round to the far side of the waist, while your right hand strokes up the abdomen. Keep pressure gentle as you glide down the side, and firmer as you pull in at the waist and stroke up the abdomen.

3 Sweep your left hand up the side of the waist and your right hand across the abdomen. Your arms will cross as you stroke round in a circle.

4 Lift your left hand over your right arm and place it gently on the abdomen to start again. Keep the return movement smooth and rhythmic, so that it feels like one continuous circle. This soothing movement can relieve a stomach ache.

Rotary pressures

Make a series of small circular pressures following the outline of the large circle that you made in the previous two moves. Press down with your hand and circle gently, then release the pressure and glide smoothly on about 3 cm (1 inch). You can press with any part of your hand – the palm, the fingers, or the heel – whatever fits the area most comfortably. The pressure should be rhythmic and firm; if it's too deep it can be painful, and if it's too light it can be ticklish. Work round the circle two or three times.

I often compare circular pressures to the gentle waves of the sea – undulating, calm, and rhythmic.

Add to your repertoire

IN YOUR ABDOMINAL MASSAGE *you can include many of the techniques you have already learned plus some new ones. Here is a selection of movements that follow on from the previous sequence. You can use all, none, or just some of these movements before going on to the closing phase of the abdominal massage.*

Kneading

Knead the whole area, starting with the hip on the side of the body furthest from you.

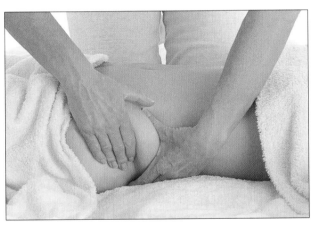

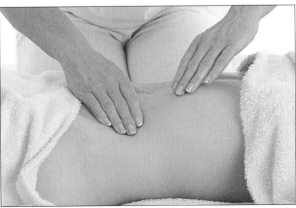

1 With your hands facing each other and your elbows sticking out, alternately squeeze and release the flesh – there is usually a good handful to get hold of. Use deep and stimulating actions to work the whole hip thoroughly.

2 Work up the side of the waist and gently across the abdomen. If your partner is on the small side, you may find it easier to use just your fingers and thumbs rather than the whole of your hands. Lift, press, and squeeze the flesh – without pinching – in several rows.

> **Trivia...**
>
> Massage is an old remedy for constipation. Medical books of the 19th century frequently advocated its use. One extr suggestion of the time was to cure constipation by rolling a cannon ball over the abdomen!

Side stroking

This soothing stroke is very calming after vigorous kneading action.

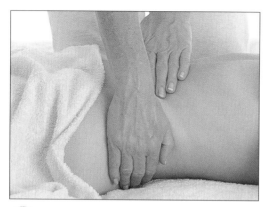

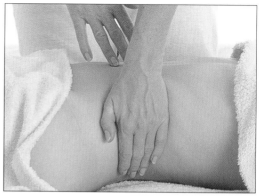

1 Keeping your hands relaxed, stroke slowly up the side of the waist. One hand follows the other as you stroke rhythmically and lazily in to the navel.

2 Lift your first hand off as you reach the navel and repeat. When working on the side nearest to you, either lean down and push up with your hands, or twist round to pull up with your hands.

Criss-crossing

This is a comforting stroke that combines continuous gliding movements with gentle squeezes. Start with your hands on either side of the waist, then pull up at the sides, and glide across the abdomen. Make a definite contrast between pulling up firmly and stroking across very gently. Repeat this movement at least six times.

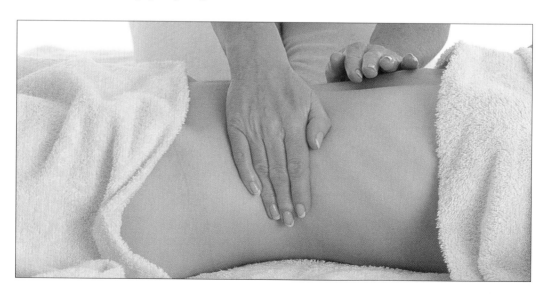

Back lifting

This can be a difficult move on a heavy person, so you should avoid it altogether if your partner is large or if you have back problems.

1 Turn to face towards the head, and stroke up the abdomen. Glide your hands down the sides, then slide your hands behind the waist to make firm circular pressures beside the spine.

2 As you glide round to the front again, pull back firmly to lift the body slightly. Keep your arms straight and take the weight on your legs with one knee up so that you don't strain your back.

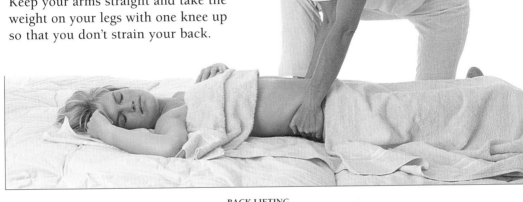

BACK LIFTING

Indian flower seller

I learned this slow, deep movement from a flower seller in India, who used it to relieve a terrible stomach ache I had. Place one hand on top of the other, fingers just below the navel, and use your palms to stroke up extremely slowly. Maintain a deep pressure until you reach the navel, then release the pressure and glide back. When using this movement, watch your partner's face to make sure it is not causing any discomfort.

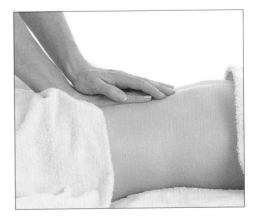

Never use the Indian flower seller movement on a pregnant woman or anyone with a hernia – it is too strong and deep.

Finishing off

ALTHOUGH A VERY BASIC abdominal massage only takes 5 to 10 minutes, if your partner seems to be enjoying it you can extend it so that it lasts as long as you like by repeating some or all of the movements described above. Eventually, however, you will want to end it and move on to another part of the body; from this point on you need to concentrate on gentle, stroking moves. You can try the techniques below or return to any of the initial circle stroking movements.

Feather stroking

Repeat the first stroking movements, then turn to face across your partner's body, and flow smoothly into circle stroking. Stroke clockwise in a circle, one hand following the other. Gradually stroke more and more gently until you are barely touching the skin. Continue for as long as you like.

The final touch

This simple technique has a dramatic effect, leaving your partner feeling relaxed and light. It is also a great move for finishing off a back massage.

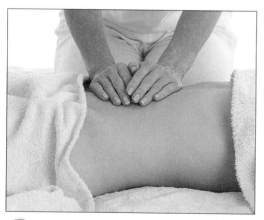 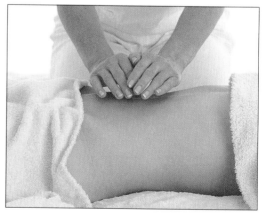

1 Cup your hands over the navel to trap some air underneath. Hold them still for a few seconds and you may feel heat gathering within. Now ease the warmth into the body by lightly flattening your hands against the abdomen.

2 Relax your hands and then lift them very, very slowly away from the body. You must not rush this movement so take your time. As your hands leave the body, your partner may feel a floating sensation as if you are drawing out tension.

QUICK CHECKLIST FOR ABDOMINAL MASSAGE

If you don't want to read through all the detail, use this short list to remind yourself of the steps in abdominal massage

1 Stroke up the abdomen, out over the ribs, and up at the sides

2 Single-handed circle stroking

3 Double-handed circle stroking

4 Undulating circle pressures

5 Kneading

6 Side-stroking

7 Criss-crossing

8 Stroking

9 Final touch

INTERNET

www.massagenet.com

MassageNet is US web site that contains editorials on relevant topics, product and training resources, and a discussion forum on all aspects of massage.

A simple summary

✔ Although many people feel apprehensive about having an abdominal massage, it is worth persuading them to overcome their anxieties for the benefits they will receive.

✔ An abdominal massage can be very effective in helping to relieve stomach aches caused by tension, indigestion, or periods, and can also alleviate constipation.

✔ Most of the moves in an abdominal massage can be done on a pregnant woman but follow the specific instructions in Chapter 17 rather than those given here.

✔ You can extend an abdominal massage by repeating some or all of the moves described here.

Chapter 15

Face and Head

A GOOD FACE MASSAGE can soothe away anxiety, headaches, and exhaustion, and replace them with a feeling of serenity and wellbeing. It can leave people looking and feeling years younger. By stimulating circulation, a face massage gives a healthy, vibrant glow to the complexion, and by relaxing taut muscles, it rids the face of weariness. Head massage is the perfect complement to face massage, and the result is relaxation in every part of the body. A thin layer of muscle covers the skull, which tightens when we are tense, leading to headaches and stress. A head massage can relax this muscle and generally ease tension and anxiety throughout the body.

In this chapter...
✓ Stroke away your worries
✓ Eye relief
✓ Looking a-head

TRY A FACE MASSAGE FOR A NATURAL LIFT

Stroke away your worries

A FACE MASSAGE can literally stroke away tension. For the best effect, your hands must be relaxed, and the movements should feel flowing and confident. Remember that the face is particularly sensitive, so be sure to use enough lubrication that you avoid dragging the skin. Also check that your hands are completely free of rough skin and that your nails are short so that they don't scratch your partner's face.

You need experience to give a good face massage, so you need to practise. Try out the movements on your knee and on your own face.

Stroking

This rhythmic stroke covers the entire face and spreads the oil. Use a fine face oil, or an enriched face cream, and kneel behind your partner's head.

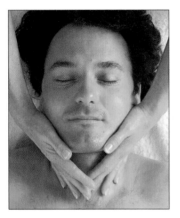  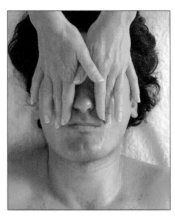

STEP 1   STEP 2   STEP 3

1. Start with your hands at the base of the neck, then sweep them up to the chin, using the whole surface of your hands. Pause for a moment.

2. Stroke out under the jaw to the ears, moulding your hands to the contours of the face. Pause for a moment with your palms resting over the ears, then glide your hands back down under the chin.

3. Stroke with your fingertips from the chin, round the mouth, to the nostrils. Continue stroking up the sides of the nose, pausing just below the eyes, then glide out under the cheekbones and up to the temples, and return to the chin.

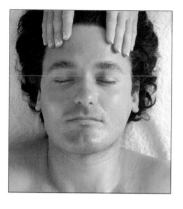

4 Stroke up the front of the face again, but this time continue up to the bridge of the nose. Pause, then stroke out across the forehead to the temples. Pause and press, then glide down to the chin. Repeat steps 1–4 at least four times.

Never give a full face massage o someone who is wearing contact lenses. Ask your partner to remove their lenses before you start, or take care to avoid to eye area.

Cupping the face

Cup your hands over your partner's face, with the palms on the forehead and your fingers over the mouth. Hold them there for a moment. Then, press down very gently. Following this, release the pressure and draw your hands out to the sides. Pause here for a moment, then repeat the whole sequence.

When cupping the face, I imagine that my hands are magnets and that I am drawing all the tension out of my client's face.

Neck and jaw

Now move down to pay attention to the neck and jawline.

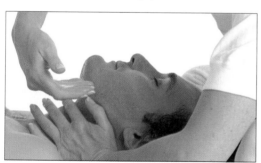

STEP 1

STEP 2

1 Working with both your hands on one side, stroke with one hand firmly up the neck from the shoulder to the ear. Then, lift your hand away and start stroking with your other hand on the same side. Repeat this move six times on each side.

2 Continue stimulating the jawline by patting and slapping under the chin. Use the ring and middle fingers of each of your hands to slap under the jaw. This is a bouncy percussion movement, which should stimulate but not sting.

A cheeky little massage

Now move up the face slightly to the cheeks.

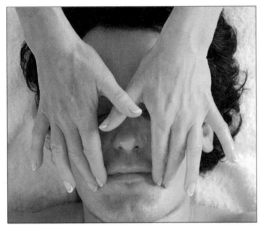

STEP 1

1 Make small, upward circular movements around the mouth with the tips of your middle fingers. Work with both hands, crossing your thumbs to equalize the pressure of your hands.

2 Then make these circles around the chin and on the *mandible*, paying particular attention to the mandibular joint (just in front of the ears) as this area is often very tense. Ask your partner to clench his or her teeth to locate the area.

> **DEFINITION**
>
> *The lower jawbone is known as the **mandible**. It is the largest and strongest facial bone, and the only moveable bone in the skull.*

3 Stroke with your fingertips from the lower lip, under the cheekbones, to the ears. Then, still with your fingertips, stroke from the upper lip to the ears. These movements help to prevent lines round the mouth.

STEP 4

4 With your hands facing each other on one cheek, loosely roll your fingers up under the cheekbone with one hand following the other. This releases tension in the jaw. Repeat on the other side.

Men don't usually think of having a face massage, although they can benefit just as much as women. It is such a simple way of removing worry and tension that I think every man should be persuaded to try.

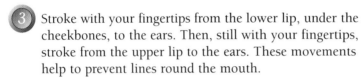

Trivia...

The effect of a face massage can be dramatic. One of my clients opted for a regular face massage instead of having a face lift, thus avoiding the risk of surgery and the inconvenience of being in hospital to recover (and probably a small fortune as well).

Soothing the forehead

Massaging the forehead and around the eyes is most rewarding. Tension and headaches can be soothed away almost miraculously, to be replaced by a relaxed smile.

 Put your hands across your partner's forehead, and press firmly with the first two fingers of each. Make zigzag strokes with your hands moving towards each other. Start with a small movement, then enlarge it to cover the whole forehead.

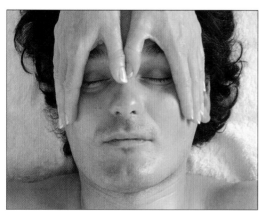

STEP 2

2 Place your thumbs on the bridge of the nose, stroke out to the temples and press gently. Repeat the stroke a little higher up and gradually cover the whole forehead up to the hairline.

3 Make circular pressures all over the forehead with your fingers or thumbs. Work with both hands simultaneously from the centre to the temples, with smooth, rhythmic pressures.

Eye relief

ALTHOUGH THE EYES *themselves are extremely sensitive, there are a number of massage moves that are perfectly safe – circular strokes, squeezing the eyebrows, and light pressures. A lot of tension is carried around the eyes, which often gives them a heavy, weary look. This can be lifted by using a combination of the gentle massage techniques below.*

Circling the eyes

Starting at the bridge of your partner's nose, stroke firmly out along the eyebrows with your fingertips. Circle on the temples, then glide back very lightly under the eyes to the nose. Try this with your hands moving out simultaneously, then alternately. This is amazingly relaxing, and will obliterate your partner's anxiety and tension.

Squeezing the eyebrows

This is a good contrast to the previous stroking sequence. Squeeze the eyebrows between your thumbs and forefingers, starting at the bridge of the nose and working out to the temples. Press gently at the temples before returning your fingers to the starting point, without touching the eyes, then repeat.

Pressing the eyes

When you feel more confident about massaging the face, and your fingers are dextrous, you can try lightly massaging the eyelids. Practise on yourself first.

1 Start by placing your fingers across the forehead, then slide them down until the middle and ring fingers rest lightly on the eyelids. Pause for a moment, press very gently, then separate the fingers and glide them out across the eyes. Press gently on the temples.

2 Now try massaging the eyes. Use your ring fingers to make very light circular pressures all over the eyelids.

Surrounding each eye, just below the skin's surface, there is a large ring of muscle called the orbicularis oculi. It roughly follows the edge of the eye socket in the skull, although at its lower edge it reaches down to the cheek bone. This muscle often gets tense and taut.

Finishing touches

As you approach the end of the face massage, you should go back to stroking. Place one of your hands across the forehead and stroke up towards the hairline, moulding your hand around the forehead. Lift your hand away and begin stroking with your other hand, returning the first hand to start again. For the final touch, cup your hands over the forehead. Hold them still for a couple of seconds, then slowly and gently press down. Hold the pressure for a moment then release it very gradually, so that your hands lift slowly away from the forehead. This simple technique seems to consolidate the whole face massage, and it feels as though you are pulling out the last vestiges of tension from the body.

QUICK CHECKLIST FOR FACE MASSAGE

Use this list to remind yourself of the steps in a face massage.

1. Stroking, then cupping the face

2. Stroking the neck and jaw

3. Patting and slapping the chin

4. Circular movements around the mouth and chin

5. Stroking the cheeks

6. Stroking and circular movements on the forehead

7. Circular pressures round the eyes; then lightly touching the eyelids

Trivia...

Japanese hairdressers always finish their haircuts with a massage. Apart from releasing tension from the head, neck, and shoulders, the Japanese are also well aware of the immense benefits to hair quality and condition.

Looking a-head

WHEN YOU HAVE FINISHED massaging your partner's face, remain in a kneeling position behind the head, and flow smoothly into the head massage. A head massage is remarkably soothing when done correctly, and its benefits can extend to all parts of the body. You do not need to use oil for a head massage, but if there is any remaining on your hands following the face massage, just check that your partner doesn't mind having a small amount of oil in his or her hair. You could mention its marvellous conditioning properties!

Hair condition can be improved through massage, and it's even possible that hair growth is stimulated by reducing the tension in the scalp and improving the circulation. My clients who self-massage twice a day tell me they have noticed a definite improvement in texture.

Rotary pressures

Use the pads of your fingers to make small circles all over your partner's scalp. Start at the front and work your way over the whole head. Make extra moves in the hollows at the base of the skull at the back of the neck. Try to move the scalp around to release tension in the underlying muscles.

To be certain that you are actually massaging the scalp, rather than just messing up your partner's hair, try it on yourself first. The cardinal rule is that you will not hear the scrunching of hair if you are doing it properly.

Pressures to the ear

Squeeze your partner's ears all over, and make small circular pressures between your thumbs and forefingers. Then, with your ring fingers, slowly explore all the crevices, and trace all round the ear.

PRESSURES TO THE EAR

Neck stretch

Place your hands behind the neck, with your little fingers on the skull and the others facing each other behind the neck. Gently and steadily pull the head towards you to stretch the neck. Keep the neck straight, and stretch it slowly and smoothly.

NECK STRETCH

Hair pulling

Although hair pulling may sound like something you might have done to torture your younger sibling when you were a child, it's actually not painful when done correctly. Start by simply stroking your partner's hair, then grasp a bunch at the roots and pull it towards you – it's important that you pull from the roots and not from further up the hair shaft (which would be painful). Release your grasp and slide your fingers up the hair. Use your hands alternately as you pull and glide up the hair. This movement gives the lovely feeling of literally pulling away all the tightness in the scalp.

The final touch

To finish the head massage, place your hands on either side of the head, with your fingers covering the ears and the heels of your hands by the temples. Gently press your hands towards each other and hold for a couple of seconds. Release the pressure very slowly, then slide your hands up the sides of the head and glide them gently off the top. Repeat this movement a couple of times.

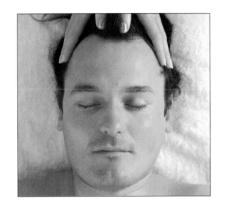

QUICK CHECKLIST FOR HEAD MASSAGE

If you want a reminder of the steps in a head massage, try using this list:

1 Small circular pressures over scalp

2 Squeezing ears

3 Stretching neck

4 Pulling hair

5 Pressing and gliding off top of head

INTERNET

www.cmhmassage.co.uk

Find out about face and head massage at this site.

A simple summary

✔ Face massage can alleviate anxiety, headaches, and exhaustion.

✔ By releasing tension and improving circulation, a face massage can actually leave a person with a young, fresh complexion.

✔ Face massage is easily done as self-massage and can be enormously beneficial.

✔ Head massage is a perfect way to complete a face massage.

✔ The hair can benefit greatly from head massage.

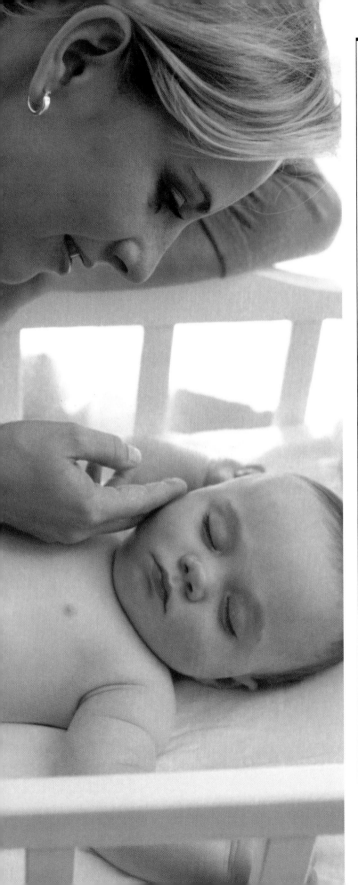

PART FOUR

AN EARLY ENCOUNTER WITH MASSAGE

MASSAGE FOR ALL OCCASIONS

NO MATTER WHAT YOUR AGE, CONDITION, OR PROFESSION, there's a type of massage out there for you. An active, kicking baby *in the womb* can be soothed through a mother's abdominal massage. Stress levels *in the office* can be reduced through back massages and holds. Dull skin  and tired eyes can be revitalized with regular facial massages, and a little sensual massage can remind us how nice it is to touch and be touched.

In Part Four I'll be covering all aspects of everyday life where massage can be used to soothe or stimulate, relax or *revive*. Whatever the desired result, it's all at your *fingertips!*

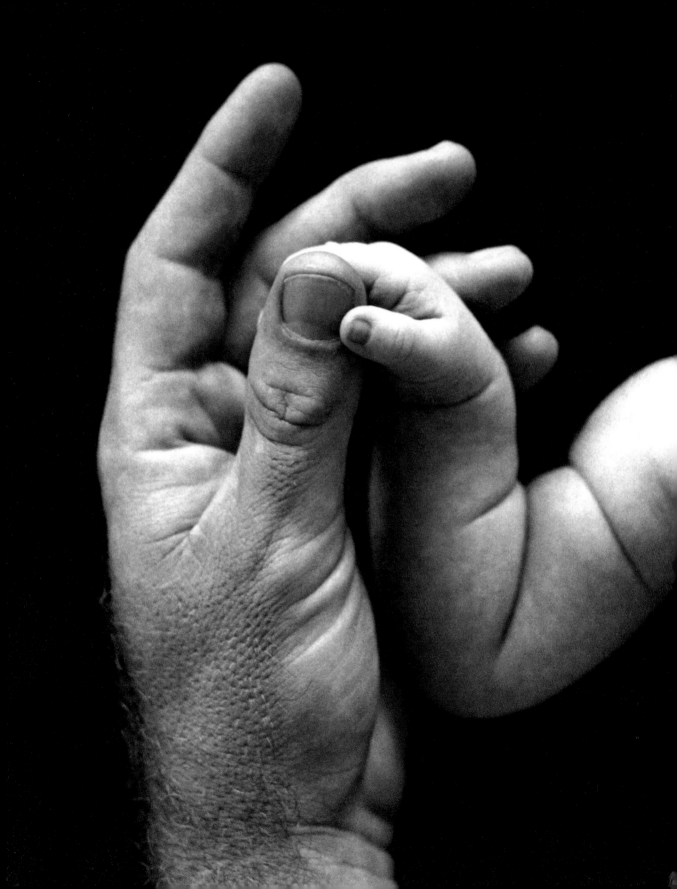

Chapter 16

The Cycle of Life

THERE IS NO STAGE OF LIFE at which a person cannot benefit from massage – babies, children, adolescents, mothers-to-be, the middle-aged, and the elderly can all experience the therapeutic and relaxing powers of massage. Massage improves circulation, relaxes muscles, aids digestion, relieves aches and pains, and speeds up the elimination of waste products. These physical benefits, combined with the psychological benefits of feeling cared for and cosseted, quickly produce a marvellous feeling of wellbeing.

In this chapter...
✓ The first years
✓ The childhood years
✓ The fertile years
✓ The menopause
✓ The elderly
✓ The bereaved

WE CAN BENEFIT FROM THE POWER OF TOUCH AT ANY AGE

The first years

IT'S THE MOST NATURAL THING in the world for new parents to stroke, cuddle, and rock their babies, and massage is no more than an extension of this desire to hold, touch, and provide comfort. Not only is massage a pleasurable, bonding experience for both parents and child, it also encourages the baby to be responsive and sociable. Calm, soothing strokes help to ease anxiety and minimize crying; research has shown that massage can boost a baby's immune system, lower stress levels, relieve colic, and encourage sleep. Agitated babies can be quietened and lulled to sleep with a massage. Although a relatively new idea in developed countries, baby massage is commonplace in countries with more traditional cultures, such as India and Africa.

Did you know?

In 1986, at the Miami Medical Center in the US, premature babies were given three 15-minute massages a day for 10 days. They averaged a 47 per cent greater weight gain per day than infants who were not massaged, and were more alert and active. The massaged babies stayed in hospital for an average of 6 days less than other babies.

Preparation

There are no special techniques and no definite sequence for massaging a baby; it's just a question of adapting a massage to fit the tiny body, and making sure that your baby is enjoying the experience. Establish contact and watch your baby for cues on his or her likes and dislikes.

Start with your baby facing you so that you establish contact. Focus your eyes on the area you are going to massage before you introduce your hands. Make sure you are responsive to your baby throughout.

Stroke with your fingertips or your thumbs whenever the area you are working on is too small for the whole surface of your hand. Keep all your movements slow and smooth; let your hands be your guide and do whatever comes naturally. Begin by using the pads of your fingers to stroke slowly and gently. As both of you gain confidence, you can increase the rhythm and depth of the movements. You will soon learn your baby's likes and dislikes.

Use a light, unscented, cold pressed vegetable oil, such as almond or sunflower, for the whole massage, including the baby's face.

As babies feel the cold more than adults, be sure that the room is kept warm. If you massage your baby on the floor or on a raised surface, such as a bed or table, make sure the area is well padded with cushions and towels. Alternatively, you can do the massage sitting up with your back well supported and your baby on your lap. The best time to massage is between feeds, after a bath, or simply when you both feel the need for closeness. The length of the massage depends entirely on how long your baby enjoys it.

Head and face

This is an ideal place to start your baby's massage as you can maintain eye contact as you stroke.

1. Cup your baby's head gently in your hands. Hold it there for a few seconds, then very gently increase the pressure of your hands. Release, then working from the centre outwards, make gentle circles to cover the whole head.

2. Support one side of the head with one hand and, with the thumb and fingertips of your other hand, gently squeeze and pull the ear. Swap hands to support the other side of the head, and work on the other ear.

3. With the flats of the fingers or the thumbs, stroke from the centre of the forehead out to the hairline, then down to each ear. Stroke from the nose out to the ears, from the nose up to the forehead, and over the chin and jaw.

Did you know?

In a study at Touch Research International in Miami, babies were either rocked or massaged. The rocked babies subsequently woke up when they were put down to sleep, but the massaged babies, who were alert during the massage, fell asleep quickly and soundly when they were put into their cots.

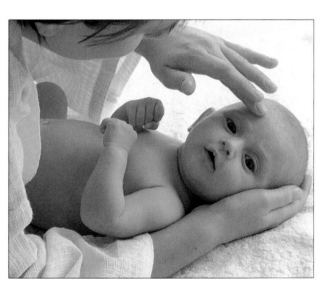

4. Now make soft, spiralling circles with your fingertips, circling the areas of the face that you have just stroked. Finish by holding the head in your hands again for a moment or two.

Arms and hands

Pour some oil onto your hands, place them on your baby's chest, and let the warmth gather.

1 Stroke the left arm a few times. Then, gently roll it backwards and forwards between your hands.

2 Rhythmically stroke one of your hands after the other down the left arm, then gently squeeze and twist the arm as you work down to the hand. Next, make soft circles around the elbow with one hand while the other hand supports the arm. Then stroke the hand, from the wrist to the fingers.

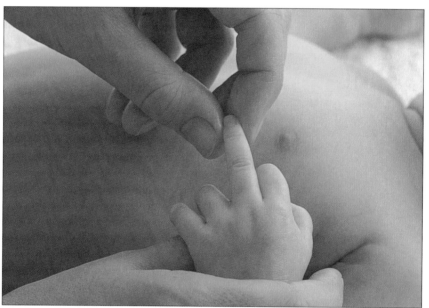

3 Play with each of the fingers in turn, rotating and loosening the joints. Work between the knuckles and all over the palm, making bunny hop movements with your thumbs.

4 Now rub the left arm quite briskly from the top to the bottom. This is a lovely energetic movement that will leave your baby gurgling with delight. Finish with soft feather stroking with your fingertips down the arm. Then move across to work on the right arm and repeat steps 1–4.

5 When both the arms have been massaged, try some passive movements. Stretch the arms in and out, across the chest, either one after the other or both at the same time.

Abdomen

Massage of the abdomen can really help babies suffering from colic. By increasing the circulation and stimulating peristalsis, it can help your baby expel gas and can relieve constipation.

1. Start with some circle stroking. Hold both hands over the stomach, then stroke one of your hands down and round in a clockwise direction, followed by your other hand. As one hand meets the other wrist, lift it over and complete the circle on the other side. One hand will, therefore, form complete circles while the other will form half circles.

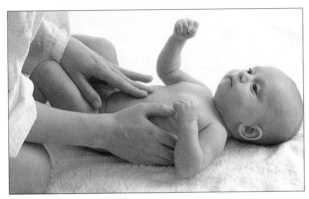

2. With one hand as support, describe little circles all over the abdomen with the fingertips of your other hand. Start on the left side, and work in a clockwise direction around the area.

3. Bring the knees up, over the stomach, and place the soles of the feet together. Relax the abdomen by rotating his or her legs around in a clockwise motion. Try and keep the pelvis still as you circle the legs around. Then stretch out the legs, going backwards and forwards.

Legs and feet

Most babies love to have their legs and feet massaged. The strokes and movements encourage elasticity, flexibility, and co-ordination.

1. Stroke down the left leg from the hip to the foot. Then sandwich the leg with your hands and gently rock it up and down, and from side to side.

2. Gently squeeze and twist all the way down the leg to the toes, using either one or both of your hands. Then work up and down the leg with an energetic rubbing action.

3. Support the calf with one of your hands, and hold the ankle with your other hand. Slowly rotate the ankle, then move on to work the foot.

4. Stroke from the ankle to the toes, then gently squeeze and rotate each toe. Repeat steps 1–4 on the right leg.

Back

To massage your baby's back, lie him or her along your legs or on the floor. Alternatively, sit your baby up on your lap, leaning forwards onto your arm.

1. Begin with criss-cross stroking across the back. Use one hand if your baby is sitting, or both hands if he or she is lying down.

2. Stroke gently down the back with the palm of your hand.

3. Make tiny circles with your fingertips, up and down the back on either side of his or her spine.

4. Finish by stroking your fingertips very lightly down the entire back.

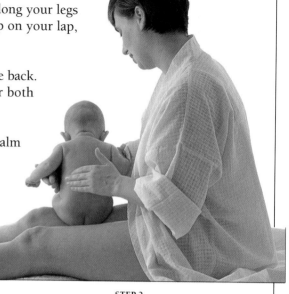

STEP 2

Passive movements

Babies love having their limbs played with so at the end of the massage try doing these gentle movements.

1. Hold the feet and bend and stretch each leg. Some babies like to have this done very fast.

2. Hold the hands and cross the arms over the chest.

3. Take the arms out to the sides and stretch them out gently.

4. Bring the arms up in front of his or her face, then cross them over again.

5. Take the arms up above his or her head and stretch them again gently.

INTERNET

www.iaim.org.uk

www.iaim-us.com

The International Association of Infant Massage aims to promote nurturing touch and communication through training, education, and research. The IAIM recruits and trains instructors to teach parents and carers the theory, skills, and techniques of parent–infant bonding through infant massage.

The childhood years

MASSAGING CHILDREN *is just as easy and rewarding as massaging babies. Children of all ages thoroughly enjoy massage and they respond well to the relaxing strokes. There are no particular rules to follow when massaging a child. Experiment with all the moves you have learned to find out what your child likes best. Younger children tend to be more ticklish than adults so you may have to leave out certain sequences or parts of the body. Adolescents may be reluctant to be massaged so you may need to keep repeating the offer.*

Did you know?

The beneficial effects of massage on children were noted as long ago as 1895 according to this quote from Dr Stretch-Dowse in his Lectures on Massage: "The most sullen and morose child seems gradually to be imbued, under the influence of massage, with the attributes of a docile, willing, and kindly disposition."

Younger children

Being active, exploratory souls, younger children may become restless quite quickly, so keep your massage sequence short. You can make your massage part of a game or a restful part of a rough and tumbles session. Your child need not undress – you can massage through light clothes.

1. Gently stroke your child's abdomen, and glide your hands up over the chest. Smooth, rhythmic stroking around the navel can be very soothing if your child complains of a tummy ache. Always stroke clockwise to follow the way food moves through the digestive system.

Never do an abdominal massage immediately after your child has had a meal.

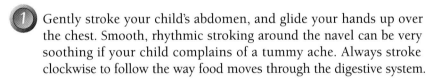

2. Stroke up the back and glide down the sides. Gently knead the shoulders, then stroke out over the tops of the arms.

3. Stroke and squeeze down the legs, then massage the feet. Try hacking the soles: hold one foot up with one of your hands, and hack lightly with the other hand.

4. To massage the hands, squeeze and rotate each finger in turn, then stroke the palm. With pre-school children, you can make this into a counting game.

Older children and adolescents

As children grow up, there often comes a time when physical contact with them is greatly diminished. Massage is a great way to bridge this gap and stay in close contact. Children who no longer wish to be cuddled enjoy the formality of a massage, and a caring touch can encourage them to voice thoughts and concerns that may otherwise be difficult to express. If a child has had a bad day at school, or an argument with a friend, or is bad-tempered, frustrated, or irritable for any reason and doesn't want to talk about it, massage can relieve all the tension.

Adolescence is a difficult time, both physically and emotionally, and the need for touch is by no means diminished. Massage can help meet adolescent touch needs without upsetting their move towards independence. On top of all the hormonal changes that occur at this time, it is also peak exam time. Here again, massage has a part to play through its ability to calm, soothe, and improve physical and mental wellbeing, all of which can remove some of the stress of exams.

> ## Did you know?
> In a 1998 study, 28 adolescents with attention-deficit hyperactivity disorder were given either a massage or relaxation therapy for 10 consecutive school days. The massage group were happier and fidgeted less following the sessions whereas no differences were seen in the other group. At the end of the period, teachers reported more time on task and better classroom behaviour in the massage group.

Appeal to your child's interests

If your child is shy and conservative, it helps if you introduce massage in a way that will appeal. For example, if reading is a major occupation, try a face and shoulder massage; adolescent girls may be more interested if you introduce hair and beauty aspects; if you have an active child who enjoys cycling or football, offer a leg massage. Afterwards, ask for a massage in return.

1 Begin by slowly stroking the thigh. Ask your child to bend one leg, then stroke one of your hands after the other firmly up the thigh towards the body. As each of your hands reaches the top of the thigh, return it to the starting position and repeat. Try to achieve a good flowing rhythm.

2 Repeat step 1, but flex your fingers so that you create a deep raking movement as you stroke down the thigh.

3 Try hacking the outer thigh: lightly strike the flesh with the sides of alternate hands. Keep your wrists loose and relaxed so that your fingers knock together. Finish this stage of the massage with gentle stroking.

4. Continue on the calf with criss-cross stroking. Mould your hands on the back of the lower calf, and pull them firmly towards you so that you squeeze the flesh. Push your hands gently back to the starting position and repeat. Work up the whole calf.

5. Now repeat steps 1–4 on your child's other leg.

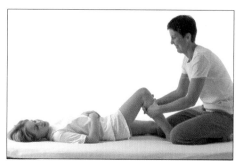

STEP 4

Adolescents may be very resistant at first to having a massage. It is extremely important to respect their wishes and keep your massage to the parts of their body they are comfortable having touched. They may also wish to remain clothed, at least for the first couple of sessions.

Children giving a massage

From as young as 3 years, children are fascinated by watching massage, and are just about ready to give one. They like to feel that they are doing something for someone else, and making that person feel better.

It's easy for a young child to massage your back. By just sitting or kneeling on you, the pressure of his or her body can feel wonderful, particularly on the lower back. Kneading comes readily to a young child – it's just like playing with modelling clay. The vigorous movement is also an excellent way to burn up excess energy. You can also get your child to walk slowly up and down your back, which is a great way of relieving tension and is perfectly safe as long as your child is light and avoids your spine and you don't have a back problem.

Some simple techniques

By the age of 5 or 6 years, a child can give a really good massage. Let's start with the back.

1. Ask your child to kneel behind you (you can be sitting or lying down) and to flex their fingers so that they can stroke down your back with deep, rake-like strokes. Your child can also try kneading your shoulders by squeezing and releasing them.

2. Then get your child to hack or pummel your shoulders. This is simple and fun and has the added attraction of making a lovely noise – in fact, it's probably the only time he or she is allowed to hit you. Ask your child to use the sides of the hands or loose fists to pat your shoulders and upper back. Make sure that the strokes are light and brisk, and that your spine is not struck.

The fertile years

MASSAGE CAN BE BENEFICIAL *to women during pregnancy, labour, and childbirth to reduce tension, anxiety, and pain. Massage can also be used as an aid to conception, and again after delivery to help relax the mother and renew her energy, and help the body regain it's shape.*

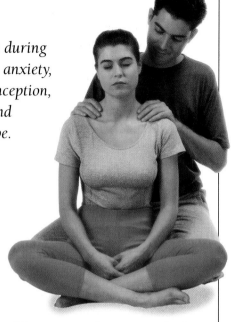

Pre-conception

There is anecdotal evidence that massage has a part to play in the expanding area of infertility treatment. The use of massage seems to lead to increased self-worth and aids relaxation in women having fertility treatment; it also improves staff/patient relationships and communication. Partners can learn to massage too, which gives them a feeling of involvement in a situation in which they may feel helpless.

■ **Partners can become involved** *and perhaps even assist in infertility treatment through the use of massage.*

Pregnancy

During pregnancy, massage can help soothe jangled nerves and alleviate common complaints such as backache, tension in the shoulders, and aching legs and feet. I continue to massage my clients throughout pregnancy and try to encourage their partners to do the same. It is a wonderful way for the father to stay involved with the pregnancy. Gentle, calming strokes stimulate the circulation without putting strain on the heart, and can help reduce blood pressure, thus calming both mother and child.

It is essential that you check with a doctor or midwife before using massage during pregnancy.

INTERNET

www.bmtc.co.uk

The British Massage Therapy Council is a professional organization representing massage associations and schools, promoting high standards in massage therapy practice and training, and the promotion of massage as a therapy.

Lower back

You need to spend time making sure that your partner is comfortable; some women like to kneel resting on a pillow but others will be happier sitting in a chair and leaning forwards; some will prefer lying on their sides.

Start the massage with soothing back strokes.

1 Place both your hands on your partner's lower back, on either side of the spine, and stroke firmly up to her shoulders. Squeeze the tops of her shoulders.

2 Stroke down each of the arms as far as you can reach, then glide back up the arms and down the sides of her body. Stroke around the hips, over the thighs, down the calves and feet, and around the buttocks to the starting position on the back. Repeat this several times, aiming for a single, unbroken stroke that flows effortlessly over the whole body.

Upper back

Now proceed to work on the upper back. For this sequence, your partner may prefer to sit up or lie on her side.

1 Begin with some circle stroking on her left shoulder blade. Stroke one hand after the other in a large circle and, as one hand meets the other wrist, lift it over and complete the circle on the other side, while your other hand continues stroking. Aim for a smooth movement.

2 Knead the top of the left shoulder by rhythmically squeezing and then releasing the flesh with alternate hands. Next, try skin rolling, using your thumbs to roll the flesh up the shoulder blade towards your fingers to create a squeeze at the top of the shoulder. This warming action helps to break down tension in the area.

3 Support the front of the body with your right hand and, with the fingertips of your left hand, apply deep, circular pressures along the left shoulder blade, pushing up and under the bone. Finish the massage sequence by stroking your hand gently over the whole area.

4 Repeat steps 1–3 on your partner's right shoulder.

Abdomen

Massaging the stomach with soft, gentle movements is a lovely way to feel close to both mother and child; it can also benefit both of them as soothing strokes have been reported to calm active, kicking babies. During the first 20 weeks of pregnancy, it is possible to perform the following massage with your partner lying on her back. During the second half of the pregnancy, the weight of the fetus in this position can constrict circulation so it is safer and more comfortable for your partner to lie on her side with her legs bent forwards. Place pillows under her head and between her knees for support.

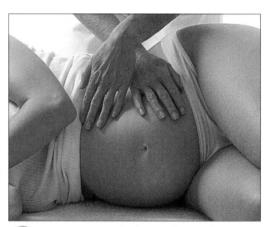

1 Side stroking is a particularly effective movement to do during pregnancy, as there is such a large surface area to work on. Kneel behind your partner, and stroke one hand after the other very gently up and over the stomach. The hand nearest to the hips can continue the stroke around the lower back before lifting off the skin and repeating the movement.

2 Now try very light circle stroking. Use both hands to trace a large circle around the abdomen, one hand following the other in a clockwise direction. As your arms cross, lift one hand over the other, making a complete circle with one hand and a half circle with the other. This movement is so superficial that it should feel no more than a caress. You can also try using one hand to circle smaller and smaller until you are just circling around the navel.

On no account use heavy pressure on the abdomen of a pregnant woman as it would cause discomfort – stick to gentle stroking movements.

Face

During a lull in contractions, a gentle face massage can be calming and reassuring. The most relaxing techniques are those that focus around the eyes and on the forehead. Stroking up the forehead into the hairline is one of the best ways of reducing tension.

Scented oils can really help during labour and childbirth. Lavender has a sedative and soothing effect so it is a particularly good choice. Add a few drops to your massage oil, and ask the midwife if you can use an oil burner or vaporizer so that the fragrance fills the air.

Feet

Although you can use any of the foot massage techniques outlined in the pregnancy section of this chapter, the two discussed below have been found to be the best to help relieve the pain of contractions.

1. Support her foot with one hand and stroke the sole firmly with the heel of your other hand.

2. Apply deep pressures, with your thumbs in a line down the centre of the sole to the heel.

For pain relief, you can also try putting pressure on the shiatsu point on the outside of the little toe, at the base of the nail.

After childbirth

Following the mental, emotional, and physical strain of childbirth, mothers need to be nurtured. Massage is a perfect way to relax the mind and body, renew energy, encourage deep sleep, and help the body regain its shape. I first became interested in massage because my mother was always in such a wonderful mood after having a massage.

Following are a few abdominal massage techniques that I learned from midwives in India and Sarawak.

Did you know?

Research at Queen Charlotte's Hospital, London, in 1999, on mothers with postnatal depression showed the benefits of massage. Mothers were taught to massage their babies. After five sessions it was found that there was an increase in bonding between mother and baby, and the mothers were less depressed.

Only do abdominal massage after the mother's postnatal check-up (generally 6 weeks after the birth). In the East, massage is traditionally done by the local midwife who knows the woman's condition.

1. Support your partner's abdomen with one hand and make a "V" shape between the thumb and fingers of your other hand. Stroke up from the pubic bone towards the navel with the "V", imagining that you are scooping everything back into place. Glide back and repeat three times.

2. Place one of your hands on top of the other and stroke very, very slowly and deeply up the abdomen. When you reach the navel, release the pressure and glide gently back. Repeat three times.

3. Gently circle around the abdomen, using soft and moulding hands.

Never undertake abdominal massage after a Caesarian without first checking with your doctor.

The shoulders and neck often get very tense as a result of breastfeeding. Loosen tight muscles with circular thumb pressures. Support one of your partner's shoulders with one hand and work the thumb of your other hand all around the neck and shoulder blade, avoiding the spine. Repeat on the other shoulder.

STEP 1

The menopause

THE CESSATION *of menstruation bringing an end to a woman's childbearing years is known as the menopause. It is a natural phase in a woman's life but, as with many other life transitions, it can be difficult. The majority of women start the menopause in their mid-forties to early fifties, but occasionally it starts earlier. It generally takes place over a year, but physiological changes and symptoms may last longer.*

The menopause does not mean that a woman loses her youthfulness or sexuality overnight – in fact, many women feel they have acquired a new maturity and they feel more self-aware and confident. However, there are associated physical and psychological symptoms, which most women experience to a greater or lesser extent. The most common physical symptoms of the menopause are hot flushes, night sweats, disturbed sleep, headaches, aches and pains, and dizziness. Psychological symptoms include mood swings, tension, anxiety, and depression. Weight gain and dry skin can lead to low self-esteem.

■ **In addition to** *its undoubted physical benefits, massage can also help relieve some of the psychological symptoms of menopause.*

A simple comfort

Many of my clients have found that massage can help them through this time. It gives support and can relieve some symptoms. Feelings of anxiety and depression can be lifted; insomnia can be alleviated; headaches and aches and pains can be helped. Dry skin can be combated by massaging with rich, emollient oils and creams. Hot flushes can be soothed with a cold compress, which has been soaked in water containing chamomile oil. Self-massage on face and body can also help reduce tension.

The elderly

IT IS NEVER TOO LATE to improve your health and quality of life, and massage can play a part in achieving this goal. Massage stimulates the circulation so that aches and pains are diminished, joints and muscles are loosened, and greater mobility may be possible. In addition, the relaxing effects of massage induce a feeling of wellbeing and an optimistic outlook on life. Massage may also reduce the need for painkillers as it triggers the release of endorphins.

In many respects, massaging an elderly person is no different from massaging anyone else, but there are a few things that you should bear in mind. An older person's bones are not as strong as a younger person's and he or she is more likely to have osteoarthritis. The circulation tends to be less efficient, leading to cold, and sometimes painful, hands and feet. The skin is thinner and less elastic, and is more easily damaged. You might need to find alternative positions as, for example, an elderly person might find lying face down uncomfortable. Extra padding may be needed for comfort and support.

As elderly people often have multiple medical problems, it is particularly important that you check beforehand that none of the conditions precludes doing a massage.

Head

Gentle stroking of the head and scalp can be very soothing. It also conveys care, concern, and empathy – emotions that are often lacking in an elderly person's life, particularly if he or she is living alone or in a residential home.

Hands and feet

Pay particular attention to these areas because massage can increase circulation to them, and increase joint flexibility and mobility. Massage the hands or feet with the person sitting in a chair. Support the arm or leg that you are massaging so the person can relax. Begin gently and slowly, only increasing the pressure if desired. Using gentle movements, rotate, flex, and extend the wrist and ankle joints to improve flexibility. Don't assume, however, that a gentle massage will always be preferred. Firm pressure in stiff parts of the body may be greatly appreciated.

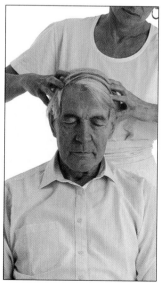

A SOOTHING HEAD MASSAGE

The bereaved

MASSAGE IS A DIRECT and powerful form of communication that can show care and provide comfort at times when words are inadequate. Bereavement is one such time, and the benefits of massage can be enormous.

Many bereaved people keep their emotions bottled up, especially in developed countries where grieving takes a more introspective form than in many Eastern cultures. Massage can work as a safety valve by releasing physical and mental tension, which can in turn shorten the grieving process. You do not have to do a full body massage to show that you care. Simply stroke the hands, or massage the neck and shoulders.

For some bereaved people, massage is not the answer as it can bring to the fore too many painful emotions. You must always respect an individual's wishes.

A simple summary

✓ Age holds no barriers to receiving massage – anyone from the very young to the very old can benefit.

✓ Massaging babies can minimize crying, boost their immune systems, lower stress levels, and encourage sleep; it also strengthens the bond between parents and child.

✓ For children and adolescents, massage is the perfect way to maintain close contact, especially during the "difficult" teen years.

✓ Massage during pregnancy, labour, and childbirth has many benefits ranging from reduction of tension to pain relief in labour.

✓ Elderly people can receive the same physical and mental benefits from massage as younger age groups.

✓ Massage can help many people cope with the pain of a bereavement.

Chapter 17

This Sporting Life

MASSAGE HAS A LONG HISTORY as a way of enhancing athletes'
performance and preventing sports injuries. Regular massage
helps sportspeople as diverse as athletes, football players, and ballet
dancers to keep physically, mentally, and emotionally healthy. It improves
performance by keeping muscles at the peak of their flexibility and
strength, and reduces stiffness and muscle soreness. Sports massage also
eases anxiety, keeping the athlete alert, yet calm. Regular sports massage
provides improved speed, strength, flexibility, and quicker post-event
recovery. Sports massage can be used both before and after an event.

In this chapter...
✓ Ready, steady, go
✓ After the event
✓ What's the problem?
✓ Help yourself

SPORTS MASSAGE CAN IMPROVE ATHLETIC PERFORMANCE AS WELL AS EASE ACHES AND PAINS

Ready, steady, go

MASSAGE CAN BE EXTREMELY BENEFICIAL for athletes, or indeed anyone involved in athletic activity. Two to three days before a sporting (or other) event, give your partner a massage to help him or her feel relaxed and supple.

A full body massage is ideal but, if you are short of time, massage the main muscles your partner will be using. Use rocking and kneading movements and, instead of finishing your massage with soporific stroking, use a stimulating movement, like pummelling, to increase blood supply. Athletes also benefit from a light, stimulating massage an hour or so before an event. Use calming strokes instead if your partner is anxious.

Many of my clients are involved in sport or dance and they all claim that after a massage their minds are clear and relaxed, and their performances are greatly improved.

PRE-EVENT MASSAGE

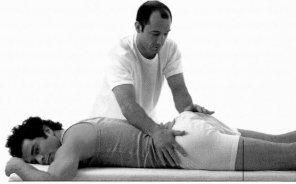

1 Applying deep tissue pressure

Begin by using gentle movements to prepare the buttock area for deep tissue work. Then use elbow pressure to soften tight muscles and promote mobility around the hip, particularly on the posterior muscles. Use your body weight for this, with one hand holding the ankle, and your other elbow and forearm carefully pressing into the buttock muscles.

2 Restoring blood flow

After deep tissue work, softer massage techniques help to restore blood flow to the area. Rhythmically grip and gently knead different sections of the buttock muscles to soothe the area that you have been working on and to create a softening effect.

After the event

DURING EXERCISE, *waste products such as carbonic acid and lactic acid are released into the muscles. It is the accumulation of these wastes that can cause muscular tension, stiffness, and pain. The* **lymphatic system** *drains them out of the body, but this can take several hours or even days.*

With its pumping and stroking action, massage can improve lymphatic flow and speed up the elimination of wastes and thus help to prevent stiffness. Massage improves the blood flow and brings fresh oxygenated blood to the area. Deeper movements can also soften and lengthen tense, contracted muscles.

DEFINITION

The **lymphatic system** *is a complex network of vessels and glands (nodes) that carry fluid (lymph) from body tissues to the blood system. It has a dual role – it drains excess fluid into the bloodstream to keep a constant balance of fluid within the body, and the lymph glands produce lymphocytes that help fight infection.*

The best techniques to use are those that encourage blood and lymph to drain towards the body. Use light pressure at first, and gradually increase it, always staying within your partner's "comfort zone".

3 **Shaking it up**

The hamstring muscles (at the back of the thigh) benefit from being vigorously shaken to loosen them up. Place your leg on the massage table or couch and use it to support the leg. Use one of your hands to hold the foot and the other to pull the thigh muscles slightly away from the bone, shaking the muscles rhythmically. This technique has a relaxing effect, both mentally and physically.

Squeezing a limb correctly is similar in effect to squeezing a sponge to extract water. As you squeeze, you encourage the circulation so that waste products from the muscles are flushed into the lymphatic system, and oxygen-rich blood is shunted into the muscle.

POST-EVENT MASSAGE

The techniques below, employed soon after an athletic or sporting event, will help prevent stiffness and injury.

1 Working the arms

Support the arm with your hand to enhance lymphatic drainage. Squeeze the arm muscles with your free hand as firmly as is comfortable for your partner. Stroking can also be performed from this position. Finish this stage by holding the hand and shaking the whole of the arm.

2 Stretching the latissimus dorsi

Reposition yourself so you are behind the head. Hold the right forearm with your left hand and rotate it at the elbow. With your right hand placed on the upper body, stretch the latissimus dorsi muscles (the main muscles on either side of the spine in the middle of the back) by pulling the forearm. Use your whole body to put strength and weight into the pulling action.

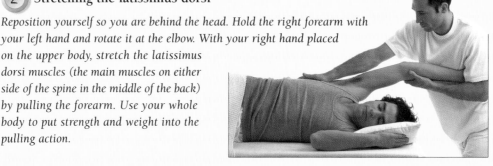

3 Stretching the rhomboids

To stretch the rhomboideous (main upper back) muscles, ask your partner to roll over onto his or her side. Place one of your hands under your partner's arm and the other over his or her shoulder. Tuck your fingers into the shoulderblade and stretch the muscle up towards you, while rocking the shoulder gently backwards and forwards.

If your partner's muscles are too tender for a sports massage, try using manual lymphatic drainage, which is a very gentle technique that is also very effective.

What's the problem?

ANYONE WHO DOES REGULAR exercise or participates a lot in sport is naturally at greater risk of injury than someone who leads a more sedentary existence. Very few athletes, footballers, rugby players, cricketers, cyclists, or dancers escape the occasional injury that requires treatment. Fortunately however, most injuries are minor and the soothing effects of massage can ease the pain and stimulate the healing process. Massage can speed up the return to full physical fitness, which can be crucially important for professionals.

If your injured partner has excessive swelling, increased temperature, or great pain, treat with basic first-aid and seek medical assistance urgently.

Cuts and bruises

Work very gently around a cut or bruise, stroking towards the nearest lymph nodes. Very gently stroke the flesh above and to the side of the injury. Ask your partner to tell you if there is any tenderness or discomfort. If there is, work further away from the injury.

Never work directly on an injury. Do not massage around an open wound, or on a bruised area unless you know the cause of the bruising.

Trivia...

Massage was used at the Olympic Games in Australia in 2000. A total of 220 massage therapists worked with the all-volunteer medical services team in Sydney. Up to 400 massages were given each day.

Cramp

If you are prone to cramp during or after exercise, massage can definitely help. A cramped muscle is tightly contracted and the blood supply to it is reduced. Massage stretches the muscle and improves circulation, leaving it more flexible. The following instructions are for self-massage.

- **Hamstring cramp** – lie on your back and raise the affected leg. Stroke the back of your thigh firmly, then knead it. Finally, stroke the area again to soothe it

- **Calf cramp** – sit with the affected leg straight, and bend your foot up so that you stretch the calf muscle. Then knead the muscle firmly, working up your leg. When you feel the muscle relaxing, soothe it by rhythmically stroking down the whole leg

● **Foot cramp** – grasp your toes, and gently but firmly bend them back while holding your heel with your other hand. Then stroke and knead the sole of the foot. You can do the same movements through your trainers if you get cramp during an event

GENTLY BENDING THE TOES BACK TO COMBAT FOOT CRAMP

Strains and sprains

Very gentle massage can be used to ease the pain and swelling caused by both sprains and strains. A sprain is caused by the abnormal wrenching and twisting of a joint. A strain is a torn or stretched muscle.

At the first opportunity, place a cold compress, such as an ice pack or a packet of frozen peas (wrapped in a tea towel or something similar), on the injured area to reduce inflammation.

The ankle is the most commonly sprained part of the body. If the ankle is very swollen and painful, consult a doctor before massaging to rule out the possibility of a dislocation or fracture. Very gentle massage can help to reduce swelling and relieve pain. Massage for at least 10 minutes, and repeat several times a day. Continue this treatment for about a week or until the injury is healed.

1. Start by gently stroking up the thigh towards the lymph nodes in the groin.

2. Stroke up the sides of the calf to the knee, and glide gently back down to the ankle.

3. Stroke extremely gently with short upward movements all around the ankle using your thumbs.

A sprained wrist can be treated in much the same way, stroking gently towards the lymph nodes in the armpits and the elbow.

Never attempt to massage a sprained knee without first obtaining a doctor's consent.

Aching feet

It is estimated that the average person walks about a 1,600 km (1,000 miles) in a year, so it is staggering to imagine what ground a runner or ballerina must cover. It is hardly surprising, therefore, that so many people suffer from aching feet. Badly fitting shoes or trainers, foot injuries, and corns, callouses, and bunions can all exacerbate the problem.

Foot massage can relieve aches and pains, and gentle exercise can help strengthen the muscles to lessen future problems. Try rolling your foot on a ball or practise picking up pencils with your toes.

Help yourself

*THERE ARE VARIOUS simple techniques that are eminently suitable for pre- and post-event self-massage. Before the event, self-massage complements stretching; use direct pressure on **trigger points** and any tight areas. Post-event self-massage can help combat muscle stiffness and fatigue.*

DEFINITION

*Small areas of tenderness within muscles are called **trigger points**.*

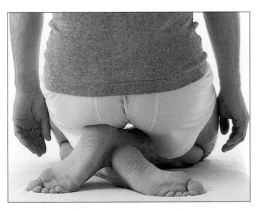

STRETCHING THE SHINS

Shins

Kneel with your ankles crossed. Place your hands on the floor for balance if you feel wobbly. Your bodyweight will stretch the area above your ankles. Rock forwards and change the angle of your ankles until the stretch feels effective.

■ **Dancing is an extremely athletic pursuit**, *and the dancer is subject to all kinds of aches, pains, strains, and sprains. Judicious use of massage can be very helpful in the relief and prevention of these potential pitfalls.*

Calves

While seated on the floor with your legs bent in front of you, clasp the toes and ball of one foot with your hands and pull back towards you. This stretches the foot and calf muscles, aiding flexibility. Repeat on the other foot.

Feet, thighs, and hips

With your feet tucked under you, raise your body so that your weight is transferred through your arms. Shift your bodyweight until you feel it passing through your knuckles. Then massage into the soles of your feet with your knuckles. If you push your hips forward, this also becomes an effective stretch for the quadriceps muscles (the large muscles at the front of the thighs) and the front of the hips.

INTERNET

www.massageaus.com.au

Massage Australia represents the interests of massage therapists practising in Australia, and their web site offers information on massage courses and events all over Australia.

MULTIPURPOSE MASSAGE: FEET, THIGHS, AND HIPS

A simple summary

✔ Before a sporting or dancing event or exercise, massage can enhance performance and improve mental and emotional wellbeing.

✔ Post-event massage helps to rid the body of a build-up of waste products that can cause pain and stiffness, and make the person more susceptible to injury.

✔ Massage can be used to relieve the pain and swelling of minor injuries.

✔ Various self-massage techniques that complement the main sports massage can be employed for general suppleness, and for relieving minor problems such as cramp.

Chapter 18

Business Before Pleasure

TWO OF THE GREATEST SOURCES OF STRESS today are work and travel. Impossible deadlines, tight budgets, and long hours at a VDU combine to make our workplace a very stressful place indeed. Massage can help relieve many of the physical symptoms caused by stress. And travel has become less pleasurable thanks to problems such as heavy traffic and airport delays. Whether you are a well-seasoned traveller or just do the daily school run, massage can alleviate some of the strain.

In this chapter...
- ✓ *Stress relief in the office*
- ✓ *Beat your VDU*
- ✓ *Travel by car*
- ✓ *Plane and simple*

DRIVING TO WORK CAN BE STRESSFUL – TRY A MASSAGE WHEN YOU GET THERE!

Stress relief in the office

TOO MUCH WORK, *not enough time, poor remuneration, and all sorts of other work-related pressures (e.g., noise, poor lighting, and seating arrangements) all conspire to make office life a stressful experience. Massage in the workplace – or on-site massage, as it has become popularly known – is becoming widespread with the realization that such a high percentage of days are lost through stress-related illnesses.*

The techniques described here help to release the tension that can accumulate in the back and shoulders, ease aches and pains in the hands and arms after intense computer work, and, above all, help to lower stress levels.

On-site massage can be done just about anywhere, is easy to learn, and only takes about 15 minutes – a small sacrifice for the good it can do. A simpler, shorter sequence can be used as self-massage.

Initial hold

Ask your partner to loosen any tight clothing before you start. Get him or her to straddle a chair. To get your partner used to your touch, rest your palms on the shoulders. Breathe calmly, focusing on your partner, then slowly apply pressure to the shoulders to relax them. Hold for about 10 seconds, then release and stroke the shoulders and back.

■ **On-site massage** *is quick and easy to perform. All you need is 15 minutes, a chair, and knowledge of a few easy-to-learn massage techniques.*

Upper back

One of the greatest areas of tension, particularly in people who spend their lives hunched over a desk, is the top half of the back.

1 **Heel pressures**: place the heels of your hands on either side of your partner's spine at the top of the back and apply an even pressure. Hold for a few seconds, release, and repeat at intervals down the back.

2 **Kneading**: squeeze and release the muscles on the tops of the shoulders with alternate hands, pushing the flesh rhythmically from side to side. Work down the tops of the upper arms.

3 **Deep pressures**: support the area with your left hand and carefully apply pressure with your right forearm elbow all around the right shoulder blade. Keep your arm relaxed so that you do not jab the flesh, then repeat on the left shoulder.

4 **Circular stroking**: stroke one hand after the other in a circle around each shoulder blade in turn to soothe the area after the elbow pressures. Lean your bodyweight into the heels of your hands as you stroke upwards, and release the pressure on the downward movement.

5 **Half Nelson**: to create a deep stretch, ask your partner to place the left hand behind the back, then use your left forearm to ease the arm back. With the heel of your right hand, or your thumb, make deep pressures under the shoulder blade. Repeat on the right shoulder.

6 **V-strokes**: support the forehead with one hand and, with the other, make a "V" shape between your thumb and forefinger; stroke from the base of the neck to the skull in a scooping movement. Then, with your hands in the same position, tilt the head slowly backwards and forwards to stretch the muscles.

Arms and hands

The arms and hands are often tense, aching, and overworked, particularly in people who do computer-based work.

1 **Shaking:** support the right wrist with both hands. Gently shake the arm up and down and from side to side to encourage the muscles to let go. Slowly increase the speed and force of the shaking as your partner relaxes.

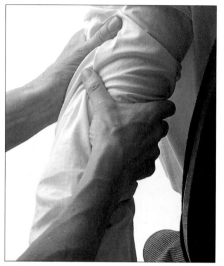 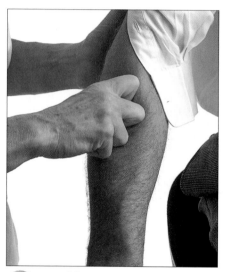

2 **Kneading:** place one hand on either side of the right arm, near the shoulder. Squeeze and release the flesh with alternate hands, working down the arm to the wrist.

3 **Knuckle pressures:** hold the top of the right arm with one hand and roll the knuckles of your other hand in a strong, circular motion, working up the forearm.

4 **Stretching the fingers:** grip any two fingers at the base, then squeeze and pull them, working down to the fingertips. Then repeat on the remaining fingers.

5 **Flexing the wrist:** support the palm of the hand with your fingers and bend the wrist backwards and forwards.

6 Repeat steps 1–5 on the left arm.

INTERNET

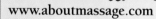

www.aboutmassage.com

Search on this site for information and tips on different techniques, schools, associations, research, and benefits of massage.

Lower back

It is very common for people in sedentary jobs to suffer from lower back pain.

If your partner is wearing a belt, remove it before starting on these lower back exercises so that you can work freely in the area.

1 **Circular stroking:** begin by rhythmically stroking with one hand after the other in a circle around the *sacrum* to soothe the area.

2 **Pressures:** apply deep, static, and circular pressures with the fingers of one hand all around the sacrum, while the other hand supports the back. You can vary the movement by using your thumbs or the heels of your hands to apply pressure.

> **DEFINITION**
>
> The **sacrum** is the bony triangle at the base of the spine.

3 **Sawing:** use the sides of your hands to rub the sacrum backwards and forwards in a sawing motion. This is a fast, warming movement that relaxes tense muscles. Follow with gentle stroking to soothe the lower back.

Never put pressure on the spine itself.

Final touches

To leave your partner in a state of deep relaxation, stroke your fingertips as lightly and slowly as possible from the top of the head to the lower back, then across the shoulders, down the arms, and off at the hands.

Alternatively, if your partner needs to be feeling alert and ready for work, use hacking or pummelling movements to wake him or her up. With relaxed wrists, pound the tops of the shoulders, using alternate hands in a light, swift action.

Self-massage

The full on-site massage can be adapted so that you can do it yourself should the need arise when there is no-one else around to massage you.

1 To induce calmness, practise slow, deep abdominal breathing. Place one hand on your chest and the other on your abdomen. Breathe in through your nose and allow the abdomen to expand. Then exhale through your nose, feeling your abdomen sink down. The hand on your chest should remain still.

2 Loosen your collar, if necessary, and mould your hands over your shoulders. Exhale, letting your head drop back, and slowly draw your fingers down over your collar bones, stroking deep into the muscles to relieve tension.

3 Place your left hand on your right shoulder by the neck and gently squeeze the flesh between your palm and fingers. Hold for several seconds, then release. Work along your shoulder and the top of your arm, wherever you feel tautness. Stroke the whole area and repeat on your left shoulder.

4 Place the fingers of both your hands at the base of your skull on either side of your spine. Apply slow circular pressures, working down your neck and out across the back of your shoulders.

5 Support your left elbow with your right hand and firmly drum the fingers of your left hand across your right shoulder blade. Then stroke the whole area to soothe it. Repeat on your left shoulder.

6 Place both hands on the back of your head, interlacing your fingers. Drop your head forwards, allowing the weight of your elbows to pull your head gently down. You should feel a stretch down the back of your neck.

7 To banish any last vestiges of tension, lift your right shoulder and slowly rotate it backwards. Repeat with your left shoulder, then rotate both shoulders together, keeping your arms loose and relaxed.

Beat your VDU

SIMPLE SELF-MASSAGE STROKES help ease the eyestrain and stiff hands and arms that can follow hours spent working at a computer. Doing these exercises will greatly reduce your chances of developing repetitive strain injury (see below). Take a 10-minute break every hour at work and spend about 5 minutes on your face and a couple of minutes on each hand. The exercises can also be done at home.

Relaxing the face

The following exercises will soothe your face muscles and help you keep going all day.

1. First release any tautness in your face. Cup your hands over your eyes and enjoy the relaxing darkness. Hold for several seconds

2. To alleviate headaches and eyestrain, apply small circular pressures to your temples with the middle two fingers of both your hands

3. Combat the effects of frowning by rubbing your fingers in a scissor-like action across the middle of your forehead and out to either side

Trivia

One of the earliest descriptions of RSI is in a 17th century publication: Hunter's Diseases of Occupations. *The symptoms were attributed to the constrained sitting position and the excessive mental effort involved with the occupation – which, surprisingly enough, was writing!*

Repetitive strain injury

RSI, or repetitive strain injury, is an occupational hazard of any repetitive work, and recently it has achieved notoriety in the workplace, probably because computer-based work has become so widespread. RSI causes pain in the forearm, wrist, and hand, and can arise in workers with jobs as diverse as knitting and road drilling; even massage therapists get RSI!

As an added precaution against developing RSI, make sure you adjust any equipment you use so that you don't have to twist your neck or hunch your shoulders while working.

Various massage techniques can help relieve the muscle tension that is the cause of the pain. Deep kneading of the shoulders and the trapezius muscle can reduce tension in the head, neck, and shoulders. Deep pressures on the forearm muscles can be very beneficial. Self-massage on the hands and forearms can also provide instant relief.

SOOTHING THE HANDS AND WRISTS

Follow the steps below to revitalize your hands and wrists after a hard day's work:

1 **Stroke your palms**

Relax each hand by stroking across one palm with the heel of your other hand. Glide back, repeat, then work from the fingers to the wrist.

2 **Stretch your fingers**

Stretch each of your fingers by holding at the base and pulling firmly. Slide and twist your grip up the finger, then let go at the top.

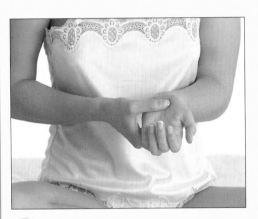

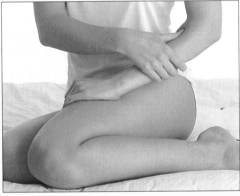

3 **Use thumb pressures**

To ease the palm and relieve headaches, turn one hand over, and with relaxed fingers make circular thumb pressures around the base of the thumb and all over the palm.

4 **Massage your forearms**

Massage your forearm with knuckling and circular thumb pressures. Then stroke the whole area up to the elbow.

Travel by car

AS MORE AND MORE PEOPLE *take to the roads, travelling by car is becoming increasingly frustrating and stressful, particularly for commuters and parents taking their children to school. Travelling long distances along motorways has the added factor of drowsiness, which needs to be dealt with to avoid the risk of accidents.*

■ **Don't let your commute** *bring you down. Use self-massage to de-stress and avoid frustration.*

Reviving self-massage

Try these self-massage techniques when it all gets to be too much on the road.

Don't try to do any self-massage techniques while you are driving. Either wait till you stop at traffic lights or pull over off the road.

● Relax tense hand muscles by supporting one palm with the fingers of your other hand and, with your thumb, stroke from each knuckle in turn down the furrow to the wrist. Repeat on the other hand

● For instant invigoration, stimulate circulation in your scalp and alleviate tension headaches by making firm circular movements with your fingertips. Work up from your forehead and all over your head

● Release taut neck muscles by making firm circular pressures at the base of the neck – on either side of the spine and along the base of the skull

● If your eyes are aching, try using palm pressures: put the palms of your hands onto your eyes, hold them there for a minute and enjoy the darkness. Then massage around the eyes and squeeze your eyebrows between your forefinger and thumb to relieve eyestrain

If you start to feel drowsy when driving, pull over at the next safe stopping point. Get out of the car, stretch your limbs, and pummel yourself all over with loose fists. People might think you are crazy – or that you have missed your junction – but that's a small price to pay to avoid falling asleep at the wheel.

Car sickness

If any of your passengers suffer from car sickness, get them to chew fresh root ginger 30 minutes before setting off and at intervals during the journey. Pressing on the middle of the inner wrist three finger-widths below the top crease for 10–15 seconds also helps.

Plane and simple

IN RECENT YEARS, travelling by plane has become an option for many more people rather than being the reserve of those who could afford to travel to far flung corners of the world. Consequently, the incidence of people suffering from the minor problems associated with flying has increased dramatically. Anxiety is a common problem, pressure changes affect the ears, and cramped conditions lead to stiffness and other problems.

Feeling at ease

Once you have reached your seat, follow these steps so that you begin your journey in a relaxed state.

 To distribute your weight well, tilt back your seat and place a small pillow behind the middle part of your back. Rest your feet on your hand luggage under the seat in front.

2 If you need to calm your nerves, close your eyes and stroke your fingers from the bridge of your nose, over your eyebrows to your temples.

3 Calm a nervous stomach by stroking around the navel in a clockwise direction with one hand following the other. Try to keep the stroke as smooth and fluid as possible.

To avoid becoming dehydrated, drink non-carbonated mineral water throughout the flight. And carrot juice has been found to prevent oxygen deprivation during flights, so pack some in your hand luggage.

Relieving blocked ears

Blocked ears during air travel can be annoying at best and painful at worst. Try these exercises to help combat the problem.

1 First, remove the neck pillow. Using the fingers of both hands, apply small circular pressures to the front of your ears, just above your jaw bone. This has a stimulating effect and helps to relieve pressure in the ears.

2 Place your index fingers behind each ear, keeping the remaining fingers in front of your ears. Make slow downward semi-circular movements with your fingers in an anticlockwise direction to improve lymphatic flow and soothe any discomfort.

Release trapped air in the ears by sucking boiled sweets, chewing gum, or swallowing hard especially when taking off and landing.

Maintaining good circulation

In recent times air travellers have become aware of the potential dangers of not maintaining good circulation throughout the flight. As well as getting up and moving around every so often, try the following techniques to keep the blood pumping.

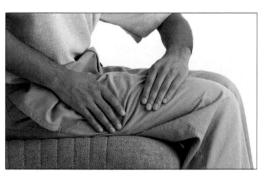

1 With alternate hands, gently grasp and release the flesh on your thigh. Repeat several times, then stroke one hand after the other up your thigh. Repeat on your other leg.

2 Squeeze each side of your calf with the palms and fingers of alternate hands. Stroke the calf. Repeat on your other leg.

3 To improve circulation in your ankles and help ease swelling, circle the fingertips of both hands around the bone on either side of your ankle. You may need to lift up your foot to reach it. Repeat on your other ankle. You can also try rotating your foot.

Combatting jet lag

If you are travelling a long distance and across time zones, you are likely to suffer from disorientation as your body clock struggles to adjust to its new environment. Calming or energizing massage relieves the lethargy or insomnia that often occurs, and helps to regulate sleeping patterns.

■ **Always one step behind?** *Jet lag can be a hindrance when on holiday, but on business trips it can be disastrous. Massage can help ensure you get sufficient rest, avoiding lateness and potential embarrassment.*

a Encourage sleep when you are travelling by closing your eyes and stroking one hand after the other up your forehead from the bridge of your nose to your hairline. Enjoy the deep sense of relaxation

b To revive a tired face, stretch your lips over your teeth to form an "O" shape, and apply circular pressures with the index and middle fingers of each hand around your mouth and chin. Then make exaggerated "aah, ooh, ee, uuu" sounds

Tips to help prevent jet lag include setting your watch to the local time, adjusting your eating patterns to suit the new environment, and trying not to sleep during daylight.

A simple summary

✔ On-site massage is enormously beneficial for relieving stress caused by work-related factors.

✔ Massage for work stress can be done by yourself, by a colleague, or by a company-subsidized professional on-site massage therapist.

✔ It is important to take precautions, including massage and regular breaks, if you have an occupation that carries a high risk of repetitive strain injury.

✔ Many simple massage techniques can be used to avoid and relieve some of the stresses of travel.

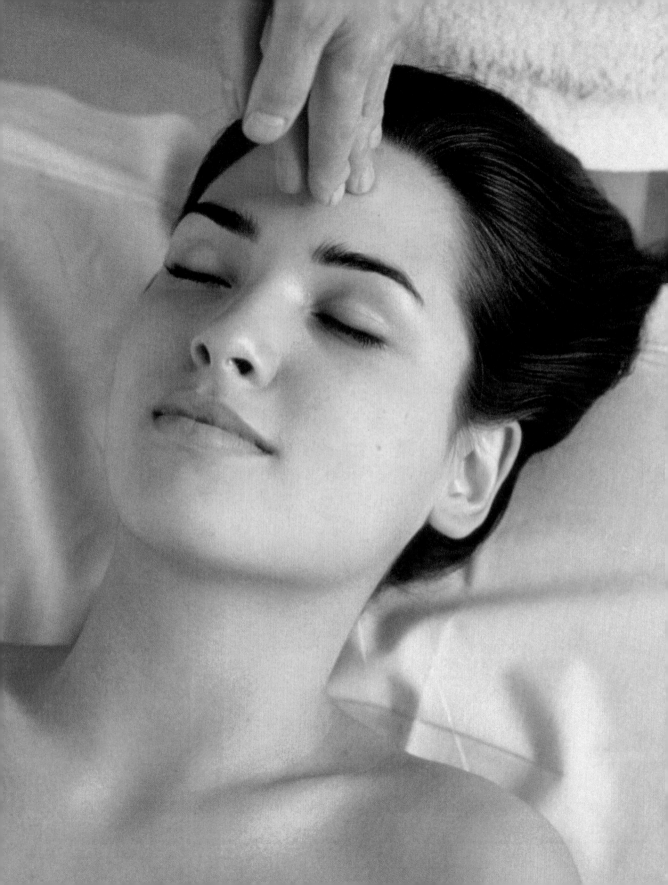

Chapter 19

Beautify Your Body

I HAVE BEEN CONSULTED by many men and women who feel that their looks have deteriorated, when in fact the problem was that they were not making the most of themselves. We all know that if you feel good, you look good, and that's where massage comes in. Its relaxing effects can brush away tension – so often the cause of facial lines, its toning and stimulating effects can firm up those flabby parts of your body, and its "feel good" factor will encourage a positive attitude towards how you look.

In this chapter...

✓ Saving face massage

✓ Massage those figures

✓ Enhance your extremities

✓ Home health spa

RELAX, THINK GOOD THOUGHTS, AND ABSORB THE BEAUTIFYING BENEFITS OF MASSAGE

Saving face massage

I BELIEVE FACE MASSAGE is the most beneficial of all massage. In just 10 minutes, it can leave the receiver looking 10 years younger and feeling stress free. Although wrinkles are an inevitable part of aging, massage can ease away fine lines so that your skin looks smoother and firmer, and it can help to prevent new lines appearing. I call this routine a natural face-lift.

Trivia...
A quote from the famous French novelist, Jean Cocteau (1889–1963), sums up the wonder of face massage for me: "A blemish in the soul cannot be corrected in the face, but a blemish in the face, if corrected, can refresh the soul."

Soothing, superficial strokes

For massaging the face it is very important to choose the oil blend that suits your partner's skin type (see chart opposite). Apply it with soft, moulding hands.

When massaging the face, your touch needs to be gentle yet confident, deep but not heavy.

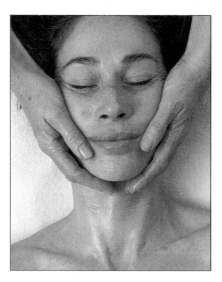

1 Stroke both hands up the neck to the chin and then from the chin to the ears. Pause, then glide back down to the chin and stroke up beside the nose. Pause again, stroke under the cheekbone to the temples, then glide back and stroke up the bridge of the nose and across the forehead to the temples. The movement should be gentle and flowing.

2 Rest your thumbs on the bridge of the nose (the "third eye" area) and stroke your fingers around the chin and jaw and up to the temples. Use your bodyweight to lean into the stroke. Repeat several times.

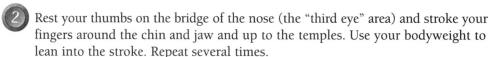

CHOOSING THE RIGHT OIL

Different oils suit different skin types so choose the best one for your partner's skin.

For oily skin:

2 drops orange essential oil
1 drop lemon essential oil
1 drop geranium essential oil
10 ml soya oil or grapeseed oil as carrier

For sensitive skin:

2 drops chamomile essential oil
1 drop lavender essential oil
10 ml sweet almond oil or grapeseed oil as carrier

For dry skin:

2 drops neroli essential oil
1 drop frankincense essential oil
1 drop rose essential oil
5 ml sweet almond oil and 5 ml jojoba as carrier

Mix oils in a small, dark, sterilized bottle, shake, and seal.

Chest and neck

The chest and neck should be included in your face massage; they are as prone to the effects of aging as the face itself.

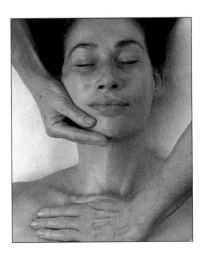

1 Rhythmically stroke up one side of the neck, with one hand following the other, at least 10 times. Then continue on the other side by gliding your top hand around the jaw and stroking your bottom hand across the chest. Now stroke up this side of the neck in the same way. Repeat several times, so that one hand strokes around the jaw as the other sweeps across the chest. Aim for seamless movement.

2 Begin as in step 1, by stroking one hand after the other up the side of the neck. Then adapt the movement slightly by stroking your top hand up the side of the face and across the forehead as your lower hand sweeps across the chest and up the neck to meet the top hand at the jaw. Stroke up the side of the neck 10 times, then repeat the whole movement, making the sequence as smooth as possible.

At first, stroking the face and chest at the same time can be difficult – a little bit like rubbing your stomach and patting your head at the same time. However, with practice it becomes much easier, and it's worth making the effort because it feels wonderful.

Jaw and chin

A good massage of the jaw and chin will relax your partner and help to release tension.

1 Lodge your fingers under the chin and use your thumbs to circle along the jaw. Circle one thumb in a clockwise direction and the other in an anticlockwise direction, applying a slight lift as your thumbs circle towards one another.

2 Stroke one hand after the other up the left cheek from the chin to the ears. Repeat on the right side. Then extend the stroke so that you circle each hand around the chin before stroking up the cheek. This is a lovely, rhythmic stroke.

3 With your thumbs stabilized on the forehead, apply circular pressures over the chin and jaw with your fingertips. Start gently, then work deeper. Ask your partner to clench his or her teeth so that you can locate the tension area.

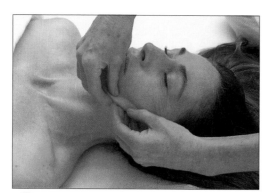

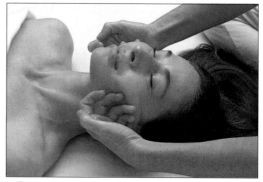

4 Using the fingers and thumbs of alternate hands, knead the jaw, working from the left ear to the chin. Squeeze and release the flesh slowly and gently, then repeat on the right side.

5 Finish with knuckling the hands on each cheek to release any jaw tension. Roll your knuckles in a strong, circular motion, rotating your wrists up and out towards the ears.

Mouth and cheeks

Move on to the mouth and cheeks, using gentle but firm movements.

1 Place one thumb on top of the other, and rest them both on the bridge of the nose for support. Gently stroke your ring fingers from the centre of the mouth to each corner. Slowly introduce your second fingers, followed by your index fingers. Repeat across the upper lip, then on the lower lip.

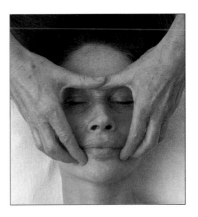

2 Keeping your hands in the same position, use the tips of your index and second fingers to make circular pressures at the corners of the mouth. Circle in one direction then in the other, working slowly and deeply. Then work all around the mouth.

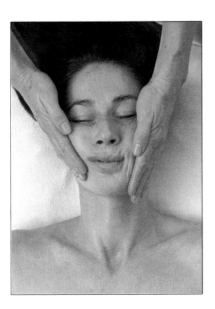

3 Support the right cheek with your right hand and make large circles with your left palm on the left cheek, working in an anticlockwise direction. Then swap sides so that you make circles with your right hand as your left hand remains stationary. Repeat several times, then rotate both hands alternately, applying more pressure on the upward movement.

4 Stroke out to the ears, then use your thumbs and fingertips to squeeze and rotate each ear, working systematically to cover the whole area. This can feel surprisingly soothing.

Eyes

The eyes can be one of the first areas to show the effects of aging. Work through the following steps to help combat the onset of laugh-lines and crows' feet.

1. Stroke your second and third fingers firmly over the eyebrows from the nose to the temples, then softly under the eyes back to the nose.

2. Now use your hands alternately so that one hand strokes over the eyebrow as the other strokes beneath the eye.

3. Place your second fingers on the corner of each of the eyes. With the second finger of your left hand, stroke under the eye, up and across the bridge of the nose and towards the right eye. When it meets your right hand, stroke it back under the right eye and across the left eyebrow. Repeat with your right hand.

4. Cross your thumbs for stability, and glide your ring fingers very gently over the eyelids from the centre to the corners. Then apply gentle, circular pressures at the corners of the eyes, easing out any laughter lines.

Forehead

Round off your facial massage by performing these steps on your partner's forehead.

1. Stroke one hand after the other up the forehead into the hairline. Stroke slowly and hypnotically, making sure that your hands are relaxed. Although this may feel boring for you, the sheer repetitiveness makes it feel very relaxing for your partner.

2. Make circular pressures at the temples and all over the forehead. Start with your little fingers, then follow with each of your other fingers, experimenting with the speed, depth, and direction of the circles according to your partner's wishes.

3. To combat frown lines, place your hands across the forehead and press firmly with the first two fingers of each hand. Make zig-zagging strokes with your hands moving towards each other. Cover the whole forehead with this soft, scissoring action, varying the speed of the strokes, and concentrating on areas of tension.

4. Support the top of the head with one hand and make light, circular strokes at the bridge of the nose with the middle finger of your other hand. Gradually spiral up the centre of the forehead with your finger and, when you reach the hairline, stroke your hand in a scooping movement, up into the hair. Repeat.

5. Place both your hands on the forehead, one on top of the other, and hold them in place for about a minute. Gradually release the pressure and then lift your hands away very slowly. This hold should leave your partner feeling calm and secure.

Massage those figures

WHILE MASSAGE TO ANY PART of the body helps to firm and tone the flesh, there are specific sequences that can help with particular problem areas. Cynics might say that massage can't help you to lose weight or look slimmer, but this is not entirely true. Although massage does not break down fat, it can improve your self-image and appearance, which in turn will help you to diet. Massage gives you a positive image of your body, which encourages you to carry yourself with more confidence. Many dieters have a distorted image of their bodies and often imagine themselves to be larger and fatter than they really are. Massage can help to give you an indication of your true size.

Massage for dieting

Because massage makes you feel better and take more pride in your body, you are more likely to stick to a diet. Knowing that the person giving you a massage is going to notice any weight loss is another incentive. Added to this are other benefits to your appearance. By stimulating the circulation, massage tones the skin and smoothes the body. This improvement builds a positive self-image, which produces more energy, making exercising easier. This is the beginning of the upward spiral, and weight will come off more easily.

Any massage is helpful for dieters, so follow the basic sequences outlined throughout this book. However, you should spend more time on the fleshiest areas, particularly the abdomen, thighs, and buttocks; use plenty of deep stimulating movements, such as kneading and pummelling. You can easily massage your abdomen and thighs yourself and should try a few minutes of vigorous massage every day.

■ **Massage can't make you thinner,** *but it can improve the way you feel about yourself, especially when used as part of an overall weight-loss strategy.*

A dieting self-massage

Try these stimulating moves on yourself every day.

1 Lie on your back and knead your abdomen thoroughly, doing several rows of kneading across it to cover the whole area

2 Roll onto one side, then knead and pummel your hip. Repeat on the other side

3 Sit up and knead your thighs from the knee up to the top. Work vigorously on the front and outside, but more gently on the inside

4 Pummel very fast all over the front and outside of your thighs, then work more gently on the inside

Anti-cellulite massage

A sad fact of life for a large number of women is that their thighs, hips, and stomachs are particularly susceptible to fat storage. Fat deposited just below the skin in these areas often takes on an unsightly "orange-peel" or dimpled appearance and is known as cellulite – the bane of many a woman's existence. Daily self-massage can improve the overall appearance of these areas of cellulite making the skin look firmer and smoother, and even give the illusion of weight loss. If your cellulite is solid and hard, you should use firm movements to soften the area and simulate circulation. If the cellulite feels soft and watery, your movements should be more gentle to encourage lymphatic drainage.

Use an oil blend that meets your needs. Marjoram and peppermint are noted for soothing the abdomen; rosemary and geranium for their invigorating effect; and juniper helps reduce fluid retention.

Abdomen and hips

1 Sit comfortably and rest your left hand on your *diaphragm* while your right hand applies about a teaspoonful of oil with clockwise strokes around the navel. Now introduce your left hand so that both hands are circling the navel.

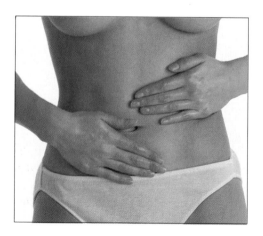

> **DEFINITION**
>
> *The area at the bottom of your rib cage just above your stomach is your* **diaphragm**.

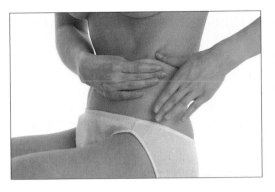

2 Knead your hips, waist, and abdomen by squeezing and lifting your flesh with one hand and releasing it into the other. Knead all over this area, wherever you can pick up enough flesh.

3 With your left hand on top of your right hand, use your fingertips to apply gentle circular pressure all around your navel.

4 Finish by gently stroking all over your abdomen and hips. This is very soothing and stimulates lymph drainage.

Avoid using anticlockwise moves when you massage your abdomen as this opposes the natural working of the intestines.

Thighs

Apply more massage oil if necessary so that your hands move smoothly over your skin.

1 Gently stroke up from your left knee, directing your movements towards your inner thigh. Then stroke from the back of your knee up to your buttocks.

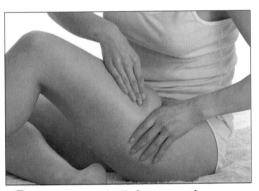

2 Knead your thigh from your knee up to the top of the leg. Use deep strokes to squeeze and lift the flesh. This stimulates the circulation and helps reabsorb excess fluid and wastes into the lymphatic system. Repeat on the back of your thigh.

3 Applying firm pressures, rotate the knuckles of both your hands all over the front and back of your thigh.

4 Place your left hand on the back of your outer thigh, and your right hand on the back of your inner thigh. Pull the flesh up to the top of your thigh, release, and cross your hands down the other side. Repeat this criss-cross movement several times.

5 Stroke very gently and smoothly from above your knee to the top of your thigh, and from the back of your knee to your buttock. This repetitive stroking encourages lymph drainage.

6 Repeat steps 1–5 on your right thigh.

Further tips to help in the fight against cellulite include: drinking at least eight glasses of water a day; eating a balanced, healthy diet with plenty of fruit and vegetables, and avoiding salt, sugar, and processed food; and rubbing the affected skin regularly, during a bath or shower, with a loofah sponge or glove.

THE SALT TREATMENT

A great way to rid your skin of the greyish tinge it acquires during the long winter months is to give your body a sea-salt scrub before a massage. This invigorating treatment effectively exfoliates the dead skin and improves the circulation. It will also enhance the massage because your skin texture will be fresh and smooth and glowing with health.

Massage sea salt onto your skin about a tablespoonful at a time. Continue until your whole body has been rubbed down, and then follow with your regular massage routine using an aromatic oil. The scrub only takes about 20–30 minutes to do, but remember to put a sheet on the floor because it's a rather messy procedure.

If you ever find yourself on a beach, you can continue your treatment there. Try scrubbing your body with seaweed, or if there's none around sand works beautifully!

Enhance your extremities

MANY PEOPLE SIMPLY FORGET *about their extremities – the hands, feet, and elbows – or choose to ignore them. However, the hands and feet are in continuous use and need to be cared for to prevent problems in the future. Self-massage of the hands, elbows, and feet is an excellent way of giving extra care and attention to the parts of the body that most need it. And pampering yourself is good for the soul.*

> ### Trivia...
> *To protect and enrich dry hands, and to prevent them from becoming old and wrinkled, ladies of the court in Elizabethan England covered their hands with extra rich cream and then cotton gloves when they went to bed at night. Lanolin makes one of the richest creams for this treatment.*

Hands

Age, hard work, water, detergents, and neglect can leave your hands rough and dry. For smoother hands, massage them in a nourishing cream.

1. Sit comfortably and apply to your right palm a little of the rich cream of your choice. Stroke it onto your left hand from the fingers to the wrist. Imagine the cream penetrating the skin – relaxing, soothing, and warming it. Repeat several times.

2. Supporting your left palm with the fingers of your right hand, use your thumb to stroke from the knuckle of your little finger down the tendon towards the wrist. Repeat, stroking down the tendons between each of the fingers.

3. Squeeze the base of your little finger between your thumb and forefinger and circle around either side of the finger, working up to and including the tip of the nail. Rub some cream into the cuticle and fingernail. Repeat on each finger and the thumb.

4. Using the knuckles of your first and second fingers, gently grip your little finger and slowly pull it as you slide up to the tip with a corkscrew-like motion that stimulates the circulation. Repeat twice on each finger and on the thumb.

5 Support the back of your left hand with the fingers of your right hand and massage the palm with your thumb. Stroke and stretch the palm and you will feel tension melting away.

6 Firmly roll your knuckle all over the palm of your hand and finish by gently stroking your wrist and then your hand with your thumb.

7 Repeat steps 1–6 on your right hand.

Elbows

With care and attention, you can transform rough, dry, and discoloured elbows. For a gentle bleaching effect, rub each elbow with half a lemon, and to reverse dryness, massage them with a generous amount of a rich cream.

Feet

Tired, aching feet can affect the way you look, feel, and move, so massaging your feet to relieve them can benefit the whole body. For the self-massage sequence below use an oil blend that best suits the way you are feeling – four drops of lavender or peppermint oil in 10 ml of sunflower or sweet almond carrier oil is good for tired feet, while three drops of rosemary and two drops of chamomile in the same carrier will help swollen feet.

1 Rest your right foot on your left thigh. Support it with your right hand while your left hand strokes the sole and top of the foot from the toes up to the ankle, spreading the aromatic oil. Use your knuckles to ripple all around the sole. Then, using your thumbs, apply deep pressure to the sole of your foot.

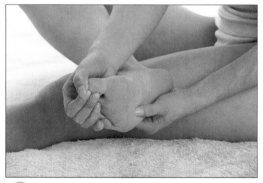

2 Massage each toe by rubbing, squeezing, and gently rolling it between your fingers. Then pinch the tip of the nail. These movements stimulate the circulation and soothe the toes.

3 Support your foot with your left hand, and clasp your toes with your right hand. Gently stretch the toes backwards and forwards to release tension and increase flexibility.

4 Using your finger, squeeze around your ankle, the Achilles tendon, and the heel. Then rotate your ankle several times.

5 Sandwich the foot by placing one hand on top and the other under the base of your toes, and rotate your hands around the ball of your foot to increase flexibility.

6 Finish by stroking up from your toes towards your ankle.

7 Repeat steps 1–6 on your left foot.

Home health spa

FEW OF US CAN AFFORD the luxury of going to a health spa but you will be surprised at how many of the treatments can be adapted for the comforts of your own home. The most simple form of **hydrotherapy** *– although you may not think of it in this way – is taking a bath; this can be both relaxing and restoring. Hot and cold compresses, and steam baths for inhalation are also basic types of hydrotherapy.*

> **DEFINITION**
>
> *Any treatment or therapy involving water is called* **hydrotherapy**.

Water affects the body in different ways according to its temperature. Hot water helps muscles to relax by raising the body's temperature; cold water helps to stimulate the circulation and reduce inflammation, and has an invigorating effect on the skin.

Revitalizing shower

Hydrotherapy techniques make a great addition to massage and can be easily incorporated into a shower or bath-time routine. This sequence will invigorate your whole body and leave your skin glowing.

For the best results, you need a shower with different flow settings. A hand-held shower will work but you will probably not feel quite as invigorated.

1. Remove dead skin with a salt scrub. Stand in the bath or shower and apply the mixture to moist skin. Massage your whole body with circular strokes. Rinse well.

2. Switch the shower to hot, and turn it to the strongest setting. Using small, circling movements, massage all around each leg with the shower jet. Then gradually work up the body, spending extra time on areas that feel tense. Massage around the chest, shoulders, and neck, and down each arm. Allow about 5 minutes in total for the hot shower massage.

3. Repeat the shower massage but this time use cold water. Use the same circling movements as before. This alternating of hot and cold water is one of the simplest ways to boost energy levels and will leave you feeling refreshed and invigorated.

4. To complete the routine, dry your skin and massage your whole body using large, circling movements with a blend of five drops orange essential oil, five drops frankincense essential oil, and 20 ml sweet almond oil as carrier. Orange oil has a mildly astringent action on the skin, while frankincense can combat dry skin.

Restorative bath

A fragranced bath, whether warming and comforting or coolly refreshing, has always been the perfect way to shed tension.

BATH BLENDS

Here is a selection of oil blends that you can use in your bath to match your mood. Blend oils in a bottle before transferring to the bath.

Relaxing blend

2 drops neroli essential oil
2 drops sandalwood essential oil
1 drop clary sage essential oil
10 ml sweet almond oil as carrier

Extravagant blend

2 drops neroli essential oil
2 drops rose essential oil
1 drop sandalwood essential oil
10 ml sweet almond oil as carrier

Invigorating blend

2 drops rosemary essential oil
2 drops juniper essential oil
1 drop geranium essential oil
10 ml sweet almond oil as carrier

For aching limbs

2 drops lavender essential oil
2 drops rosemary essential oil
1 drop marjoram essential oil
10 ml sweet almond oil as carrier

While the bath is filling with water, stimulate your skin by brushing it vigorously all over with a natural bristle brush, using brisk, circular strokes. When your bath is nearly full of warm, not too hot, water, add the oil blend of your choice. For a truly relaxing atmosphere, bathe by candlelight.

If you add essential oils to the bath when you start running it, you will lose much of their benefit as the perfumed oils will have evaporated by the time the bath is full.

You can achieve the same benefits in a shower if you mix 12 drops of essential oils into 30 ml of liquid soap and use some of this to wash your body.

After your bath, rub yourself briskly with a towel, which will stimulate your circulation as well as drying you. Then apply moisturizer if you need it.

INTERNET

www.waba.edu

This is the web site of the Worldwide Aquatic Bodywork Association, which combines shiatsu and other massage techniques with water. The site offers courses, a register of practitioners, and employment opportunities.

■ **Hydrotherapy**, *which can be as simple as taking a shower or bath, is one of the best ways of revitalizing after a hard (or any other) day.*

A simple summary

✓ Regular intensive face massage can be thought of as the equivalent of a natural face-lift.

✓ Massage can help firm up areas of your body that are affected by cellulite.

✓ Massage has an important psychological role to play in weight reduction.

✓ Combining water with massage enhances its effects even further.

Chapter 20

Sensual Massage

THERE IS A BIG DIFFERENCE between therapeutic touch and sensual touch. However, sensual touch can also be therapeutic. There is a lot of confusion in people's minds about sensuality and sexuality and many people have literally lost touch with the sensual part of their being. Sensual is literally "of the senses or sensation"; in other words, a basic instinct that is completely independent of intellectual or spiritual needs. A sensual massage can remind us of the simple pleasure of touching and being touched. Most of the techniques illustrated in the book can be adapted as part of a sensual massage – you just need the right environment, the right partner, and plenty of time.

In this chapter...

✓ Creating a
   sensual atmosphere

✓ Choosing the oils

✓ Adapting the moves

Creating a sensual atmosphere

SETTING THE SCENE *is important for a sensual massage, but it's not the be-all and end-all. As with all massage, peace, quiet, and privacy are essential – after all if the phone is ringing, children are screaming in the background, or the dog is scratching on the door, relaxation is the last thing on your mind.*

Maximize the mood

Keep the lighting low and subtle and preferably use candles. Candlelight will particularly enhance the atmosphere if you use a candle scented with a sensuous essential oil. Soft and gentle music will heighten your responsiveness, but be sure to choose something that both you and your partner like. The room should be warm, but not hot – you don't want your partner drifting off to sleep. Colours have an astonishing effect on mood – warm and sunny reds, oranges, and yellows are more relaxing than the blues and greens from the colder end of the colour spectrum. I'm not suggesting that you repaint your room but you can add touches of colour in the towels you use for the massage or add a vase of flowers to the scene.

■ **Low lighting and warm colours** *can help to create an atmosphere conducive to sensual massage.*

The massage is the thing

However, if you don't have the time to make the room special, don't worry because the surroundings are the trimmings and not the main ingredients or essence of a sensual massage. And don't forget, the benefits of spontaneity must never be underestimated.

To scent your linen, add a few drops of essential oil to the fabric softener section of your washing machine, or use rose, lavender, or orange flower water to dampen your sheets when you iron them.

Choosing the oils

WITH THE MASSAGE KNOWLEDGE you have gained so far, you will know that oil and massage go together like food and wine. The oil really helps to produce a continuous movement so that if you are receiving the massage you can't tell when one move finishes and the next starts; this will allow you to be lulled into a blissfully relaxed state. Use a little extra oil than usual when you give a sensual massage to make the movements flow. By adding fragrant essential oils to your basic massage oil you can create a whole range of effects, both therapeutic and sensual.

Stimulate those hormones

Dr Alan Hirsch, neurological director of the Smell and Taste Treatment and Research Foundation in Chicago, has found that certain oils contain aromas similar to substances in human sweat that can stimulate hormones and trigger sexual desire. Sandalwood, for example, contains *androgens*.

> **DEFINITION**
>
> **Androgens** *are sex hormones that are produced by men and to a lesser extent by women.*

■ **Your massage** *will really "flow" when you add oil to the mix.*

THERE ARE MANY OILS TO CHOOSE FROM

Which oils?

The best oils to use for sensual massage are obviously the ones you enjoy most, but in addition to sandalwood, jasmine, rose, patchouli, and ylang-ylang also supposedly have aphrodisiac properties. You can combine any of these with oils that have relaxing properties – for example lavender, neroli, and clary sage. The chart below contains suggestions for massage blends.

According to Dr Hirsch humans fall in love through their noses, not their eyes or ears. "Once we are attracted to a person's odour, even if it is below the level of conscious detection, a strong sexual and emotional bond is possible."

OIL BLENDS FOR SENSUAL MASSAGE

Mix the oils together in 20 ml sweet almond oil.

Sensuous blend

2 drops clary sage
3 drops rose
4 drops sandalwood

Stimulating blend

2 drops ylang ylang
3 drops rosemary
4 drops orange

Romantic blend

5 drops sandalwood
3 drops rose
2 drops jasmine

Luxurious blend

4 drops neroli
3 drops jasmine
2 drops rose

Adapting the moves

TO MAKE YOUR MASSAGE *sensual,*
simply approach the moves in a different way.
Strokes are the most sensuous of all massage
techniques and should be the mainstay of your
sensual massage. You can use the familiar
massage movements, but their quality and
their intention will be different.

INTERNET

www.massagewarehouse
.com

Go to this site for a catalogue
of products including essential
oils, scented candles, and
music, which can all help set
the mood for your massage.

The pleasure principle

Concentrate on the feel of your touch and respond to your partner's body, repeating
the movements that seem to give him or her most pleasure. Let your strokes linger for
longer. Use your fingertips to explore. Add to the intensity by inventing new moves and
different combinations. Concentrate on very sensitive (but not necessarily erogenous)
areas, such as the nape of the neck and the crease of the elbow. Be guided by what
you yourself like as well as by the feedback your partner gives you. Above
all, be creative: no two massages are, or even should be, the same; just do
whatever feels good.

Percussion, kneading, and deep pressures are not very suitable for
sensual massage as they tend to be invigorating, rather than relaxing.

■ **If it feels good, do it.**
Your partner's responses to your
touch will let you know if
you're on the right track.

283

■ **A simple pleasure:** *sensual massage in its purest sense is all about touching and being touched. Use long, lingering strokes, focus on sensitive areas, be creative, and let what feels good be your guide.*

Get in close

Experiment with the position of your own body as you massage your partner. You can be much closer than in non-sensual massage and you needn't worry about invading your partner's private space; while you are releasing tension from your partner's body, you are still in close proximity. This reinforces feelings of tenderness and sensuality. Try blowing on your partner's body (don't overdo the blowing as it may cause faintness), or using your hair (if it's long enough) to stroke for a heightened sensation.

■ **There are no constraints** *on body proximity in sensual massage, so get as close as you both desire.*

When you have finished massaging your partner you can swap roles and receive the same sensual treatment – unless he or she has dropped off to sleep!

Variations

Consider mutual massage, of the feet or hands, as a variation to your massage routine. Another idea is to introduce water by massaging your partner in the shower or bath.

A simple summary

✔ Stroking is the main action used in sensual massage, but other therapeutic massage moves can be adapted and included.

✔ Getting the atmosphere right can enhance the beneficial effects of sensual massage.

✔ Using fragrant oils creates a sensual atmosphere and assists in producing a massage that flows from continuous movement.

✔ There is no set formula for sensual massage – just go with the flow.

Chapter 21

Massage for Health

MASSAGE HAS A LONG TRADITION as a healing therapy, and has been used by many cultures for centuries. As well as relieving physical symptoms, massage can provide psychological benefits in a body that is slightly out of kilter or one that is struggling with a serious disease. Massage also has a role when recovery is unlikely. A terminal illness can be very frightening and lonely; massage can help by providing comfort, which can reduce anxiety, depression, and pain.

In this chapter...

✓ Stress-related problems

✓ Headaches

✓ Respiratory problems

✓ Abdominal problems

✓ Aches and pains

✓ Serious illness

MASSAGE CAN HAVE POSITIVE EFFECTS ON BODY, MIND, AND SPIRIT

Stress-related problems

AT EVERY OPPORTUNITY throughout this book I have talked about how marvellous massage can be in the management of stress. Approximately one-third of absences from work can be attributed to the effects of stress, anxiety, and depression, so it is in everybody's interest to deal with stress as quickly as possible. However, not all stress is bad as we need a certain amount to give our lives zest and excitement. It's only when demands made on us become too great that we suffer the negative aspects of stress and then seem unable to cope.

There is a strong link between stress and illness: it affects the immune system, making people more vulnerable to infection; it is related to high blood pressure and heart disease; it can cause headaches and backache; and there are even suggestions that there may be a link with cancer, due to the effects of stress on the immune system. So by relieving stress not only will you feel better, but you are also reducing your chances of developing other problems in the future.

Massage for stress-related problems

The best way of relieving stress, anxiety, and depression is with a full body massage. This will induce a sense of relaxation, and relaxing is the thing that most stressed people find impossible to do. You should concentrate on the areas your partner likes best. Keep the massage as flowing and rhythmic as possible, as that will sweep away the tension that is causing the physical problems.

To enhance the relaxing effects of the massage, try adding a calming essential oil to your massage oil. You may also try using the oils in a relaxing bath as well.

Did you know?

Although stress seems to be a disease of the 20th century, a Victorian doctor made the following observations in 1887: "The mind, which before massage is in a perturbed, restless, vacillating, and even despondent state, becomes after massage, calm, quiet, peaceful, and subdued; in fact, the wearied and worried mind has been converted into a mind restful, placid, and refreshed."

KNEADING AWAY TENSION

ESSENTIAL OILS FOR STRESS RELIEF

● Roman chamomile, frankincense, lavender, marjoram, and sandalwood are soothing

● Clary sage, geranium, rose, and jasmine have antidepressant properties

● Orange, neroli, and petitgrain are used to combat anxiety and insomnia

Stress-induced insomnia

Insomnia often occurs as a result of stress, and massage can help you break the vicious cycle of tiredness and inability to sleep. Give the massage regularly at bedtime until you have broken the habit. Your partner should lie on a bed so that if he or she succumbs to sleep during the massage you can leave him or her happily dozing. Ideally, you should do a complete body, face, and head massage, which takes about 1½ hours.

If you don't have much time, you will get the quickest results by concentrating on the back, abdomen, feet, and face. You can massage all four areas in any order, or just one, depending on how quickly your partner relaxes. Follow a basic back massage routine but avoid stimulating movements, such as pummeling and energetic kneading, and spend a long time on soothing strokes such as the cat stroke. For the abdomen, feet, and face, give slow and gentle touches on each area. Shiatsu massage can also be helpful in treating insomnia.

I have numerous clients who, through regular massage, have stopped using prescription medicine and consider that massage is the very best medicine – as effective as drugs or alcohol without any of the side effects.

Self-help for stress-related problems

There is a lot you can do for yourself if you are feeling stressed, anxious, depressed, or if you are having trouble sleeping. One of the problems associated with stress is that it affects your mental health, which can cause people to suffer from low self-esteem; spending time on yourself will help boost morale. Try self-massage; if you take the time and trouble to complete the whole routine you will be amazed at how much better you feel both immediately afterward, and for hours and even days later.

Just relax

Try adding essential oil to a restorative bath and really try to relax and withdraw from all your worries; allow at least an hour, and light a scented candle. Make sure there's enough hot water for topping up. Once you start to associate a particular essential oil with a relaxing experience, such as a warm bath, in time you will find the scent alone soporific; if you put a few drops of your chosen oil onto a tissue and then place it on your pillow, you may find yourself drifting off to sleep with great ease.

Hops are renowned for their sleep-inducing effect and you can buy little pillows stuffed with them. Or try making one yourself with dried hop flowers. Other flowers and herbs such as lavender or chamomile also also have sedative effects.

Headaches

ONE OF THE MOST COMMON *symptoms suffered by humankind, headaches can range from tension headaches, usually caused by fatigue and stress, to debilitating migraines. It is thought that most headaches are caused when muscles in the back of the neck and scalp contract and constrict the blood vessels. Massage can help by relaxing the contracted muscles, thereby allowing blood to flow*

■ **Headaches** *can affect us all.*

more freely. This results in the headache lifting. Headaches can be stopped in their tracks, and even severe headaches can often disappear after only a few minutes of massage.

The causes

Headaches can be caused by a huge variety of triggers. Stress and anxiety are common, but poor posture, eye strain, fatigue, certain foods, and changes in the weather can all bring on a headache. Very occasionally there is a more serious underlying cause.

If you regularly have headaches, particularly if they are severe, you should consult a doctor.

Massage for headaches

The type of massage you use depends on the intensity of the headache and what your partner prefers. You can use very gentle feather stroking or deep firm pressure. It is generally best to start with slow, superficial stroking and then as the pain subsides and your partner relaxes and feels confident of your touch, you can apply firm pressures to key points.

Although every headache is different, I find that I get the best results by following this general pattern. Always use smooth, rhythmic, and compassionate movements.

1. Stroke up the forehead very gently and slowly, then rhythmically stroke the chest and shoulders, and up the back of the neck.

2. Apply circular pressures behind the shoulders, up the back of the neck on either side of the spine, at the base of the skull, and on the scalp.

3. Gently stroke the whole of the face from the centre out to the sides.

4. Press the bridge of the nose, then pinch the eyebrows, and press on the temples.

5. Press in the middle of the cheek, directly under the cheekbone, and then apply a line of pressures up the centre of the forehead, from between the eyebrows to the hairline.

6. Circle around the eyes, stroking out along the eyebrows and gliding back gently under the eyes.

7. Stroke rhythmically up the forehead with one hand following the other, as you did at the beginning.

If there is very little time, or I am treating a very severe migraine, I get the best results by imagining that my hands are magnets, drawing out all the tension and pain. Use the feather touch, and stroke the tension away from the head and off the body.

Many other types of massage can help relieve headaches including back, face, neck and shoulder, and hand massage. Shiatsu, reflexology, and aromatherapy may also help.

Did you know?

In a study at Knopio University, Finland, 21 women suffering from chronic tension headaches each received ten relaxing upper back massages over 2½ weeks. Researchers found that the women had significantly fewer headaches immediately after the massage period, and that the rate remained low for months afterwards.

Self-help for headaches

One of the best ways to relieve your headache is with self-massage. First massage the back of your neck and head, then concentrate on your forehead, around your eyes, and on your temples. Very gentle, light stroking on your forehead also helps to relieve even the most stubborn headache.

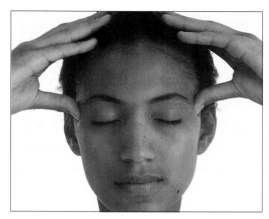

SELF-MASSAGE FOR HEADACHES

Shiatsu for headaches

Shiatsu is often very helpful, particularly for severe headaches. Many of my clients have told me that they can control headache pain by massaging *acupressure points*, particularly those found in the hands, wrists, ankles, and feet. One of the best shiatsu points to press is known as the "Great Eliminator". This is situated between the thumb and the forefinger; press around the area until you find a point that usually feels quite distinctive.

Do not press the "Great Eliminator" point during pregnancy; it's not called that for nothing!

Using oils

Massaging essential oils into the temples is also a well-established headache cure. Lavender is probably the best oil to use, although chamomile, peppermint, and eucalyptus also help to relieve tension, which helps to cure headaches. At the onset of a headache, mix eight drops of oil with 20 ml carrier oil and massage well into your temples. Another way of using aromatherapy to cure a headache is to apply a cold, wet compress containing one of the above oils to your head.

An Indian doctor told me that the fastest way to cure a headache is to put your wrists in hot water — this improves circulation and relieves the headache.

Respiratory problems

DISORDERS OF THE RESPIRATORY SYSTEM *are common – few people escape a cold or cough during the winter months – but many people are plagued with more chronic problems, such as bronchitis or asthma. Massage and aromatherapy can alleviate some of the symptoms of minor infections, and also relieve some of the stress and tension caused by longer term respiratory disorders.*

Massage for respiratory problems

For coughs and colds, try rhythmic stroking on the chest to soothe the area. Follow this with a gentle neck and face massage, and finish with gentle static pressures on either side of the nose. Catarrh and sinusitis can be relieved with massage using circular pressures at the base of the skull, followed by squeezing the eyebrows, forehead, and base of the nose; finish with gentle strokes down the nose, out to the ears, and down the neck. Chest infections, such as bronchitis, benefit from a full chest massage and, if there is much congestion, concentrate on percussive cupping movements at the base of the lungs. This is often done by physiotherapists to help shift mucus and relieve congestion.

For many asthma sufferers there is a family history of the disease and it is often associated with other allergic problems such as eczema. Triggers include allergens such as pollen and house dust mites, but stress and anxiety can aggravate attacks. Gentle massage can really help if done on a regular basis, and may even prevent or at least reduce the severity of asthma attacks.

Self-help for respiratory problems

Respiratory infections can be helped by steam inhalation; the aromatic steam can clear your nasal passages and ease breathing. Use eucalyptus, tea tree, sandalwood, bergamot, or cypress oils as they have antiseptic and decongestant properties. You can also try adding up to five drops of the same oil or combination of oils to a warm bath.

Do not use steam inhalations if you suffer from asthma – the concentrated steam may trigger an attack.

STEAM INHALATION

293

Abdominal problems

DIGESTIVE PROBLEMS *and other abdominal complaints, such as premenstrual bloating and period pains, are very common. Poor diet and lack of exercise are typical causes, but stress and other emotional factors can contribute to the problem. Massage can help to relieve the pain and reduce any stress.*

Massage for abdominal problems

Massage soothes pain, stimulates movement in the gut, and is calming, so helps to restore the normal working of the digestive tract. It can help constipation by relaxing the abdomen and by stimulating peristalsis (the rhythmic movement that propels food through the digestive tract). In people prone to diarrhoea, massage can help to relieve the stress that is so often the trigger.

To release abdominal tension, you must try to induce a relaxed state in your partner. Use calm, smooth stroking movements with both your hands. Gently stroke from the navel up towards your partner's chest. Then let your hands glide out over the ribs. Be guided by your partner about the strength of the pressure. Shiatsu and reflexology can also be used to help alleviate abdominal pain.

SMOOTH STROKING FOR ABDOMINAL TENSION

Premenstrual syndrome

Premenstrual syndrome (PMS) affects many women. Symptoms can vary from mild bloating of the abdomen to severe pain and depression, and massage can help to soothe frayed nerves and relieve swelling and pain. Shiatsu and reflexology may also help.

Self-help for abdominal complaints

There's a lot you can do to help yourself if you suffer from minor abdominal problems. For constipation, drink plenty of water and eat lots of fresh fruit and vegetables; this will help the passage of food through the intestines. Take vigorous exercise, such as running or swimming, three to four times a week. Try massaging your stomach in a clockwise direction, or apply undulating circular pressures.

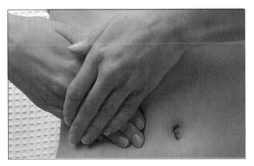

MASSAGING THE COLON AREA TO RELIEVE CONSTIPATION

Reflexology (see Chapter 24) can be helpful for abdominal problems. For constipation, work on the colon, liver, and solar plexus areas of the foot. For PMS, work on the points on the outer ankle below the ankle bone. For shiatsu (see Chapter 23), apply pressure to either side of your Achilles tendon to relieve stomach ache, or press shiatsu points such as Stomach 36 or Conception vessel 6.

Aches and pains

OF ALL MEDICAL PROBLEMS, *massage is probably most renowned for helping back pain, stiff neck and shoulders, and general aches and pains. Although the aging process contributes to some of these problems, many can be avoided by simple lifestyle changes such as improving posture, taking more exercise, drinking more water, and eating more fresh fruit and vegetables.*

Massage for backaches and pains

Back pain is one of the most commonly experienced problems, causing more days off work than any other physical symptom. Massage can help to relax stiff muscles, to locate and loosen areas of tension, and to ease stress, which is often a factor in back pain. Helpful treatments for back pain, covered elsewhere in this book, include kneading, skin rolling, firm pressures, Chinese massage, Thai massage, shiatsu, and reflexology.

INTERNET

www.americanmedical massage.com

The American Manual Medicine Association is a professional organization that promotes medical massage therapy training by establishing education programmes and creating standards. Its goal is to promote medical massage therapy as a healthcare profession and differentiate it from other forms of massage.

Massage for other aches and pains

Aches and pains become increasingly common with age, and for many elderly people the pain, swelling, and stiffness of arthritis and rheumatism is a sad fact of life. However, there is plenty of evidence that shows the benefits of regular massage in reducing pain and swelling, increasing mobility, reducing the need for painkillers, and improving mood. Some of the massage treatments suitable for aches and pains include hand and foot massage, manual lymphatic drainage, and hydrotherapy.

Self-help for aches and pain

For back pain, self-massage of the neck, shoulders, and lower back can work wonders. It will relieve pain and alleviate stress at the same time. Other self-help treatments include applying a hot or cold compress to the back, and reflexology: massage the instep to affect the back.

Never massage directly on an inflamed joint. Avoid any area that feels hot and swollen, instead massage very gently above the inflamed region.

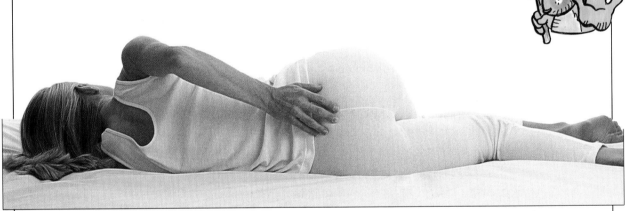

■ **To alleviate lower back pain,** *apply circular pressures and stroke the sacrum area gently.*

Other measures

Aches and pains can be washed away in a relaxing bath. Try adding a few drops of rosemary, chamomile, or lavender essential oil to your bath and benefit from their soothing properties. Regular exercise, particularly swimming, is very important to maintain mobility.

Serious illness

WHEN WE BECOME ILL, we experience not only physical discomfort but also many psychological reactions. Massage can really help, even in very serious illness, by conveying acceptance, support, care, and concern. I have worked with ill people for over 30 years, and it still amazes me that something as simple as a massage can bring such benefits.

Did you know?

In 1995, the Royal Marsden Hospital, London, conducted research in which 24 cancer patients had eight weekly massages. Compared with a control group, the massaged group had less anxiety and pain, and was more mobile.

What can massage do?

If a friend is ill, it can be difficult to know how to respond; this is particularly true in hospital where physical needs are taken care of and you are both in an unfamiliar, possibly frightening, environment. Massaging is a practical way to show that you care. Your friend may not feel like talking, or listening to you, but through touch you can reach out to show your empathy without the effort of conversation.

Massage has very specific benefits when someone is ill. It can help to control pain; it assists recovery by helping the immune system to work properly; it promotes wellbeing and reduces stress; it enables the sufferer to express his or her fears about the illness. All these benefits help speed up the recovery process.

In hospitals, we call massage the "treat" not the "treatment".

When to massage

Massage can be used on patients with heart disease (including after heart surgery), cancer, HIV infection, and AIDS. The most useful types of massage treatment for someone who is very ill are aromatherapy, self-massage, hand and foot massage, Swedish full-body massage, manual lymphatic drainage, and shiatsu.

If you are going to massage someone who is very ill, or in hospital, or recovering from surgery, always get the doctor's approval first.

297

Heart disease

Early in my career, I worked at a cardiac ward where some patients had undergone surgery and others were recovering from heart attacks; what they all had in common was a very high level of anxiety. I found that massage helped patients to sleep, and lowered their blood pressure and heart rate. As part of the rehabilitation programme, we taught couples how to massage each other so that the patients could continue to receive beneficial massage once they were home again.

After surgery, you must not massage the area around the incision site. You must wait until the wound has healed and scar tissue has formed.

Cancer

I first became interested in massaging cancer patients when a friend's mother was dying of cancer. She felt isolated, frightened, and anxious, and massage calmed her down almost miraculously. Although she had round-the-clock nursing care, the nurse was unable to comfort her emotionally. Over the last 15 years, however, I have seen massage become widely accepted as a way to improve the wellbeing of cancer patients, in hospitals, hospices, and at home. In addition to providing comfort, massage can alleviate some of the unpleasant side-effects of cancer treatments, such as pain, nausea, and tension.

■ **Massaging the hands** *relaxes the whole body, and communicates care and concern to the ill person.*

There are no special techniques for massaging someone with cancer but do make sure the person's doctor knows what you intend to do. Gentle touch is comforting; if your friend is confined to bed, a very gentle hand, foot, or face massage can be particularly soothing.

Never massage over radiotherapy entry and exit sites, and keep the massage elsewhere very gentle and soothing.

HIV infection and AIDS

Students from my massage school first worked with HIV-positive patients in the 1980s. All the patients said how important massage was to them. It made a positive contribution to their lives; as well as diminishing physical discomfort, it made them feel cared for and supported.

Relief for body and mind

I think that massage should be an integral part of our lives, to help attain and maintain good health. Whether we are suffering from a mild case of anxiety, constant stress, insomnia, backache, chronic pain, or even a life-threatening illness, massage can help – it eases our troubled minds, relieves aches and pains, and provides care, comfort, and support when we need it. In fact, one of my favourite sayings is "Life takes it out of you but massage puts it back."

Did you know?

Touch Research International in Florida conducted a study on HIV-positive men. The participants received 45 minutes of massage, 5 days a week for a month. At the end of the study, levels of the stress hormone, cortisol, had decreased, and levels of serotonin, a hormone that enhances mood, had increased. More significantly, the participants were producing more of the cells that fight invading viruses and bacteria.

A simple summary

✓ Massage should be an integral part of caring for anyone who is sick in body, mind, or spirit.

✓ Stress, anxiety, depression, and insomnia can all be helped by massage.

✓ Minor symptoms, such as headaches, colds, and stomach aches, can be helped by massage, as can more serious disorders, such as heart disease, cancer, and AIDS.

✓ Most of the massage techniques shown in this book can be used on a sick person, but be guided by common sense and the wishes of your partner, and avoid the more stimulating moves that may in effect do more harm than good.

INTERNATIONAL MASSAGE AT YOUR FINGERTIPS

MASSAGE AROUND THE WORLD

THE IMPULSE TO TOUCH in order to heal is a human instinct that applies to every culture in every country across the globe. The only way in which it differs is its particular system of application.

The art of *massage* may take on a different flavour from East to West, but the overlap in practices demonstrates how many different techniques stem from the same *influences*. As modern research confirms the power of massage, we should be humbled by the realization that this healing art form has been tried and tested throughout human history, all over the *world*. In the following pages, I will guide you through some of the oldest and most fundamental systems of massage, introducing you to both the vigorous and soothing strokes that many nations have relied on for wellbeing for thousands of years.

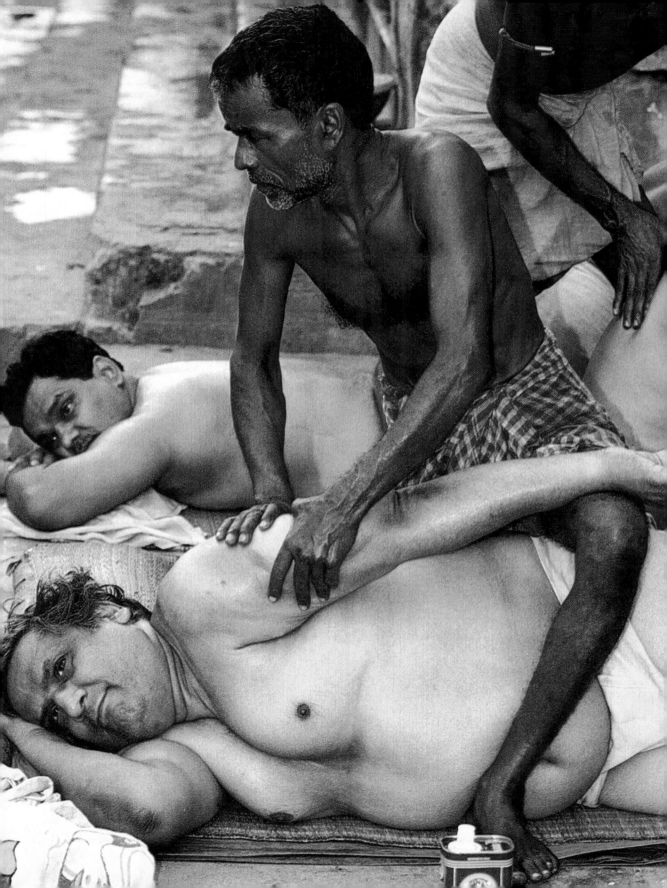

Chapter 22

Global Massage

MASSAGE IS PRACTISED all over the world by many different cultures. Simply speaking, it can be divided into two main types, or systems, depending on whether it originates from the West or the East. Most of the massage done in developed countries is based on so-called Swedish massage, which started as a form of physiotherapy in the early 19th century. A different system that involves softly palpating the skin is known as manual lymphatic drainage. The other systems mentioned in this chapter are based on oriental massage.

In this chapter...
- ✓ Swedish massage
- ✓ Manual lymphatic drainage
- ✓ Chinese massage
- ✓ Eastern head massage

IN MOST ASIAN COUNTRIES YOU DON'T HAVE TO GO FAR TO FIND A GOOD MASSAGE

Swedish massage

ALTHOUGH MASSAGE has been around for centuries in Eastern cultures, it didn't really take off in the West until the 19th century. Under the influence of a Swedish physiologist and fencing master, Pir Henrik Ling (1776–1839), a system was developed that combined massage with physical exercise. This became known as Swedish massage, and is still the basis for most massage practised in the West today.

Ling gave French terms to many of the movements he devised, and they are still in use today: effleurage (stroking); petrissage (kneading); frictions (circular pressures); and tapotement (percussion). In order to keep everything simple I will use the translations as these are the words I have used throughout the book.

Key principles

A sequence of Swedish massage usually starts with stroking, followed by kneading, friction, vibrations, percussion, stroking again, and then passive movements. It traditionally takes place on a massage couch, as it is essential for the masseur to keep a straight back. The massage usually begins on the legs and feet, followed by the hands and arms, then the abdomen and chest, and finally the back.

Upper leg

1 Place one hand behind the other on the front of the thigh above the knee. Stroke (effleurage) both your hands firmly up the thigh, and glide them smoothly down the sides. Repeat several times.

2 Knead (petrissage) the thigh with alternate hands. Work up the leg in rows.

3 Hold the leg with one hand and use the fingers of the other to make rows of circular pressures (friction) along the outer thigh, towards the hip.

4 Make a light, brisk hacking (tapotement) movement with the sides of your hands, along the outer thigh. Follow with stroking (effleurage).

Lower leg

1 Use one hand to support the right knee, and with the thumb of your other hand, make circular pressures (frictions) all around it. Follow with firm strokes from the ankle to the knee.

2 Using both your hands, knead (petrissage) the inner side of the calf. Then support the leg at the ankle, and knead the outer calf.

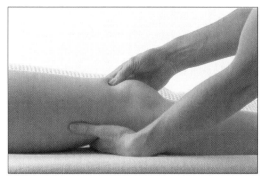

STEP 1

3 Still supporting the leg, make circular finger pressures (frictions) with your other hand along the outer calf. Finish by stroking.

Foot

Sandwich the foot between your palms, and stroke firmly downwards (effleurage) and glide back. Repeat a few times. Make circular thumb pressures (frictions) along the top of the foot with your fingers supporting the sole, then along the sole of the foot with your fingers holding the top. Massage each toe and finish with gentle stroking (effleurage).

Passive movements

Clasp the toes with one hand and give the ankle some support with the other. Slowly rotate the foot a few times, then flex the toes gently backwards and forwards. Holding the ankle with one hand, raise the leg and bend the knee forwards, supporting the thigh with your other hand. Straighten the leg and repeat the movement several times.

■ **This 19th-century** *French engraving depicts the application of the Swedish system of massage.*

305

Arms and hands

Follow the sequence for legs and feet, adapting the movements for the smaller surface area of the arms, working down towards the hands.

Chest

1 Place your hands side by side, just below the collar bone, and stroke (effleurage) firmly down the chest. Fan out to the sides, gliding towards the shoulders. Stroke over and behind the shoulders, and up the back of the neck to the base of the skull. Glide your hands down the sides of the neck to start again. Repeat six times.

2 Use your thumbs and fingers to knead (petrissage) the chest gently and rhythmically. Try not to pinch the skin.

3 Make circular pressures (frictions) with your thumbs on the muscles between the ribs. Start at the sternum and work out in a series of rows towards the shoulders. Vary the pressure according to your partner's needs. Finish with more stroking (effleurage).

Avoid any firm movements on the sensitive tissue around the breasts.

Abdomen

1 Place a small pillow under the knees to relax the abdomen. Facing across the body, place one hand on the lower ribs and the other below the navel. Stroke (effleurage) your lower hand slowly and lightly around the navel in a clockwise direction.

2 Use the fingers of one hand to apply gentle, circular pressures (frictions). Work around the navel, increasing the pressure as your partner relaxes.

3 Using flat palms, knead (petrissage) the top of the abdomen by rhythmically pushing the flesh from one hand to the other. Then knead each side of the abdomen with a deeper movement.

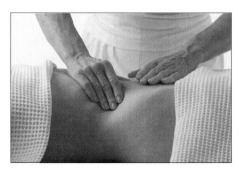

STEP 3

4. Place one palm on top of the other, below the rib cage on the left side of the abdomen. Contract your upper forearm to create a trembling movement (vibration) in your hands, then slowly pull your hands towards the pelvis and continue around in a clockwise direction.

Back

1. Start with some gentle fan stroking (effleurage). Place your hands on the lower back, on either side of the spine, and stroke firmly upwards. When you reach the lower ribs, fan your hands outwards and down the sides. Repeat.

2. Face your partner's body, then knead (petrissage) grasp, squeeze, and release as much flesh as you can with alternate hands. Start on the far hip, then work up the side of the back and across the shoulders towards you. Work twice around the back.

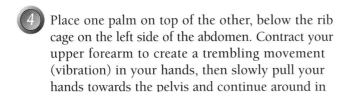

Did you know?

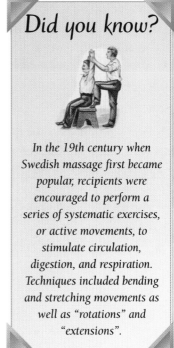

In the 19th century when Swedish massage first became popular, recipients were encouraged to perform a series of systematic exercises, or active movements, to stimulate circulation, digestion, and respiration. Techniques included bending and stretching movements as well as "rotations" and "extensions".

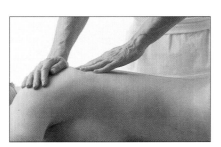

3. Support the left shoulder blade with your right hand and make circular pressures with the fingers of your left hand in the groove beside and away from the spine. Work all the way down the side of the back. When you reach the hips, release, glide up, and start again on the right side of the back.

4. Loosely cup your hands. With your fingers pointing downwards, rhythmically and lightly pat your hands alternately over the buttocks. This percussion (tapotement) movement should make a loud, hollow sound. Continue over the back, taking care to avoid the kidneys. Finish by stroking one hand after the other down the back.

Manual lymphatic drainage

DEVELOPED IN THE 1930s by a Danish massage therapist, Dr Emil Vodder, manual lymphatic drainage (MLD) is a gentle, but amazingly powerful, technique that consists of slow, delicate, repetitive movements. Dr Vodder and his wife discovered that gently palpating and moving the skin could stimulate the lymphatic system and improve congested conditions. This led them to develop a system to treat the whole body.

Consult a qualified medical practitioner if there is a serious or persistent condition, such as swelling that occurs in heart failure, cancer, or thrombosis.

Why MLD?

Healthy connective tissue nourishes every body cell, but when it is congested, cell nutrition and the flow of waste products to the bloodstream slows down. When the lymphatic system is stimulated by MLD, this stagnation is reversed, the body functions more healthily, and the immune system is strengthened.

MLD is an extremely versatile treatment. It can help to reduce swelling and bruising, minimize scarring, speed up healing, relieve sinus congestion, reduce water retention and cellulite, help ease arthritic pain, and is useful as a first-aid treatment for minor burns, knocks, and grazes.

Whatever the condition you are treating with MLD, always begin on the neck. This area has the greatest concentration of lymph nodes in the body, containing approximately 30 per cent of the total.

Self-treatment

Stationary circles are the easiest and best movements to use in self-treatment. The following treatment is designed to reduce puffiness and firm the skin. There is no need to use oil. The movements should be repetitive and gentle, so that the skin is moved superficially.

INTERNET

www.wittlinger-therapiezentrum.com

The Dr Vodder School of Austria site offers courses and information on the original method of MLD as devised by Dr Vodder in the 1930s.

THE PRINCIPLES OF MLD

MLD has many applications, from self-help treatment for minor swellings, to professional treatment for chronic *oedema*. The lymphatic system consists of clusters of lymph nodes (or glands), which are connected to one another by lymph vessels. Lymph nodes occur in clusters mainly around the neck, armpits, and groin; they contain white blood cells that help to fight infection by filtering out bacteria. The lymphatic system also keeps the fluid levels within the body constant.

DEFINITION

The medical term for an accumulation of body fluid within the tissues is **oedema**. *It may be visible, as in a swelling, and may be localized, for example at the site of an injury, or generalized, as in some heart conditions. The ankles are common sites of oedema.*

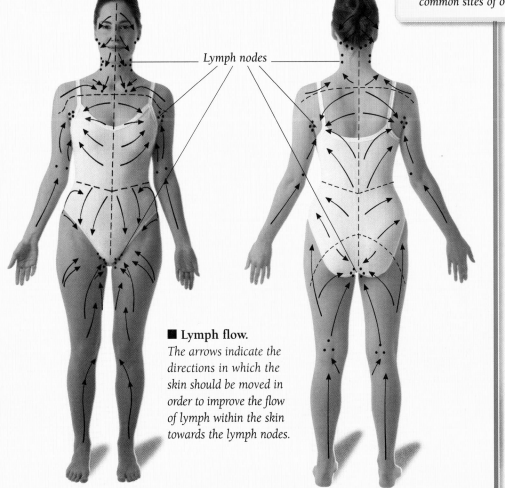

Lymph nodes

■ **Lymph flow.**
The arrows indicate the directions in which the skin should be moved in order to improve the flow of lymph within the skin towards the lymph nodes.

Neck and shoulders

Raise your elbows so they are at right angles to your body, and place your hands on either side of the neck. Straighten but relax your fingers, and use the middle part to gently circle the skin back and down. Release, and let the skin gently pull your fingers upwards to complete the circle. Repeat four times, then move your hands a finger's width down your neck and repeat another five times. Now cross your arms in front of your chest and make five stationary circles at the tops of your shoulders, bringing the skin towards your collar bone. Repeat the entire sequence three times.

NECK AND SHOULDERS

Face and jaw

Place your hands on either side of your chin, and make five stationary circles at three overlapping positions, working towards your ears. Move the skin down towards your body and release out towards your ears. Repeat the sequence three times. Then make stationary circles over the rest of your face, using the length of all your fingers on the flatter areas, and one or two fingers on either side of your nose.

Eyes

If you have puffiness or discoloration under your eyes, make stationary circles in three positions along the edges of the semicircles just above your cheekbones, starting beside your nose. Use the pads of your fingers and apply half the pressure used elsewhere. Finally, make stationary circles down each side of your face and repeat step 1 three more times.

For MLD to work successfully, it must be used on a regular basis.

Treating a partner

The slow and repetitive moves of MLD can have an incredibly soporific effect and may be used as a calming technique, sending your partner to sleep within minutes. MLD takes practice to master, but you can use the following key movements as an introduction and keep practising on your partner until you feel the moves are really flowing and you can see the results. Stationary circles are used mainly on the face and other sensitive areas; pump and scoop techniques on the limbs; and rotary movements on larger, flatter areas, such as the back and abdomen.

Stationary circles

Place your fingers on either side of the jaw, and complete five stationary circles at three overlapping positions, working towards the ears: move the skin gently towards the body, then out to the ears, then allow the skin to pull your fingers back. Repeat three times.

Place your fingers on either side of the mouth, and make five stationary circles with relaxed, straight fingers. Continue on the rest of the face.

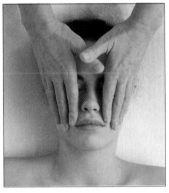

STATIONARY CIRCLES

Pump and scoop

Before working on the leg, clear the groin area with stationary circles towards the body. Then bend the knee and place one hand on the front of the leg and the other on the back.

For the pump action, use the hand at the front of the leg to stretch the skin gently out towards each side. Then ease the skin up towards the body.

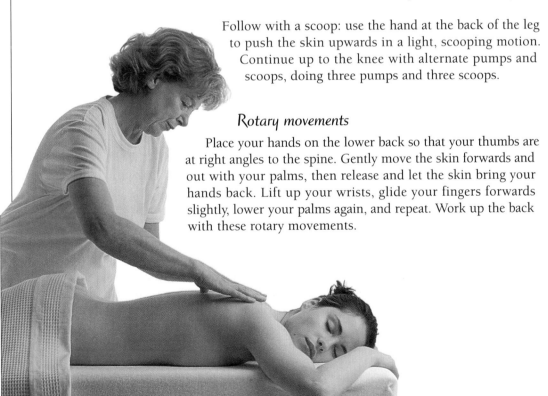

Follow with a scoop: use the hand at the back of the leg to push the skin upwards in a light, scooping motion. Continue up to the knee with alternate pumps and scoops, doing three pumps and three scoops.

Rotary movements

Place your hands on the lower back so that your thumbs are at right angles to the spine. Gently move the skin forwards and out with your palms, then release and let the skin bring your hands back. Lift up your wrists, glide your fingers forwards slightly, lower your palms again, and repeat. Work up the back with these rotary movements.

ROTARY MOVEMENTS

Chinese massage

IN CHINA, MASSAGE *is one of the therapies, along with acupuncture and herbal medicine, that has been around for centuries and is still an essential part of Chinese medical care today. Different systems co-exist, including* tuina *("pushing and grasping") and* anmo *("pressing and rubbing"), and there are numerous regional styles. In the warm south, massage technique is usually gentle and slow, while in the colder north it is strong and vigorous. Traditionally massage is performed through clothes, so there is no need for oil.*

■ **A street masseur** *in Beijing, China's northeast, gives a vigorous treatment. In the warmer south, massage is more gentle.*

Qi energy

In traditional Chinese medicine, the energy that flows along the meridians is known as *qi* (also known as *chi*) and the aim of treatment is to create an unobstructed flow of *qi* in the body. There are 12 regular meridians, each one influencing a major organ and its associated functions. Another two meridians trace the midline of the front of the body, *Ren* (Conception vessel) and the back of the body, *Du* (Governing vessel).

In a healthy person, *qi* is balanced between the opposite but complementary qualities, *yin* and *yang*. *Yin* signifies dark, cold, and passivity, and the meridians run along the front of the body, the abdomen, and the insides of the arms and legs; *yang* signifies light, warmth, and activity, and the meridians run mainly on the back and the outsides of the arms and legs. The aim of a massage is to balance the body into a cohesive, energetic whole.

Traditionally, a Chinese masseur practises techniques on a sacking bag of rice. When a person manages to reduce the bag of rice to one of flour, the technique is considered to be mastered.

THE MERIDIANS

Traditional Eastern medicine is based on the belief that life energy flows along channels, or meridians, within the body. Part of oriental diagnosis and healing involves working with the health-restoring energies within the patient. The idea is that the healer doesn't actually do the healing but that the patient is self-healed. The meridians channel the flow of energy, or *qi*, through the body. *Yin* meridians tend to run along the front of the body, and *yang* meridians along the back.

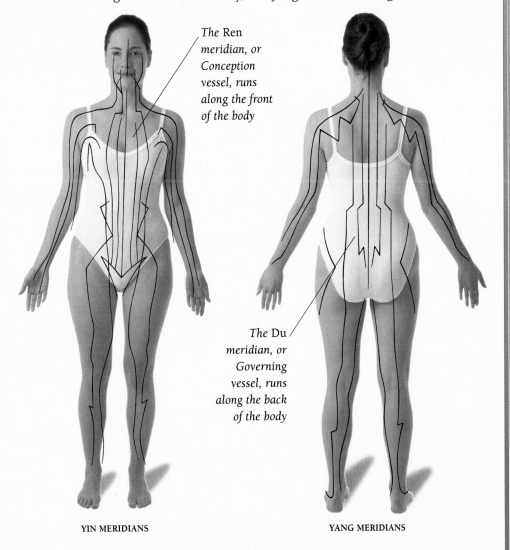

The Ren *meridian, or Conception vessel, runs along the front of the body*

The Du *meridian, or Governing vessel, runs along the back of the body*

YIN MERIDIANS

YANG MERIDIANS

Back massage

I will only go through the stages of back massage here, although you can adapt the moves to use on any part of the body.

Although a back massage can be performed through clothes, some of the steps are easier if you work directly on the flesh. Make sure your partner is wearing something loose that can be lifted up easily.

1. Place one hand on the sacrum. Stroke your other hand in a swift, smooth action up the right side of the back and around the shoulder. Glide back, then stroke up the left side of the back and shoulder in the same way.

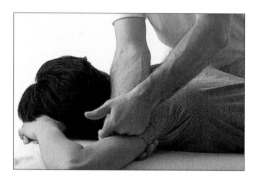

2. Hold the top of the arm with one of your hands and place the knuckles of the ring and little finger of your other hand on top of the arm. Roll your wrist obliquely away from you, then roll it back onto the knuckles. Work all over the upper arm and shoulder, then repeat on the other side.

3. Place your thumbs and fingertips around the muscles that run down either side of the spine in the small of the back. Then, keeping your hands still, slowly rock the body. Rock for about 30 seconds, then squeeze the flesh between your fingers and thumbs, and push your hands together to create a compression. Hold for 5 seconds.

4. Loosely clasp your hands and rest your forearms on the upper and lower back. Then circle your forearms in an anticlockwise direction, using your body weight to achieve a deep pressure. Cover the whole area.

5. With your forearms in the same position, roll one of them briskly up and down the back, while keeping your other arm still. Make sure that your body weight is evenly distributed by keeping your feet apart. Then use your other forearm to roll up the back.

STEP 4

6 Place your thumbs on top of each other, just beside the spine on the side nearest to you. Press down and stroke your thumbs towards the spine. The technique, which has a strong, toning effect on the muscles, requires some practice. Stroking away from the spine relaxes taut muscles. This movement can also be done on the legs and feet.

7 Squeeze the flesh on the sacrum between your thumbs and the sides of your index fingers, and roll the flesh up the back by "walking" your thumbs forwards. When you reach the middle of the back, glide back and repeat this movement three times. Then squeeze the flesh on the sacrum again, but instead of rolling it, pull it up sharply. Release and repeat all the way up the back.

When done correctly, squeezing the flesh and pulling it up sharply often causes a popping sound.

8 Press your palms and fingertips together and lift your elbows out to the sides. Then, starting on the buttocks, make a hacking movement with your hands, trying to create a loud clacking sound as your fingers knock together. Work up the back.

Do not work the spine and kidney area when hacking the back.

STEP 8

9 In traditional Chinese massage, this vigorous movement is used with a special warming ointment or oil. Place one hand on top of the back as a support, and make a strong, quick, sawing movement with the side of your other hand, up and down the side of the spine. Repeat on the other side of the spine.

315

Eastern head massage

ALTHOUGH I WAS TAUGHT this technique in India, it is commonly used in many Eastern countries. In Japan, China, Singapore, and Turkey as well as in India, barbers and hairdressers will automatically offer a reviving scalp massage. The 10-minute massage outlined here is quite energetic and best done on dry hair. Walk around your partner as you do it.

Do not perform a vigorous head massage on wet hair, as it can stretch and break individual hairs.

■ **Barbers and hairdressers** *routinely offer customers a head massage in many Asian countries.*

The 10-minute head massage

1. To bring awareness to the area, rest your hands lightly on either side of the head with your fingers pointing upwards. After about a minute, slowly press your hands towards each other and lift slightly, then repeat.

2. Support the head with your left hand and use the palm of your right to apply circular pressures all over the scalp. Press into the scalp so that the skin, and not the hair, is moved. This movement feels good around the temples. Repeat with your left hand, then use the palms of both your hands together.

3. With relaxed, curled fingers, make circular pressures all over the scalp, from the forehead to the nape of the neck. Keep your fingers firmly in place.

4. Support the head with your left hand again and use the flat fingers of your right hand to rub lightly and swiftly backwards and forwards, starting behind the right ear. Work up and across so that you cover the whole of the head. Then repeat with the fingers of your left hand, using your right hand to stabilize the head.

5. With the fingertips of your right hand, make short, zig-zagging movements over the scalp while your left hand supports the head. Begin by working slowly and lightly, then build up a faster, deeper action. Your partner will either love it or hate it!

STEP 4

6 To release tension in the neck, support the front of the head with your left hand and use the side of your right hand to rub backwards and forwards across the base of the skull in a sawing motion. Then knead the base of the neck.

To understand the full impact of each massage technique, practise on yourself.

STEP 7

7 Support the head with your left hand and press the palm of your right hand firmly onto the head. Jiggle the skin on the spot. Work all over your partner's head, then change hands. This movement feels particularly good on the sides of the head. Rest your left hand on the head and with your right, clasp a handful of hair at the roots and twist it around your fingers. Gently pull the hair, hold for a few seconds, then release and repeat with alternate hands.

8 To finish the massage, stroke the fingers of alternate hands gently through the hair, taking care not to pull it. Then stroke your fingertips as lightly as possible all over the head.

A simple summary

✓ Most of the massage practised in the West is based on Swedish massage, which was devised by a Swedish physiologist in the early part of the 19th century.

✓ Another type of massage of European origin – manual lymphatic drainage – has many therapeutic and healing uses, as it stimulates the lymphatic system to remove excess fluid and waste products from the body more efficiently.

✓ The majority of Eastern types of massage are based on the traditional Chinese concept of body meridians through which life energy flows.

1067

Chapter 23

The Japanese Art of Shiatsu

SHIATSU IS AN ORIENTAL THERAPY, also known as acupressure, in which various disorders are treated by pressing on the skin at precisely located points. Although considered a Japanese type of massage, shiatsu actually has its origins in traditional Chinese medicine. It is based on the Eastern principle that the energy of life flows though longitudinal meridians in the body. The aim of treatment is to apply pressure at certain points along these meridians to maintain harmony and good health.

In this chapter...
✓ Look back in time
✓ Practice makes perfect
✓ Back to front
✓ Common complaints
✓ Quick-cure shiatsu

THE ART OF SHIATSU HAS BEEN PRACTISED FOR CENTURIES IN JAPAN

Look back in time

SHIATSU, LITERALLY TRANSLATED as *"finger pressure", was introduced into Japan about 1,500 years ago. It has its roots in traditional Chinese medicine and, like Chinese massage, is based on the theory that energy flows through meridians in the body.*

■ **An early** *19th-century photograph illustrates the practice of* **anma**, *the precursor to shiatsu. It shows a technique still used in shiatsu today.*

Humble beginnings

For hundreds of years, the most common form of Japanese massage was anma, which was used as a form of relaxation. At the beginning of the 20th century, however, the therapeutic potential of shiatsu was rediscovered, and it enjoyed a renaissance as a result of Tamai Tempaku's work and inspiration. Shiatsu was further popularized by Tokujiro Namikoshi, who from the age of seven, was able to alleviate his mother's debilitating rheumatoid arthritis with massage. After training, he went on to open the Japan Shiatsu Institute in 1940. For the next two decades, shiatsu was thought of as anma massage, but in 1964, it was given official recognition in Japan.

Tokujiro Namikoshi said: "The heart of shiatsu is like pure maternal affection; the pressure of the hands causes the spring of life to flow." Shiatsu is used in Japan by professional therapists to diagnose and treat ailments, and it is taking over as one of the fastest growing areas of complementary medicine in many Western countries.

Key principles

Shiatsu is based on the same principles as traditional Chinese medicine, according to which the life energy (*ki* in Japanese, *qi* in Chinese) circulates around the body through meridians. There are 14 meridians, each of which is associated with a major organ. Some practitioners work on whole meridians, while others focus on specific shiatsu points. There are about 600 points arranged symmetrically on the meridians on the body.

Stimulating the acupoints externally by finger pressure and massage is said to influence the flow of ki, dispersing energy from where there is an excess (jitsu) and replenishing areas that are depleted (kyo). This is said to re-establish balance and restore health.

MAIN SHIATSU POINTS

Some of the most commonly used shiatsu points are labelled below:

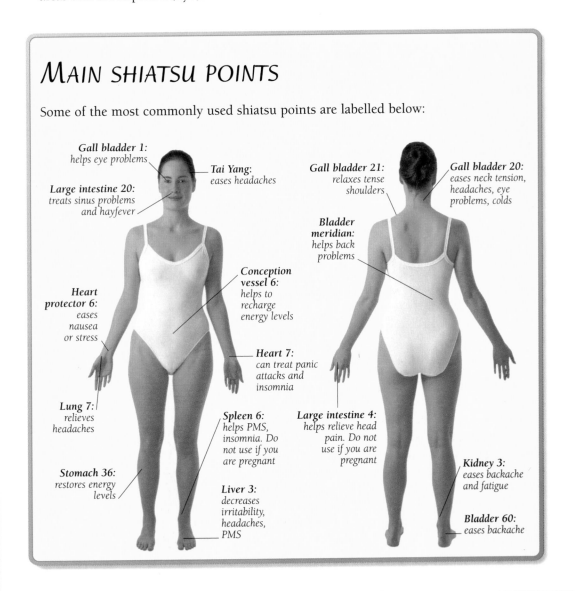

Gall bladder 1:
helps eye problems

Tai Yang:
eases headaches

Large intestine 20:
treats sinus problems
and hayfever

Gall bladder 21:
relaxes tense
shoulders

Gall bladder 20:
eases neck tension,
headaches, eye
problems, colds

**Bladder
meridian:**
helps back
problems

**Conception
vessel 6:**
helps to
recharge
energy levels

**Heart
protector 6:**
eases
nausea
or stress

Heart 7:
can treat panic
attacks and
insomnia

Lung 7:
relieves
headaches

Spleen 6:
helps PMS,
insomnia. Do
not use if you
are pregnant

Large intestine 4:
helps relieve head
pain. Do not
use if you are
pregnant

Kidney 3:
eases backache
and fatigue

Stomach 36:
restores energy
levels

Liver 3:
decreases
irritability,
headaches,
PMS

Bladder 60:
eases backache

Practice makes perfect

THE MOST IMPORTANT THING *about shiatsu is using your body weight correctly to apply pressure. As you can imagine, to get this right requires considerable practice.*

On the courses I teach, the students spend their first 5 minutes crawling around the room on all fours. This is a simple way of teaching them how to relax their weight onto their hands, which is a key to applying pressure correctly in shiatsu.

Applying pressure

Shiatsu is usually performed on the floor. Do not prod your partner's skin, but relax with your arms straight, and lean slowly in with your body weight. In this way, you can apply very deep pressure without causing pain. Hold the pressure for about 5 seconds, so that you have time to tune into your partner's body and so that your partner becomes aware of his or her own body and gradually relaxes.

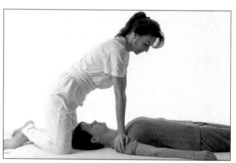

■ **Use your bodyweight** *to apply deep pressure, but lean in slowly.*

The supporting, or "mother", hand is a very important concept in shiatsu, and means that one hand is active while the other is receptive and "listens" to the body, therefore encouraging a flow of *ki*. Try to establish a rhythm and work slowly, so that you stay still for a while with each pressure.

You can use shiatsu pressures simply on their own or in combination with another massage sequence.

Understanding meridians

If you are having trouble with the concept of meridians, you can discover the appropriate places to apply pressure by exploring your partner's body with your hands. Meridians are usually longitudinal lines, so glide your thumb along the limbs, abdomen and back, and feel for indentations, or points, that seem to "want" to be pressed. Most points give a radiating sensation when pressed, rather like a dull, but pleasurable, ache. As you practise, work systematically moving from one acupoint to the next. Apply the pressure on the point as your partner breathes out. Release the pressure as your partner breathes in, and move on.

Practising shiatsu pressure techniques

Different parts of the body require different degrees of pressure, which can be achieved using the following techniques:

a **Ball of thumb:** use the ball of your thumb and rest your fingers on the skin to help give a steady, even pressure. Do not use the tip of your thumb, because your nail, however short, will gouge the skin

b **Elbow or forearm:** make sure that your arm and hand are relaxed so that you apply a gentle pressure, not a hard prod. This is useful on large, muscular areas

c **Two thumbs:** for extra depth on the shoulders, buttocks, back, and soles of the feet, put one thumb on top of the other

d **Thumb and fingers:** treat smaller areas, such as the arms, by squeezing them between the thumb and fingers

e **Two fingers:** put your index finger on top of your middle finger for greater depth. This is useful if your thumbs are sore or tired

f **Heel of hand:** to give a more general stimulation to the acupoint, use the heel of your hand

Back to front

NOW THAT YOU ARE FAMILIAR with the pressing techniques, you are ready to start the shiatsu massage. It is most effective to treat the whole body, to harmonize energy, which takes between 45 minutes and an hour.

Back of body massage

As with many massage routines, you should begin the shiatsu sequence on your partner's back. Continue by treating the back of the body before moving onto the front.

Back

Place the heels of your hands on either side of your partner's spine towards the top of the back, and relax your fingers. Lean your body weight onto your arms. Hold for 5 seconds, then sit back, glide your hands a little further down, and repeat the pressures.

Hips

You may find it comfortable to kneel astride your partner's legs. With the heels of your hands, apply pressures to the soft, hollow areas in the sacrum, at the base of the spine, moving your hips forwards when you lean into a pressure. Work down to the middle of the buttocks then repeat the pressures with your thumbs.

Buttocks

Now swivel your hands so that your fingers are pointing inwards, and place the heels of your hands in the hollows on the side of each buttock. Lean forwards, keeping your back straight, and slowly squeeze the buttocks between the heels of your hands. Release, then repeat the pressure two or three times.

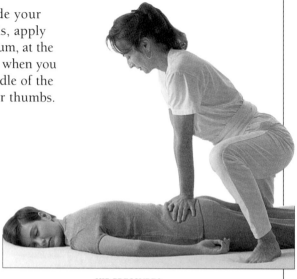

HIP PRESSURES

Backs of legs

Face the legs and place your right hand on the sacrum. This is the "mother" hand, a support only. With your left hand, make palm pressures down the back of the leg nearest to you, avoiding the knee area. When you reach the foot, squeeze the Achilles tendon between your thumb and fingers for 5 seconds. Repeat on the other leg.

When working on the backs of the legs, your partner may be more comfortable if his or her feet are flat and slightly pigeon-toed.

PRESSURE TO THE SHOULDERS

Shoulders

Kneel behind the head and place your "mother" hand on top of the back. With your other elbow, apply pressures around the shoulders, avoiding the spine, and keeping your hand relaxed so that you do not cause pain. Alter the angle of your elbow to vary the strength of the pressure, and work all over the muscle between the shoulder blades. Then swap hands and work with your other elbow.

Front of body massage

Ask your partner to turn over and lie on his or her back, as now you are ready to begin massaging the front of the body. Start with the chest.

Chest

Kneel with one knee on either side of the head, and place the heels of your hands in the hollows between the collar bone and shoulder joints, fingers facing outwards. Bring your hips forwards and lean into your partner's shoulders for a few seconds. Make palm pressures across the chest to the sides of the body, followed by gentle thumb pressures between the ribs.

THUMB PRESSURES TO THE FACE

Face

Still kneeling behind the head, make thumb pressures all over the forehead and along the eyebrows. Then place your thumbs in the hollows just to the side of each nostril and make a series of pressures under the cheekbones. This helps to clear the sinuses.

Arms and head

Place one of your partner's arms out to the side, at right angles to the body, and place your "mother" hand around the top of the shoulder. Shape your other hand around the top of the arm, and make palm pressures all the way down to the wrist. Repeat on the other arm.

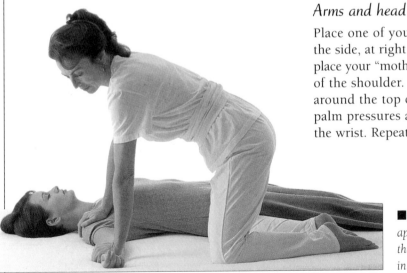

■ **While the active** *hand applies pressures to the arm, the supporting hand remains in contact with the shoulder.*

Abdomen

Rest your "mother" hand on the ribs, and make palm pressures with your other hand clockwise around the abdomen. Then place your hands just below the navel, with your fingers interlaced, and rock the stomach in a soothing, wave-like motion.

Common complaints

IDEALLY, SHIATSU IS USED to help attain and maintain good health. However, even if you are in good health, you may not escape the odd bout of being off-colour. I will now take you through some self-help shiatsu techniques that can be used to relieve, or in some other way help, various symptoms and minor conditions. Remember that if your symptoms are severe or recur, you should see your doctor or a qualified shiatsu practitioner.

Headaches

For a shiatsu-based headache cure see Chapter 21. Shiatsu can also be used to relieve migraine and sinus headaches.

Migraine

1. Press below the end of your eyebrow and level with the corner of your eye, simultaneously on both sides of your face (Gall bladder 1).

2. Press at the base of your skull and to each side of the spine (Bladder 20).

3. Pinch the web of skin between your thumb and forefinger, first on one hand, and then on the other (Large intestine 4).

4. Press in the depression formed by the two tendons at the base of your thumb, first on one hand and then on the other (Large intestine 5).

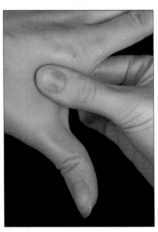

■ **Migraine can be relieved** *by pressing the web of skin between thumb and forefinger.*

Sinus headache

1. Press in the middle of each eyebrow and between your eyebrows (Extra points).

2. Press on the centre of the lower edge of the eye socket (Stomach 1).

3. Pinch both sides of your hand just below the knuckle at the base of your little finger (Extra point); do the same on your other hand.

Insomnia

If you sometimes have trouble sleeping, try the following routine before you go to bed.

1 Sit comfortably with one knee bent and the other leg straight. Rest one of your elbows on your knee and apply pressure with your thumb to the bridge of your nose, leaning your body weight onto your thumb. Hold the pressures for 10–15 seconds (Extra point).

2 Measure four fingers's width up from the inside of your left ankle bone, and place your right thumb on this spot. Apply pressure for 10–15 seconds, then repeat on your right ankle (Spleen 6).

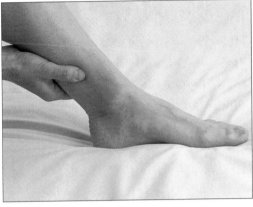

SHIATSU FOR INSOMNIA

3 With your right thumb, press the depression on the side of your left wrist, below the little finger. Hold for 10–15 seconds. Repeat on your right wrist (Heart 7).

Sciatica

A form of nerve pain, sciatica may be felt anywhere along the course of one of the *sciatic* nerves, but is most commonly felt in the buttocks and thighs. Sciatic pain can sometimes be eased by pressing with your thumbs on certain shiatsu points. Hold the pressure for about 10 seconds then move onto the next point.

> **DEFINITION**
>
> *The two largest nerves in the body are the **sciatic** nerves. They run from the base of the spine down the backs of the legs to the feet, and form the main nerve in each leg.*

1 Press on either side of your spine at the small of the back (Bladder 24).

2 Press at the back of your thighs directly under your buttocks (Bladder 36).

3 Press in the middle of the back of your thighs (Bladder 37).

4 Press in the centre of the hollow on the side of your buttocks (Gallbladder 30).

5 Press halfway down the side of your thigh (Gallbladder 31).

6 Press halfway down the back of your calf (Bladder 57).

Quick-cure shiatsu

IN ADDITION TO the well-established cures for minor ailments as described in the previous section, there are a number of really quick, on-the-spot, shiatsu relievers for other minor ailments that can hit anyone literally at any time. You can perform most of these pressures very discreetly, wherever you happen to be when the problem develops.

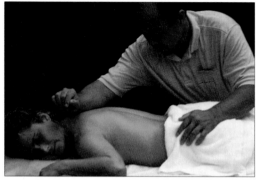

■ **Shiatsu** *is becoming increasingly popular as an alternative medical treatment in the West.*

When using Shiatsu quickcures, remember that you are treating the symptom and not the cause of the problem. If the symptom returns, you should consult a doctor or a shiatsu practitioner.

Common cold

1. Press on the web of skin between your thumb and forefinger (Large intestine 4).

2. Press on the indentations at the base of your skull (Governing vessel 15 and Gallbladder 20).

3. Press at the base of your neck, on either side of the vertebrae and about three finger widths below (Bladder 12 and 13).

Stomach ache

1. Press three finger widths below your navel (Conception vessel 6).

2. Press in the groove on the outside of your shin bone, four finger widths below your knee (Stomach 36).

Toothache

Press on the web of skin between your thumb and forefinger (Large intestine 4).

Menstrual pain

Squeeze on either side of your ankle just behind the bony prominence, and on the inside of your leg about four finger widths above the prominence (Kidney 3, Bladder 60, and Spleen 6).

Aching legs

Put pressure in the groove on the outside of your shin bone, four finger widths below your knee (Stomach 36).

Hangover

Press on the crown of your head (Governing vessel 20).

Lack of energy

1. Press just below the ball of the foot in the centre of your sole (Kidney 1).

2. Squeeze the middle of the palm of your hand (Heart constrictor 8).

3. Press in the groove on the outside of your shin, four finger widths below your knee (Stomach 36).

INTERNET

www.shiatsu.org

The official web site of the Shiatsu Society, UK. An umbrella organization, it sets standards in training and maintains a register of qualified practitioners.

A simple summary

✓ Although associated with Japan, shiatsu has its roots in traditional Chinese medicine, and adopted the Chinese theory of meridians.

✓ Shiatsu can relieve various ailments by applying pressure to points along the meridians to influence the flow of life energy and restore bodily wellbeing.

✓ Mastering shiatsu requires much practice, a knowledge of acupoints, and an understanding of meridians.

✓ Shiatsu can be used as a self-treatment for a range of minor symptoms.

Chapter 24

Reflexology

MASSAGING THE FEET IS ANOTHER ancient art that has evolved and become more sophisticated for the 21st century. As with Eastern therapies, reflexology is based on the philosophy of *qi*. Reflexologists believe that the feet (and hands) are mirrors of the body and there is a map that shows you which part of the foot corresponds to which part of the body. By stimulating reflex points on the foot (or hand) you can relax and balance the whole body and treat a range of minor disorders. Even though there is no scientific explanation for why or how reflexology works, the benefits to the receiver are very positive.

In this chapter...
- ✓ *How it started*
- ✓ *Your life in your feet*
- ✓ *How do you do it?*
- ✓ *Helping yourself*

331

How it started

FOOT MASSAGE is one of the most ancient forms of massage, said to have originated in China over 5,000 years ago. There is also evidence that it was practised in ancient Egypt: tomb paintings have been excavated showing people manipulating other people's feet.

THE MASSAGING OF HANDS AND FEET FROM THE PHYSICIAN'S TOMB, SAQQARA, EGYPT, 2300 BC

Zone therapy and reflexology

In 1915, Dr William H. Fitzgerald, an American ear, nose, and throat specialist, introduced the concept of "zone therapy". According to his theory, energy flows through ten vertical zones that run from the head to the feet; five zones to the right of an imaginary line that runs through the centre of the body, and five on the left side. Pressure on a reflex point in the appropriate zone area on the foot can treat symptoms emanating from organs in that particular zone. Fitzgerald was suitably humble about the healing powers of zone therapy: "Zone therapy is not a cure all but a valuable adjunct to therapy".

This concept was taken a step further in the US in the 1930s by Eunice Ingham. Her so-called compression massage maintained that all parts of the body could be treated by pressing relevant areas of the feet. She was responsible for developing a map of the feet to show the location of reflex points, and for developing techniques for stimulating them. In the 1960s, reflexology was introduced into the UK, and is now a hugely popular form of complementary medicine in many parts of the developed world.

The foot is the most familiar part of the body used in reflexology, but in fact the whole body has reflex points as we know from acupuncture points and pressure points. The hand is another popular area for reflexology, and maps similar to the foot chart have been drawn up for these areas.

Your life in your feet

THE FOOT IS A COMPLEX STRUCTURE *with an extensive nerve distribution. Many of the nerve endings in the feet correspond to acupuncture and shiatsu points, and it is thought that by stimulating these points endorphins are released.*

The sensory cortex in the brain is the area responsible for receiving touch and pressure signals from nerves within the skin.

The majority of the nerves of the body are found in the feet, hands, and face, thus making massage to these areas particularly effective.

Sole searching

An easy way to remember the location of the reflex points is to visualize a picture of the body superimposed on the soles of the feet (see overleaf). The big toe corresponds to the head, the inside edges of the feet correspond to the spine, and the reflex points for the main organs are located roughly according to their positions in the body. Although most of the reflex points are on the soles of the feet, there are some on the top of the foot and around the ankles.

A disorder in any part of the body is reflected by sensitivity in the corresponding area of the feet. Reflexologists do not claim to diagnose illness, but a good therapist can usually tell where there is a weakness in the body. When there is an imbalance in the body, granular or crystalline deposits will accumulate on the relevant reflex point, making it feel tender to the touch. Hard skin, corns, bunions, and infections can all be interpreted as external manifestations of problems in the corresponding area of the body.

Therapeutic benefits

Although science cannot explain how reflexology works, it has been found by many to be a very successful therapy. Massaging the feet in this way is incredibly relaxing, which in its own way has beneficial effects on health. It can reduce muscular tension, thus enabling blood to circulate freely, distributing nutrients to the cells and removing waste products more efficiently.

Did you know?

In China, studies have been carried out combining reflexology with medical treatment on children with chest infections. The studies show that reflexology can not only shorten the duration of the disease but can prevent complications. In addition, it can improve the functioning of the immune system, speed up recovery, and reduce the recurrence of the disease.

REFLEX POINTS

The reflex areas of the soles, top, and sides of the feet correspond to the different organs, glands, and parts of the body. The right foot corresponds to the right side of the body and the left foot to the left side of the body.

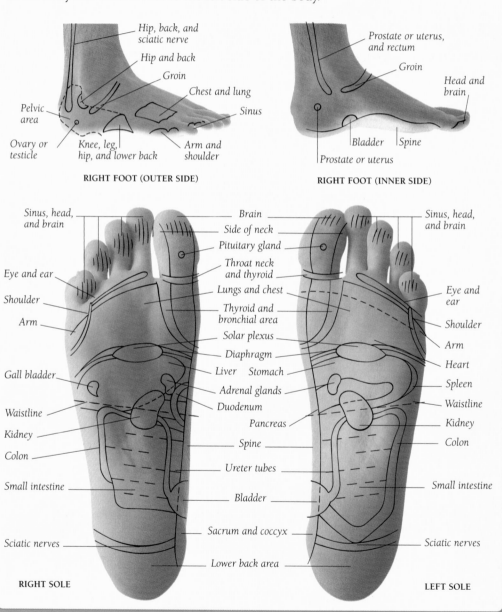

RIGHT FOOT (OUTER SIDE)

Hip, back, and sciatic nerve
Hip and back
Groin
Chest and lung
Sinus
Pelvic area
Ovary or testicle
Knee, leg, hip, and lower back
Arm and shoulder

RIGHT FOOT (INNER SIDE)

Prostate or uterus, and rectum
Groin
Head and brain
Bladder
Spine
Prostate or uterus

RIGHT SOLE

Sinus, head, and brain
Eye and ear
Shoulder
Arm
Gall bladder
Waistline
Kidney
Colon
Small intestine
Sciatic nerves

Brain
Side of neck
Pituitary gland
Throat neck and thyroid
Lungs and chest
Thyroid and bronchial area
Solar plexus
Diaphragm
Liver Stomach
Adrenal glands
Duodenum
Pancreas
Spine
Ureter tubes
Bladder
Sacrum and coccyx
Lower back area

LEFT SOLE

Sinus, head, and brain
Eye and ear
Shoulder
Arm
Heart
Spleen
Waistline
Kidney
Colon
Small intestine
Sciatic nerves

How do you do it?

YOUR PARTNER SHOULD SIT *comfortably with his or her legs supported with a cushion under the knees. Although your partner can lie completely flat for the treatment, I prefer to prop up my clients so I can maintain eye contact and can tell whether an area of the foot is sensitive. Sit or kneel at your partner's feet – choose the most comfortable position for yourself. Work over the whole foot for a really relaxing result and to promote and maintain good health.*

Locating problem areas

As you work, you may come across particularly sensitive areas that may indicate a problem in the corresponding part of the body. A problem area may feel as if there are granules under the skin. Give extra attention to these areas to disperse the granules in the feet and reduce congestion elsewhere. In this way, you can treat a variety of complaints ranging from headaches and backache to digestive problems, constipation, sinusitis, and insomnia.

Pressures on problem areas may feel painful, so watch your partner's face to make sure you are not causing pain. It is better to treat a disorder by working gently and repeating the treatment several times, rather than overworking sensitive areas all in one go.

The technique

In reflexology, apart from the initial soothing strokes you do not massage the feet; instead, you apply precise pressure with your thumb or forefinger to each specific point. You can use either a static pressure or a "walking" technique, in which you bend and then straighten your thumb to move it forwards. Hold the foot firmly with one hand, and work with your other thumb, using the edge of the thumb, just by the nail. Press firmly for about 3 seconds, then move on. Work systematically first on the right foot and then on the left.

Do not use oil for reflexology as this will make your fingers slip. Just lightly dust your partner's feet with talcum powder or use nothing additional.

A complete reflexology treatment takes between 45 minutes and 1 hour. It is very important to have short nails for reflexology.

The reflexology sequence

I am going to show you a brief sequence as a simple introduction to reflexology. You can build on this to expand the massage into a full reflexology session.

1 **Passive movements**: begin the sequence by rolling and twisting the foot from side to side between your palms. This will help to relax and warm the foot before you start on the pressure techniques.

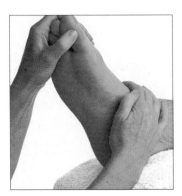

2 **Diaphragm**: support the top of the foot with your right hand and "walk" the thumb of your left hand along the diaphragm line, just under the ball of the foot.

3 **Spine**: use your thumb to apply static or "walking" pressures from the heel of the foot to the big toe, while your other hand supports the top of the foot.

4 **Head**: work up each toe in turn, starting with the big toe and finishing with the little toe. Use your fingers to support the toes and your other hand to support the top of the foot.

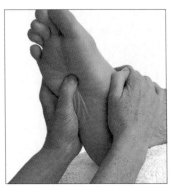
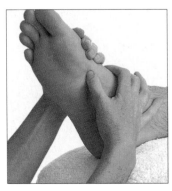

| STEP 2 | STEP 3 | STEP 4 |

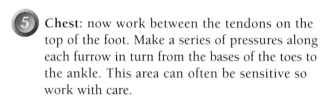

The big toe has many pressure points that affect the head, and treating this along with the other toes will help anyone with congested sinuses. A friend of mine who used to suffer from chronic sinusitis now has regular treatments before the hayfever season.

INTERNET

www.aor.org.uk

The site for the Association of Reflexologists is a mine of useful information about reflexology. It includes articles and research and you'll also find details on schools and practitioners.

5 **Chest:** now work between the tendons on the top of the foot. Make a series of pressures along each furrow in turn from the bases of the toes to the ankle. This area can often be sensitive so work with care.

6 **Digestive system:** apply pressures in diagonal lines from the waistline to the diaphragm line, then from the heel to the waistline.

7 **Reproductive organs and back:** support the foot firmly and make pressures all around the ankle with your thumb. Then work all over the heel to prevent or treat lower back pain. Take extra care in these tender areas. Finish by stroking the foot gently from the ankle to the toes.

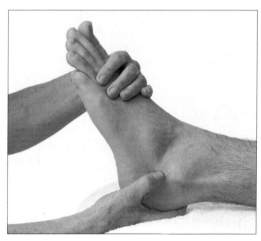

STEP 7

During a treatment, your partner may feel a temperature change, and afterwards he or she may feel tired. Encourage your partner to drink plenty of water and to take things quietly for a while after the end of the session.

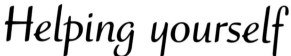

Helping yourself

ALTHOUGH IT IS INEVITABLY *a little less relaxing than receiving a treatment from someone else, it is quite possible to give yourself an effective reflexology treatment.*

■ **Feel your way** *through the reflex points on your feet and you'll soon come to understand the relaxing, if not necessarily healing, power of reflexology.*

Either sit comfortably with one foot resting on the thigh of your opposite leg, or lie down with one leg bent, and rest the opposite foot on your raised thigh. Slowly explore your whole foot, following the sequence on pp. 336–37. Pay extra attention to any sore or sensitive areas: build up pressure on them gradually, and return to work on them several times, trying to dispel the soreness.

Reflexologists recommend that you work on your feet once a week to promote good health. A healthy body is reflected in healthy, pain-free feet, so you should start looking after your feet today.

Using your hands

Although your feet are more sensitive than your hands, you can try doing reflexology on your own hands. There are similar reflex points on the hands but they are usually deeper and less sensitive than those on the feet. However, the advantage of hand reflexology is that it can be practised at any time – at work, on the train, or while watching television – and is ideal for relieving stress.

Here are a couple of examples:

1. **Sinuses:** with the thumb of one hand, "walk" several times up each finger and down the thumb. Repeat on your other hand. This will ease congestion.

2. **Colon:** massage with one of your thumbs across the palm of your other hand. Do this several times before repeating on your other hand. This stimulates the intestines and helps relieve irritable bowel syndrome.

HAND MAPS

Although the reflex points on the hands mirror those found on the feet, they have less depth and so there are no maps for the sides of the hands. As you can see from the diagrams, most of the reflex areas are found on the palms of the hands.

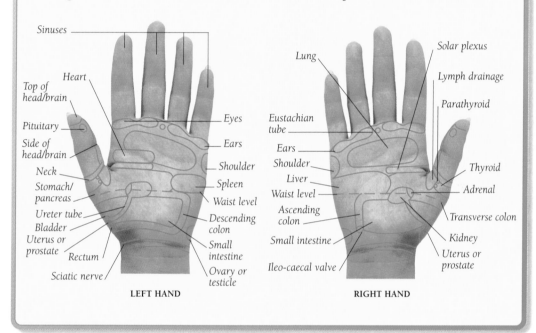

LEFT HAND

Sinuses
Heart
Top of head/brain
Pituitary
Side of head/brain
Neck
Stomach/ pancreas
Ureter tube
Bladder
Uterus or prostate
Rectum
Sciatic nerve
Eyes
Ears
Shoulder
Spleen
Waist level
Descending colon
Small intestine
Ovary or testicle

RIGHT HAND

Lung
Solar plexus
Lymph drainage
Parathyroid
Eustachian tube
Ears
Shoulder
Liver
Waist level
Ascending colon
Small intestine
Ileo-caecal valve
Thyroid
Adrenal
Transverse colon
Kidney
Uterus or prostate

A simple summary

✓ Reflexology is based on the philosophy that every area of the body is represented by a site on the foot and that by massaging particular areas, various problems can be alleviated. Though less sensitive, there are similar reflex points on the hand.

✓ A trained reflexologist can detect problem areas by feeling for granulations under the skin.

✓ Self-reflexology is a simple option that can be useful when a trained reflexologist or a willing partner is not to hand.

Further resources

Organizations

Aromatherapy Organizations
Council (AOC)
    PO Box 19834
    London SE25 6WF
    020 82517912
    www.aoc.uk.net

Association of Reflexologists (UK)
    27 Old Gloucester Street
    London WC1N 3XX
    0870 5673320
    www.aor.org.uk

Association of Remedial Masseurs
(Australia)
    PO Box 440,
    Ryde
    NSW 1680
    (02) 9807 4769
    www.remedialmasseurs.com.au

Australian Natural Therapies
Association
    PO Box 856
    Caloundra, Qld 4551
    (toll-free) 1800 817 577
    www.anta.com.au

The Australian Traditional
Medicine Society
    Unit 12/27 Bank Street
    Meadowbank, NSW 2114
    (02) 9808 6800
    Email: enquiries@atms.com.au

British Complementary Medicine
Association (BCMA)
    PO Box 2074
    Seaford
    East Sussex
    BN25 1HQ
    0845 3455977
    www.bcma.co.uk

British Massage Therapy Council
    17 Rymers Lane
    Oxford OX4 3JU
    www.bmtc.co.uk

General Council for Massage
Therapy
    46 Millmead Way
    Hertford
    SG14 3YH

International Association of Infant
Massage (UK)
    56 Spansholt Road
    Barking
    Essex IG11 7YQ
    www.iaim.org.uk

International Society of
Professional Aromatherapists
(ISPA)
    ISPA House
    82 Ashby Road
    Hinckley
    Leicestershire LE10 1SN
    01455 637987
    www.the-ispa.org

International Therapy
Examination Council (ITEC)
    10–11 Heathfield Terrace
    London W4 4JE
    020 89944141
    www.itecworld.co.uk

National Association of Holistic
Aromatherapy
    PO Box 17622
    Boulder
    Colorado 80308 7622
    USA
    www.naha.org

Research Council for
Complementary Medicine
    Suite 5
    1 Harley Street
    London W1G 9QD
    www.rccm.org.uk

Shiatsu Society (UK)
    Eastlands Court
    St Peter's Road
    Rugby CU21 3QP
    01788 555051
    www.shiatsu.org

Touch Research Institute
    University of Miami School
    of Medicine
    PO Box 016820
    Miami
    Florida 33101
    USA
    www.miami.edu/touch-research

Books

Aromatherapy Massage
by Clare Maxwell-Hudson, Dorling Kindersley, 1994

The Art of Swedish Massage
by B. Ravald, Bergh Publishing Group, 1982

Baby Massage: The Magic of the Loving Touch
by A. Auckett, Thorsons, 1982

Beard's Massage (4th edn.)
by G. De Domenico and E.C. Wood, W.B. Saunders, 1997

The Book of Massage
by L. Liddlell, Ebury Press, 1984

Carrier Oils
by L. Price, Riverhead, 1999

Chinese Massage
Shanghai College of Traditional Chinese Medicine, 1983

Chinese Qigong Massage
by Y. Jwing-Ming, Paul H. Compton, 1992

The Complete Book of Massage
by Clare Maxwell-Hudson, Dorling Kindersley, 1988

Healing Massage Techniques
by F. Tappan, Appleton & Lance, 1988

Healthy Pleasures
by R. Ornstein and D. Sobel, AddisonWesley, 1989

Infant Massage: A Handbook for Loving Parents
by V. McClure, Souvenir Press, 2000

Introduction to Dr Vodder's Manual Lymph Drainage
by H. Whittlinger and G. Whittlinger, Haug Publishers, 1982

Loving Hands
by F. Leboyer, Alfred Knopf, 1979

Massage and Aromatherapy
by A. Wickers, Chapman & Hall, 1996

Massage for Healthier Children
by M. Sinclair, Wingbow Press, 1992

Massage and the Original Swedish Movements
by K.W. Ostrom, Octagon Press, 1991

Massage for People with Cancer
by P. McNamara, The Cancer Support Centre, Wandsworth, 1995

Massage. The Ultimate Illustrated Guide
by Clare Maxwell-Hudson, Dorling Kindersley, 1999

Milady's Theory and Practice of Therapeutic Massage
by M. Beck, Milady, 1994

Mind Body Medicine
by D. Goleman and J. Gurin, Consumer Report Books, 1993

Molecules of Emotion
by C. Pert, Simon & Schuster, 1997

Mosby's Fundamentals of Therapeutic Massage
by S. Fritz, Mosby Lifeline, 1995

The New Massage
by G. Inkeles, Allen & Unwin, 1980

Pocket Massage for Stress Relief
By Clare Maxwell-Hudson, Dorling Kindersley, 1996

The Relaxation Response
by H. Benson, New York Times Books, 1984

Remedial Massage Therapy
by M. Cash, Ebury Press, 1996

Save your Hands
by L. Greene, Infinity Press, 1995

Shiatsu
By T. Namikoshi, Japan Publications, 1972

341

Shiatsu Theory and Practice
by C. Beresford-Cooke,
Churchill Livingstone, 1995

Therapeutic Massage
by E. Holey and E. Cook,
W.B. Saunders, 1997

Therapeutic Touch
by D. Kreiger, Prentice Hall
Press, 1979

Timeless Healing
by H. Benson, Simon &
Schuster, 1996

Touching. The Human
Significance of the Skin
by A. Montagu, Columbia
University Press, 1978

Touch Therapy
by T. Field, Churchill
Livingstone, 2000

Understanding Sports Massage
by P. Benjamin and S.
Lamp, Human Kinetics,
1996

Magazines

Aromatherapy
WV Publications and
Exhibitions
57–59 Rochester Place
London NW1 9JU

Aromatherapy World
ISPA House
82 Ashby Road
Hinckley
Leicestershire LE10 1SN
www.the-ispa.org
(Journal of the International
Society of Professional
Aromatherapists [ISPA])

The International Journal of
Aromatherapy
Harcourt Place
32 Jamestown Road
London NW1 7BY
www.harcourt-
international.com/journals/ijar

Massage & Bodywork
28677 Buffalo Park Road
Evergreen
CO 80439–7347
USA

Massage Magazine
1636 W.1st Avenue
Ste 100
Spokane
WA 99204-0620
USA
www.massagemagazine.com

Massage & Health Review
Massage Therapy Institute
of Great Britain
PO Box 2726
London NW2 3NR

Massage Therapy Journal
820 Davis Street
Evanston
IL 60201
USA
(the official publication of
the American Massage
Therapy Association,
AMTA)

Massage on the Web

THE INTERNET is a good place to browse for information on massage or massage-related topics. If you want to learn more about the benefits of a particular massage stroke, or order some essential oils, or find out where your nearest qualified massage therapist can be located, it's all here. Many of the web sites listed are linked to the principal massage organizations.

www.aboutmassage.com

Search here for anything massage related, including techniques, schools, associations, research, and benefits of massage.

www.americanmedicalmassage.com

The American Manual Medicine Association is a professional organization that promotes medical massage therapy training by establishing education programmes and creating standards.

www.amtamassage.org

At the web site of the American Massage Therapy Association (AMTA) you'll find an online massage room, as well as massage-related information.

www.anta.com.au

The Australian Natural Therapies Association (ANTA) has a listing of natural therapists throughout Australia on their web site.

www.aoc.uk.net

The web site of the Aromatherapy Organizations Council (AOC) – the UK governing body for aromatherapy.

www.aor.org.uk

The web site of the Association of Reflexologists (AOR), which represents over 6,000 members in the UK. The site provides lists of these professional practitioners as well as details of almost 100 accredited schools and colleges.

www.a-t-c.org.uk

The Aromatherapy Trade Council (ATC) is the authoritative body of the UK aromatherapy essential oils trade. You'll find lists of approved essential oils suppliers at this site.

www.backpain.org

The site of a UK charity that helps people manage and prevent back pain by providing advice and promoting self help.

www.baldwins.co.uk

G. Baldwin & Co is one of the oldest herbal suppliers in the UK. Check out its online store.

www.bartleby.com.107/189.html

Go to this incredibly resourceful site and you'll have *Gray's Anatomy of the Human Body* at your fingertips.

www.bcma.co.uk

The British Complementary Medical Association represents around 25,000 complementary medicine practitioners within 11 branches of therapy, including massage.

www.bmtc.co.uk

The British Massage Therapy Council is a professional organization that helps to promote high standards in massage therapy practice and training.

www.bodyworker.com/history

This site has a comprehensive list of the history of massage.

www.careeratyourfingertips.com

This site has a good section on the different kinds of massage and frequently asked questions if you're looking for a career in massage.

www.cmhmassage.co.uk

I make no apology for including the web site address of my own school of massage – The Clare Maxwell-Hudson School of Massage. You will find information on the site about the school, the teachers, courses – both for initial training and continuing education – and publications.

www.essentiallyoils.com

For all your aromatherapy needs, including essential oils, carrier oils, floral waters, cosmetic bases, bottles and jars, books, and videos. Also a mine of information with articles, comments, research, and newsletters on aromatherapy.

www.essentialorc.com

The site of the Essential Oil Research Consultants provides research information and education on essential oils.

www.fleur.co.uk

Here you'll find useful information on an extensive range of aromatherapy products, including fact sheets and health and safety issues.

www.fimed.org

The Foundation for Integrated Medicine aims to promote the development and integrated delivery of safe and effective forms of healthcare, including orthodox and complementary medicine.

www.iaim.net

The International Association of Infant Massage, which aims to promote nurturing touch and communication through training, education, and research.

www.imagroup.com

The web site of the International Massage Association (IMA). The IMA represents complementary healthcare professionals and is committed to taking complementary healthcare mainstream.

www.itecworld.co.uk

The web site of the International Therapy Examination Council (ITEC), the largest alternative therapy graduating body in Europe, with registered schools worldwide.

www.massageaus.com.au

Massage Australia is an organization representing the interests of massage therapists practising in Australia. The organization produces numerous publications, including *Massage Australia Quarterly Journal*.

www.massagemag.com

This is the online version of one of the best-selling massage magazines. It contains research articles, topical massage-related news, expert advice, information on courses in massage and other related therapies.

massagenetwork.com

The Massage Network is a link to other relevant sites. It has the capacity to search for massage therapists in a selection of countries around the world.

massagetherapyhomepage.com

The Massage Therapy Homepage is a resource for articles, education (schools and workshops), professional organizations, and other massage information.

www.massagewarehouse.com

This site stocks essential items for the professional massage therapist as well as the amateur, ranging from massage tables, aromatherapy products, and massage gadgets to books, music, and clothing.

www.miami.edu/touch-research

Touch Research Institute's web site is a fascinating mine of information about past, present, and future research that the institute is involved in.

www.mlduk.org.uk

The web site of the professional association of manual lymphatic drainage practitioners contains an international register of therapists as well as details of training courses.

www.mtwc.com

Massage Therapy Web Central is a comprehensive resource centre, book and music store, and global directory for individuals and organizations interested in the massage profession.

www.naha.org

The National Association for Holistic Aromatherapy (NAHA) is an organization dedicated to enhancing public awareness about the benefits of true aromatherapy.

www.nccam.nih.gov

Web site of the National Center for Complementary and Alternative Medicine in the US.

www.rccm.org.uk

The web site of the UK's Research Council for Complementary Medicine carries news, research, and a database of relevant articles on all types of complementary medicine, including massage.

www.reflexology.org

The Home of Reflexology web site lists most of the reflexology organizations in the world.

www.reflexology-uk.co.uk

The web site of the UK branch of the International Institute of Reflexology (IIR) contains information on regional offices, training courses, practitioners, news, books, and charts.

www.reflexologyworld.com

Reflexology World is an international web site with links to other relevant reflexology organizations.

www.remedialmasseurs.com.au

The ARM (Association of Remedial Masseurs) is a professional organization that promotes, represents, and supports the massage profession. The web site has information on the benefits of massage and a directory of Australian massage therapists.

www.scotmass.co.uk

The Scottish Massage Schools web site gives information on courses offered by massage schools in Scotland.

www.shiatsucollege.co.uk

The Shiatsu College UK is a collaboration formed in 1986 to bring together a range of teachers' experience and expertise in different types of shiatsu.

www.shiatsu.org

This is the official web site of the Shiatsu Society, UK – the umbrella organization for all types and styles of shiatsu.

www.shiatsu-therapists-alliance.on.ca

The web site of the Shiatsu Therapists Alliance, a Canadian organization that aims to inform and protect the public, provides news, reviews, research, and training information.

www.the-ispa.org

The International Society of Professional Aromatherapists (ISPA) is one of the largest and longest standing associations for professional aromatherapists with a worldwide membership. The web site also contains a directory of accredited training schools.

www.waba.edu

Web site of the worldwide aquatic bodywork association, which combines shiatsu and other massage techniques with water.

www.wittlinger-therapiezentrum.com

The Dr. Vodder School of Austria offers courses and information on the original method of MLD as devised by Dr. Vodder in the 1930s.

www.worldofmassagemuseum.com

This site has lots of great information on the history of massage.

A simple glossary

Achilles tendon The tendon at the back of the leg directly above the heel.

Acid mantle The protective coating on the skin that is inhospitable to bacteria.

Acupressure points Specific points along the meridians that are used in Traditional Chinese Medicine. Also called acupoints, they are employed in acupuncture, acupressure, Chinese massage, and shiatsu.

Adhesion The medical term for the abnormal union of parts of the body due to inflammation or a band of tissue joining such parts. Scar tissue is an example of an adhesion.

Androgens A male sex hormone that also occurs in small amounts in women.

Aromatherapy A form of relaxation therapy or treatment using scents in the form of essential oils. Often used in combination with massage.

Artery Large blood vessels with thick muscular walls that carry blood from the heart to the rest of the body.

Biceps The anatomical term for the muscles at the front of the upper arm.

Carrier oil A bland-smelling or odourless, moisturizing oil used to dilute essential oils for use in massage. Examples are sunflower oil and sweet almond oil.

Cellulite Fat deposited just below the skin in areas of the stomach, hips, and thighs that takes on an unsightly "orange-peel" or dimpled appearance.

Clavicle The anatomical term for the collarbone. It is made up of two portions that extend from the edge of the shoulder blade (scapula) at the outside to the top of the breastbone (sternum) on the inner side.

Contraindication A pre-existing medical condition or state that precludes the use of massage. The literal translation is "indicated against".

Dermis The second layer of the skin that contains most of the living elements, such as blood vessels, sweat glands, and nerves.

Diaphragm The muscle that lies between the bottom of the lungs and the top of the stomach and liver, separating the lungs and heart from the contents of the abdominal cavity. It is the main muscle involved in breathing.

Distillation The most commonly used method to extract essential oils from plant material. It involves heating the plant in steam and then cooling; the liquid that forms is mainly water with the extracted essential oil floating on top.

Effleurage Another word for stroking (from the French verb *effleurer*, meaning to brush against).

Endorphins Morphine-like chemicals with a painkilling effect that are produced by the nervous system.

Essential oil A highly volatile chemical substance extracted from the roots, flowers, leaves, or stalks of various plants. An essential oil's complex chemical make-up can include between 10 and 100 known naturally occurring compounds, as well as some unidentified elements. Every essential oil has a unique range of therapeutic effects.

Femur The anatomical term for the upper leg, or thigh, bone.

Gluteus maximus The main muscle in the buttock. It is commonly called the gluteal muscle.

The Great Eliminator In Traditional Chinese Medicine, and other Eastern medicine derived from it, the acupressure point situated on the Large Intestine meridian (LI4). It is used for pain relief.

Hamstrings The common collective name for the three muscles that sit at the back of the thigh.

Hormone A chemical released into the blood by a gland or tissue that has a specific effect on tissues elsewhere in the body.

Humerus The anatomical term for the upper arm bone.

Hydrotherapy Any treatment or therapy involving water.

Latissimus dorsi The main muscle on either side of the spine in the lower and middle back.

Lymphatic system A complex network of vessels and nodes (glands) that carry fluid (lymph) from body tissues to the blood system. It has a dual role – it drains excess fluid and proteins into the blood stream to keep a constant balance of fluid within the body and the lymph nodes produce lymphocytes to help fight infection.

Mandible The lower jawbone. It is the largest and strongest facial bone, and the only moveable bone in the skull.

Meridian One of many imaginary longitudinal lines that stretch the length of a person's body. According to Eastern medicine, energy flows along meridians and symptoms of disease arise when there is a disruption to this flow. Most forms of traditional Eastern healing, including massage, are based on this theory.

Metabolism The collective term for all the chemical processes that take place within the body to maintain it. The chemical by-products of metabolism are called metabolites, and they can cause problems if allowed to build up in the body.

Oedema The medical term for an abnormal accumulation of body fluid within the tissues. It may be visible, as in a swelling, or localized, for example at the site of an injury, or generalized, as in some heart conditions. The ankles are common sites of oedema.

Olfactory nerve The nerve that conveys smell sensations from the nose to the brain. It is one of a pair.

On-site massage Massage carried out in the workplace. On-site massage is usually done with the client fully clothed and sitting in a chair. Lasting about 15–20 minutes, it concentrates on the head, shoulders, and back.

Peristalsis The rhythmic, wave-like contraction and relaxation of muscle that moves food and waste products through the intestines.

Petrissage Another word for kneading, from the French verb *petrir*, meaning to knead.

Quadriceps The anatomical term for the four large muscles at the front of the thighs.

Reflexology A form of therapy and relaxation in which various parts of the sole of the foot or hand are pressed to relieve areas of tension in corresponding parts of the body.

Sacrum The triangular bone at the base of the spine. Made up of five fused vertebrae, it forms part of the pelvis.

Scapula The anatomical term for the shoulder blade.

Sciatic nerve One of a pair of the two largest nerves in the body. They run from the base of the spine down the backs of the legs to the feet, and from the main nerve in each leg. Sciatica is lower back pain caused by pressure exerted on this nerve.

Shiatsu A type of massage therapy that evolved in Japan. It involves applying pressure using fingers, thumbs, elbows, and even feet to key points on the body to influence and stimulate energy flow in the body.

Tapotement Another word for percussion movements, from the French verb *tapoter*, meaning to tap or drum.

Tibia The larger bone of the lower leg – the shin bone. The other lower leg bone is called the fibula.

Trapezius The muscle in the upper back that supports the neck and head.

Triceps The anatomical term for the muscle at the back of the upper arm.

Trigger point Small areas of tenderness within muscles.

Vein Blood vessels that carry blood from all parts of the body back to the heart. Veins have thinner walls than arteries as the blood they transport is under less pressure than the oxygen-rich blood leaving the heart.

Vertebra One of the 24 differently shaped bones that make up the spine. The vertebrae together form a protective covering for the delicate spinal cord and provide the supporting back bone of the skeleton.

Index

Acknowledgments

Author's acknowledgments

I would like to thank everyone who has helped with this book, especially Amina Shah and Gill Whitworth for all their support and encouragement; Philip Beach for help on the Chinese massage section; Carola Beresford-Cooke for help on the Shiatsu section; Lorna Dixon for help on the Aromatherapy section; Tim Goullet for help on the sports massage section; Annie O'Dell for help on the Reflexology section; Jackie Pietroni for help on the anatomy and physiology section; Anne Vadgama for help on the Manual Lymph Drainage section; my clients, students, and teachers for all that they have taught me; everyone at Dorling Kindersley, especially Mary Lindsay and Caroline Hunt; and finally Sandra Lousada for her beautiful photographs.

Publisher's acknowledgments

Dorling Kindersley would like to thank Barry Robson for the design of the dogs, Katy Wall for jacket design, Beth Apple for jacket text, Jenny Lane for editorial assistance, and Hilary Bird for the index.

Picture credits

The publisher would like to thank the following for their kind permission to reproduce their photographs: (Abbreviations key: t=top, b=bottom, r=right, l=left, c=centre)

Corbis: Bettmann/Corbis 70cr, 182c; Jonathan Blair 109tr; Gianni Dagli Orti 25cr; Macduff Everton 328tr; Earl & Nazima Kowall 206c, 316tf; Bob Winsett 104cr. **Mary Evans Picture Library:** 20l, 22c, 26tr, 32bc, 301cl, 305br, 307tr, 318c, 320c. **The Image Bank:** Steve Allen 28tr; M. Gratton 100c; Hans Nelemann 34c; Marvin E. Newman 55br; Chris M. Rogers 262c; Marc Romanelli 62bl, 112c; B. Schnall 71bl; Juan Silva 286c; Simon Wilkinson 269br; Yellow Dog Productions 257tr. **Ingham Publishing Inc:** 332c. **The Photographers' Library:** 140c, 248c. **Photonica:** Doug Plummer 94c; Erik Rank 330c. **Pictor International:** 64c. **Popperfoto:** David Loh/REUTERS 312tr; Bazuki Muhammad/REUTERS 300l; REUTERS/Str 302c. **Powerstock Photolibrary / Zefa:** 50c, 156c. **PWA International:** 61bl. Retna Pictures Ltd: Debbie Boccabella 92c. Science Photo Library: Dagmar Ehling 166c; Cordelia Molloy 326cr. **Corbis Stock Market:** Ed Bock 37br; Chris Collins 78c; George B. Diebold 117br; Norbert Schafer 128tr; Ariel Skelley 77cl, 105bc. **Gettyone stone:** Bruce Ayers 238c; Jon Bradley 124c; David Hanover 57tr; Serge Krouglikoff 67br; Tom Landecker 196c; Niyati Reeve 24tr. **Superstock Ltd:** 76l, 216l, 218c, 235cr, 246c, 260c, 278c. **Wellcome Library, London:** 66tr, 138l.
Sandra Lousada: Back jacket cl, 5, 7, 8, 9, 12, 15-16, 27, 42, 43, 44, 45, 46, 52, 53, 54, 58, 59, 60, 81, 82, 83, 84, 85, 86, 87, 88, 89, 90, 91, 93, 96, 97bl, br, 98, 99, 101, 104bl, 106, 107, 108, 109br, 110, 114, 115, 116, 117tl, 118, 119, 120, 121, 122, 126, 127, 128br, 129, 130, 131, 132, 133, 134, 135, 136, 137, 139, 142bl, 143, 144, 145, 146, 147, 148, 149, 150, 151, 152, 153, 155, 158, 159, 160, 161, 162, 163, 164, 169, 170, 171, 172, 173, 174, 175, 176, 177, 178, 179, 180, 185, 186, 187, 188, 190, 191tl, tr, 192, 193, 194, 198, 199, 200, 201, 202, 203, 204, 208, 209, 210, 211, 212, 214, 215, 217, 221, 222, 223, 224, 226, 227, 229, 230, 231, 232, 234-235c, 236, 240-241, 242, 244, 245, 247, 250, 251, 252, 253, 254, 256, 258, 259, 261, 264, 265, 266, 267, 270, 271, 273, 274, 277, 280, 281, 283, 284, 285, 288, 292, 294, 295, 296, 298, 304, 305cr, 306, 307cl, 307br, 310, 311, 314, 315, 316bl, 317, 322, 324, 325, 327, 336, 337, 338

All other images © Dorling Kindersley. For further information see: **www.dkimages.com**